I'm with the brand

JUST IN CASE YOU GET

THE URGE TO TEACH...

Melissa

also by **rob walker**

Letters from New Orleans

I'm with the brand

THE SECRET DIALOGUE BETWEEN
WHAT WE BUY AND WHO WE ARE

rob walker

CONSTABLE
London

Constable & Robinson Ltd
3 The Lanchesters
162 Fulham Palace Road
London W6 9ER
www.constablerobinson.com

First published in the USA by Random House,
an imprint of The Random House Publishing Group,
a division of Random House, Inc., New York

This edition published by Constable,
an imprint of Constable & Robinson Ltd, 2008

A copy of the British Library Cataloguing in
Publication Data is available from the British Library.

ISBN: 978-1-84529-887-6

Printed and bound in the EU

1 3 5 7 9 10 8 6 4 2

for Mom and Dad,
and Mick, Rick, and TeriSu:
my original influencers

I'm with the brand

contents

introduction

Imagine that you're thirsty.

That shouldn't be too hard to do – it's a basic human condition that pretty much everyone, across every culture, has experienced. It is a signal from the body calling for hydration, a fundamental human need.

But never mind what you *need* when you are thirsty. Any casual visit to a grocery store or even a gas station food mart offers a riot of choices; we all know about the awesome variety that contemporary consumer culture offers. What do you want? What are you thirsty *for*, exactly?

One day in December 2001, I traveled to Miami Beach, where the skies were clear and the weather was warm. I was there to work – to cover what was essentially a marketing stunt on behalf of Red Bull, the energy drink. At the time, the corporate owners of Red Bull were still in the early stages of introducing their product, and the idea of energy drinks in general, to the American marketplace. In other words, Red Bull offered a new answer to the question of what we might be thirsty for.

Back then, the proceedings made no sense to me at all. The marketing stunt involved a small group of extreme-sports enthusiasts who were planning to ride wind-powered kiteboards eighty-eight miles from Key West to Varadero, Cuba. I was living in New Orleans at the time, and I'd just started to see Red Bull popping up in bars in the French Quarter. So what *was* this stuff, and who was it supposed to be for – athletes or barflies? Why weren't there any ads making the answer clear? To compound the weirdness, even this kiteboarding exercise, which I had assumed was designed to attract maximum free publicity, seemed instead to be happening in a void: I was the only journalist on hand, and there were no spectators or even a sign to attract them. It seemed to me that the whole idea of selling a product involved making a case to the public about why we should buy it – why *this* was the stuff to quench our thirst. In contrast, Red Bull's marketing seemed so murky that I made up a word to describe it: *murketing*.

It turned out that the murketing of Red Bull worked. In the years since my trip to Miami Beach, the stuff has gone mainstream: Previously unknown in the United States, energy drinks are now a $3.7 billion category with hundreds of competitors, led by Red Bull. How did that happen? I don't mean in the descriptive sense of a brand's or a product's movement from one group of consumers to another, until it becomes familiar to almost everybody. I mean on an individual level. We all have our thirsts – real and metaphorical. How do we decide what will quench them and what won't? How are those decisions affected by the commercial persuasion industry and the billions it spends to influence us? And how is the relationship between us and those "branding" professionals different now from, say, in the days before we knew what Red Bull was?

That's what this book is about: the secret dialogue between what we buy and who we are, and how it is changing.

I use the word *dialogue* because what I'm talking about is not a one-way process. It's not simply about the intrinsic elements of, say, Red Bull. It's not just about what a product is made of or what it's supposed to do. Nor is it just about a brand image that is invented by experts and foisted on the masses, who swallow it whole. Any product or brand that catches on in the marketplace does so because of us: because enough of us decided that it had value or meaning and chose to participate. Because of the dialogue between consumer and consumed.

I use the word *secret* because the way that dialogue plays out is anything but explicit. It's complex, subtle, and sometimes misleading. And I suggest that it's changing because in the years since my trip to Miami Beach, where I first puzzled over how we choose to quench our thirsts, real and metaphorical, that secret dialogue has gotten murkier than ever.

Back then, the mechanics of marketing was a new subject for me. I was writing about advertising for the online magazine *Slate*, but strictly from a consumer point of view, treating ads more as an extension of pop culture than as a business. My reporting on Red Bull involved the first of what would become many examinations of product or brand success, looking at both the buyers and the sellers. And it turned out to be an interesting moment to start paying attention to the relationship between the commercial persuasion industry and the rest of us. Soon the steady march of progress that had been reshaping media and technology for years broke into a sprint, through the rapid rise of devices and innovations like TiVo, the iPod, increasingly sophisticated cell phones, YouTube, Facebook, and so on. The landscape seemed to be changing every day.

By early 2004, I was writing about all of this on a weekly basis, in a column for *The New York Times Magazine*, called "Consumed." As with my earlier commercial critiques for *Slate*, my perspective still tilted toward consumers, but I was paying a lot more attention to the commercial persuasion side of the dialogue, as well as to the marketing experts and consumer-culture observers and what they had to say about what was changing.

According to many of them, this new landscape not only had changed the commercial persuasion business, it had changed us. We consumers had become fundamentally different from prior generations. Pliable citizens of the old "passive couch-potato" nation had taken in advertising like an order: After repeated exposure to a particular thirty-second TV commercial, the consumer of the past would compliantly "go out like an android and buy Downy" or whatever, as one new-technology guru put it.

But right around the turn of the twenty-first century, this line of thinking went, a "new consumer" had started to appear. By the time I started writing "Consumed," this clever new creature had been armed with all kinds of dazzling technology, from ad-blocking gizmos to alternative, grassroots media. This added up to what professional zeitgeist watchers like to call "a paradigm shift." "Consumers don't march in lockstep anymore," one celebrated trend master declared. "We are immune to advertising," other experts announced. The mindless "mass market" had been shouldered aside by thinking individuals: "Consumers are fleeing the mainstream." Somehow we had all become more or less impervious to marketing and brands and logos; we could *see through* commercial persuasion. It's as if the fundamentals of human cognition were getting rewired, upgraded, and replaced as quickly as the latest BlackBerry variation.

The only problem with this theory was that it did not match up particularly well with the realities of the marketplace that I was writing about every week in the *Times Magazine*. That disconnect – between the theories I was hearing and the behavior I was seeing – is what led me to write this book. I have come to see the mythology of the "new consumer" as counterproductive – both for marketers and, more important, for the rest of us.

I do think there is real change going on and that it can affect everything from our sense of individuality to the way we define community (and how we balance those notions). But if you really want to understand it, then you have to start by understanding what *isn't* going to change. This is the starting point in unraveling the secret dialogue between what we buy and who we are.

   The first section of this book, then, is about what I call "the Desire Code." Cracking it involves a few steps. The first is figuring out why symbols matter to us, how meaningful symbols (logos included) get created – and how, even when we claim to be immune from such things, we often participate in that meaning-creation ourselves. The second is understanding that in the twenty-first century we still grapple with the eternal dilemma of wanting to feel like individuals and to feel as though we're part of something bigger than ourselves – and that, most of all, we all seek ways to resolve this fundamental tension of modern life. The third is seeing how the desire – the need – to resolve that tension is at the heart of the stories we tell about ourselves. The fourth is coming to grips with who we are telling those stories to (and no, it's not about keeping up with the Joneses).

   "New" consumer notwithstanding, it remains a commonplace to complain that Americans are "obsessed" with consumption or shopping. I don't think that's actually true. We certainly consume quite a bit, but to qualify as obsessed we'd have to really think seriously about why we buy what we buy. Despite all the technological progress we enjoy, we still don't really do that very often. So cracking the Desire Code helps us see our own behavior more clearly. It might even help us change it.

When marketing experts in particular talked about the birth of a new consumer, what they were really talking about was the reinvention of their own business. Many popular business gurus have become fond of declaring that the advertising business is, as one announced not long ago, "on its way to extinction." What these people mean is the end of "traditional" advertising: somebody at a big company thinking up a new slogan or jingle for a soft drink or some other product, advertisements placed in the mass media, 90 percent of the buying public promptly getting the message, and the "happy consuming engines" of the past snapping up Coca-Cola or Scope or Model A's. One reason this no longer works, we're told, is that the new consumer doesn't care what some ad tells us about who won the Pepsi Challenge or what four out of five dentists recommend. The proof is in the slowing sales of some venerable brands as well as the high failure rate of product introductions.

The trade, business, and mainstream press have each seconded this judgment. Thanks to "the explosion in information available to shoppers," *The New Yorker* argued, "brand loyalty is in fast decline," and "the customer is king." *The Economist,* too, pointed to super-informed shoppers who have acquired "unprecedented strength" in their dealings with commercial persuaders and approvingly quoted a famous ad executive announcing: "For the first time, the consumer is boss." *Advertising Age* soberly informed its readers that because of "the power of the public," consumers have lately obtained "increasing sway . . . over any product's success" – in fact, the consumer is in control.

It's one thing to conclude that the advertising business is evolving with the new media landscape. But these giddy claims go well beyond that: After all, the consumer marketplace helps shape everything from the economy to popular culture. So what would constitute proof that the consumer is "boss" and "in control" in some way that's new and unprecedented? Lower credit card balances? A conspicuous absence of logoed apparel on city streets and in malls? A disappearance of consumer fads, trends, and crazes? A decreasing amount of advertising? Shrinking landfills? Bigger and more effective boycotts of unhealthy or ethically suspect products? Increased saving rates? Maybe – but of course, none of this is happening. Instead, one thing that *did* happen between 2000 and 2006 – right as the new consumer was said to be bossing corporate America around like never before – was that the profits of Fortune 500 companies soared; indeed, companies in the "consumer staples" category of that famous index saw their profits more than double. This despite the fact that the real wages of most Americans were, at best, flat. During precisely the same period, the personal savings rate actually fell into negative territory for the first time since the Great Depression.

Meanwhile, the number of brand messages we are exposed to goes up, and so does the amount of trash we produce. And on a more personal level: Have you noticed any decrease in the number of times you buy something you were sure you would love, only to regret it later or to simply forget about it in the back of a closet? There you are, contemplating the limitless and ever shifting choices in what to drink, what to wear, what to drive, what to buy. It is literally impossible to try everything for yourself. Be honest: As you navigate this brand-soaked world, do you *feel* "in control"?

The truth is that the commercial persuasion industry, while clearly coping with change, isn't going out of business anytime soon. It's adapting. There really is a change going on, and it's happening on both sides of the dialogue between consumer and consumed. What's really changing is what I first glimpsed when I was reporting on Red Bull – we have entered the era of murketing.

A blend of *murky* and *marketing*, murketing has two parts. The first refers to the increasingly sophisticated tactics of marketers who blur the line between branding channels and everyday life. The examples are many: deals to integrate product placements and brand mentions into blockbuster movies, popular computer games, comic books, and even cult online Web video shows. Ads for television shows emblazoned on eggs. A "Got Milk?" billboard rigged to pump out the smell of cookies. Dunkin' Donuts recruiting teenagers to wear temporary tattoos of the chain's logo on their foreheads. Turner Broadcasting hiring ex-art students to place flashing signs around several cities, sparking an embarrassing and expensive spectacle in Boston when officials mistook these marketing pieces for bombs. Nissan pandering to the street-art crowd by defacing its own ads with what amounted to corporate graffiti. Toyota bankrolling underground club parties. And, of course, Red Bull sponsoring an obscure kiteboard expedition to a country that is subject to a strict U.S. trade embargo.

And so on. The upshot is that, while it's true that traditional marketing always had its limits, murketing seems to have none at all. Thus we live in a world defined by more commercial messages, not fewer.

But that's only part of the story. The other half of what murketing means is found on the consumer side of the dialogue. Sure, we tell pollsters and friends that we're sick of being bombarded with advertising, we're indifferent to silly logos, we're fed up with rampant materialism. If our behavior matched our rhetoric, it's doubtful that the "Consumed" column could have lasted six months. In reality, one of the most significant changes I've observed over the years that consumer behavior has been my primary beat is something that goes well beyond the long-standing human tendency to enjoy acquiring things.

This change is particularly noticeable among many of the younger people I've met and spent time with while reporting on things like Red Bull, or the unlikely resurgence of Pabst Blue Ribbon, or the launch of a new Toyota model that targeted members of Generation Y, among other subjects. Frequently, these smart and creative young people were quite happy to inform me that, yes, they were immune to commercial persuasion – that they saw through it, as the experts liked to say. Meanwhile, they were playing key, active roles in helping certain products and brands succeed. And what was more surprising, many of them were busily starting their own brands and making their own products. They were doing something new, but it wasn't really about resisting and rejecting branding. It was about reinventing it and maybe even revitalizing it.

They were in the vanguard of what looks an awful lot like an increasingly widespread consumer *embrace* of branded, commercial culture. More and more people of all ages are, in a variety of ways, actually participating in new forms of marketing, from signing up with "word of mouth" firms to spread the news about some new product the firm represents or submitting their own home-brew advertisements on behalf of well-known consumer brands. The modern relationship between consumer and consumed – what I'm calling murketing – is defined not by rejection at all, but rather by frank complicity.

This is something we have to come to grips with if we want to figure out how consumer culture is really evolving – and how it can evolve. That's the subject of the book's final section: how the future of consumer culture might shape – and be shaped by – businesses, communities, and individuals.

"I'm not much of a consumer."

People say that to me all the time. I guess nobody wants to define himself or herself as "a consumer," because it feels a little trivial. Still, once whoever I'm listening to has established the necessary nonconsumer credentials, what usually follows is an opinion about a product or brand that I've written about lately. If it's something that she would not personally buy, then she's amazed anyone would; if it's something that he has personally bought, then he assures me that I failed to capture the real quality or style or excellence of whatever it was.

Obviously, we're all consumers. And probably we all think we're better at playing the consumption game than most people. In one informal poll, 77 percent of those who were asked said that they are more aware of such efforts than most people are; 61 percent said their knowledge of persuasion techniques is above average; and 66 percent said they are better critical thinkers than their typical peer. If these respondents are correct, then most people are more clever than most people.

Clearly a lot of the respondents are wrong. But still, some of us *must* be better critical thinkers than others. And here I have to admit something. Having spent years as a journalist focused on marketing and consumption, and having seen an awful lot of evidence that didn't really match up with what marketers were saying about how hard it was to sell anything these days, I still believed that I was different. But there was one specific incident that finally made me reconsider what I thought I knew about consumers, marketers, and even myself. This was the news that Nike had bought Converse.

As a business journalist, I'm in awe of Nike, one of the extraordinary success stories of modern capitalism. As a consumer, well, it's not my kind of thing. To me, Nike's famous swoosh logo had long been the mark of the manipulated, a symbol for suckers who take its "Just Do It" bullying at face value. It's long been, in my view, a brand for followers. On the other hand, the Converse Chuck Taylor All Star had been a mainstay sneaker for me since I was a teenager back in the 1980s, and I stuck with it well into my thirties. Converse was the no-bullshit yin to Nike's all-style-and-image yang. It's what my outsider heroes from Joey Ramone to Kurt Cobain wore. So I found the buyout disheartening, and I wasn't alone: Shortly after the deal was announced, *The Washington Post* interviewed various dismayed anarchists and college students who vowed never to wear Chucks again.

But why, really, did I feel so strongly about a brand of sneaker – *any* brand of sneaker? I know why I rejected the swoosh. In Air Force 1's, I'd feel like a brand zombie. But what I suddenly couldn't reconcile was my belief that I could project my individuality through some *other* brand.

So when I talk about this book being inspired by the disconnect between what the experts say and how we really behave, I have to include myself.

Not long after my Chuck Taylor epiphany, scientists at the Baylor College of Medicine conducted an interesting experiment. They revisited one of the eternal thirst-quenching questions of our time: Coke or Pepsi?

In an initial round of tests, they basically re-created the famous Pepsi Challenge, which was a blind taste test. They found a slight preference for Pepsi based on taste alone, but it was so close that it was practically a draw; essentially, when the two beverages squared off solely on the basis of intrinsic sensory appeal, they were found to be about the same. This makes sense, given that (as the Baylor researchers pointed out) the ingredients are extremely similar. The next round of tests, however, included something else: "cultural information."

In this instance, the cultural information was branding. The subjects now chose between a clearly labeled drink (Coke for some subjects, Pepsi for others) and an unlabeled one. Properly labeled, Pepsi again finished in a tie with its unknown competitor. But properly labeled, Coke was the decisive favorite against its mystery rival. The Coke brand, evidently, had something that the Pepsi brand did not have – something that people liked. (In both cases, subjects were told that the unlabeled drink might be Pepsi or it might be Coke; in reality, the labeled drink was competing against itself. Thus branded Coke trounced its unbranded self.) Remarkably, all this was true even though roughly half the subjects had stated a preference for Pepsi at the start of the experiment. And according to these neuroscientists' interpretations of brain scans that they made of their subjects during the experiments, the key was that adding cultural information (in the form of the Coke brand) to the equation "recruits" different parts of the brain – where more complicated notions of the self and memories intermingle – into the decision-making process. And that's what changed their minds. "Brand knowledge," the researchers concluded, had a "dramatic effect . . . on subjects' behavioral preference."

So we can talk all we want about being brandproof, but our behavior tells a different story. This is why I have come around to the view that there is nothing to be gained by simply believing we are immune to brands. But there might be something gained in understanding why we aren't.

And that's where the story begins.

part one
the desire code

the pretty good problem

rational thinking

Imagine that you're naked.

Or maybe it's better to put it this way: Imagine that you need some sort of clothing. This may not be a biological imperative like thirst, but wearing something is still pretty much a baseline acceptable social behavior. How, then, do you choose to meet this authentic consumer need?

Cram as many responses to that question as will fit into the two million square feet of exhibition space at the Las Vegas Convention Center, and you have Magic. Magic is a twice yearly trade show for the apparel industry, a place where makers of clothes gather to display their wares for the benefit of retail buyers – the people who decide what boutiques and department stores all over the world will make available to consumers. Most every brand that you could think of is here (from Polo to True Religion Jeans, from Jhane Barnes to Timberland), along with many brands you probably could not think of.

The geography of Magic is the geography of consumer demographics: Sections are labeled Young Men's, Magic Kids, Active Lifestyle, Casual Lifestyle, Women's Sportswear, Dresses and Outerwear, and Streetwear. The mode of Magic is mercenary tribalism: buyers and sellers roaming the floor in their signifying outfits (there's a couture guy, here's a hip-hop girl, there goes a Japanese hipster kid), cutting their deals, while the trend prospectors and fashion editors study the action, looking for the smallest flicker of a pattern change in the garment zeitgeist. The language of Magic is an endless babel of logos and brands.

Part of the reason for my first trip to Magic, in early 2005, was to connect with Bobby Kim, otherwise known as Bobby Hundreds. I had met him in Los Angeles some months earlier, and he seemed likely to be a great help to me as I worked to understand what was changing in the consumer marketplace. He was twenty-five years old, a Korean American who grew up in multicultural Los Angeles and was into hip-hop, punk, and skateboarding. He was the kind of person the youth-obsessed marketing industry chases relentlessly, and he knew it. But he scorned mainstream efforts to speak to his generation. I'd been struck, for example, by an essay on his Web zine blasting the "commercialized" version of skateboarding culture that he saw in the X Games or on MTV as a "big-industry ruse."

So that's Bobby Hundreds: He is hard to impress. I'm making him sound like a cynic, but that's not the case. He's a smart guy with a lot of hustle; he has the highest standards, the greatest expectations, the biggest dreams. He's the new consumer, the nightmare of the brand managers and retail buyers who make Magic hum. We'll spend more time with him later; but for now, all you need to know is that, when Bobby Hundreds looked around Magic, it was with a knowing smirk. He saw through the whole charade – just as the experts said he should. All these brands have no meaning; each one was, he said, "just another clothing line."

If brands and logos are mere symbols, empty of meaning, then choosing among clothing lines – or anything – becomes a largely rational affair. There are probably four, or maybe four and a half, factors to consider. One, of course, is price. Another is convenience. A third is quality. The fourth rational factor, I think it's fair to say, is pleasure. The half factor is ethics, which I'll leave aside for now but return to later, in this book's final section.

Needless to say, these ideas not only collide, but bleed into one another. You can derive pleasure from the simple fact of a bargain's low price, for example. To borrow a term from economics, the goal of the rational consumer is to "maximize utility" – the usefulness, or satisfaction, a consumer derives from a given purchase. A vacuum cleaner that does a nice job on your carpets is both useful and satisfying (assuming you want your carpets clean); a vacuum cleaner that leaves the carpet looking just as filthy as it did before you bought the thing probably isn't.

It's a simple enough framework for decision making, one that marginalizes squishier ideas like brand image. It's also consistent with what twenty-first-century consumers tell surveyors about how we make decisions: We regularly claim that logos mean little or nothing to us. Those polled by GfK Roper Consulting on the subject of why they buy what they buy named "past experience" with a given brand, followed by quality, price, and "personal recommendations of others." Only about a fifth were willing to cite branding as a factor at all. Another survey, focused specifically on apparel, suggested that most consumers had wised up to all the hype about new styles and trends and that a majority agreed that "fashion is less important to me than value and comfort." Who could disagree? Of course you and I are more interested in rational concerns like "value and comfort" than on frivolous trends. "Buying a $5,000 handbag just because it's a status symbol is a sign of weakness," as one keen observer of branded culture put it. Who was that keen observer? Miuccia

Prada, overseer of the famous luxury brand. (Presumably, buying a $5,000 Prada bag is okay, if you're doing it for the *right* reasons – quality and value, for instance.)

This summarizes the thinking of those who point to the emerging superdemanding new consumer. Like *Homo economicus* – "Economic Man," the strictly rational cost/benefit maximizer of economic models – the new Consumer Economicus sorts through the explosion of available information and makes his or her best choice. Consumer Economicus is not swayed by branding, "status symbols," or anything else that smacks of phony image making.

Yet it's hard to square this with the endless choices on view at Magic. There must be a million products here, ten million. Clearly there are differences in quality, materials, cut, form. But how many differences can there be? Shirts, pants, dresses, shoes. These are the essential tropes. Are there *really* so many quality and style variations?

The answer is in the Desire Code, my name for the complex of factors, rational and otherwise, that spark us to make particular purchase decisions. The backdrop for cracking that code – and the reason it's getting more complicated to crack – is the most interesting thing on display at Magic, a thing that absolutely nobody talked about, even though it was obvious everywhere you looked: the Pretty Good Problem.

fifty-three pretty good kitchen ranges

A couple of years ago, *Consumer Reports* tested and ranked fifty-three different kitchen ranges, priced from $400 to $5,200. Of these, it found that forty-seven were, over all, "very good." Four were "excellent." The lowest composite rating, given to a $1,100 Frigidaire dual-fuel model and a $750 GE gas range, was "good." None were rated "poor" or even "fair."

Barry Schwartz is a psychology professor at Swarthmore College with a particular interest in the incredible (and at times paralyzing) abundance of options available to the contemporary consumer. He wrote a book about it, *The Paradox of Choice*. Once upon a time, the challenge for the consumer was navigating a world of faulty, shoddy, or unsafe products. But really, Schwartz argues, that's not much of an issue anymore. The fifty-three pretty good kitchen ranges are a routine example of something that he sees happening in practically every consumer category. So when *Consumer Reports*, or whatever other authority is doing the testing, studies some group of products, the conclusion is invariably that most of the choices are, you know, pretty good. All that's left is to sift among increasingly minor differences to decide which one is the *very best* value of all, by however absurdly narrow a margin. And while we may feel otherwise sometimes, the simple fact is that there are probably more pretty good products being sold in America now than at any time in history. This is a tribute to progress, but it both complicates our decision-making as consumers and makes it increasingly difficult for one of those fifty-three ranges to stand out.

While Schwartz approaches this problem from the point of view of the befuddled and overwhelmed consumer, Seth Godin is among those who look at it from the marketer's perspective. Godin is the author of many marketing- and business-advice books, including one called *Purple Cow*. The title is explained in an anecdote about driving through France with his family; at first they were "enchanted" by the "storybook cows" they saw, but within twenty minutes, the sight of these animals had become familiar, and "boring." If a purple cow were to come into view, however – "*that* would be interesting," Godin wrote.

His point was that "most products are invisible," as is most marketing, and this means things must be made "remarkable" if they are to have a chance to succeed. There has to be something there for people to talk about. The first edition of *Purple Cow*, for example, included a limited number distributed in milk carton-like containers.

It's important to parse the metaphor closely: The cow is not remarkable because it produces more milk or requires less feed or also functions as an MP3 player and digital camera. Its purpleness is not an innovation, it's a novelty. The cow – or the kitchen appliance or the garment – still functions much like all its marketplace rivals. Except that it's purple. Which is "remarkable."

the commodity t

The Pretty Good Problem is even more acute at Magic than it is in the pages of *Consumer Reports* or, possibly, the picturesque pastures of France. The more narrow the range of actual differences in commodity attributes, the more important it becomes to create a different kind of value – one that transcends the merely material. This is the goal of branding.

It's easy to think of branding as a transparent and almost pointless process: Huge companies buying TV ads to shout their trademarked names at us is pretty much the opposite of honest and authentic expression, let alone novelty. A mere logo, then, seems an unlikely way to achieve Godin's state of purpleness. But there is more to branding than that. Branding is really a process of attaching an idea to a product. A hundred years ago or more – when consumers started to choose (for instance) factory-sealed containers of flour marked Pillsbury, rather than buying flour of unknown provenance and quality out of open vats – that idea might have been strictly utilitarian and rational: trustworthy, effective, a bargain. Over time, and thanks in part to the sprawling abundance that production improvements offered, the ideas attached to products have by necessity become more elaborate and ambitious. This is why, for example, a widely discussed and award-winning campaign for Dove skin cleansers – featuring women who were decidedly less svelte than the models traditionally used in advertising images – took the form of a grandiose statement on the nature of beauty itself.

If a product is successfully tied to an idea, branding persuades people – whether they admit it to pollsters or even fully understand it themselves – to consume the idea by consuming the product. Even companies like Apple and Nike, while celebrated for the tangible attributes of their products, work hard to associate themselves with abstract notions of nonconformity or achievement. A potent brand becomes a form of identity in shorthand. It solves the Pretty Good Problem.

Here is one tool for understanding how this plays out in the market: the T-shirt. The T-shirt, really, is nothing. A former undergarment popularized as outerwear by World War II veterans who enjoyed their "skivvy" shirts on the often balmy Pacific front, it is today the plain brown cow of clothing, the sartorial equivalent of tap water. On a functional level, T-shirt innovation has not been radical compared with, say, the evolution in music-listening products. A time traveler from the 1930s might not know how to operate an iPod but could still figure out how to use the twenty-first-century T-shirt.

But speaking of music: Band logos stood out as one popular strategy for adding value to a commodity in my safari through the Magic wilderness. A dozen or more companies offered T-shirts for the Clash, Slayer, Iron Maiden, Afrika Bambaataa, Melle Mel, and a seemingly endless variety of others, from the well-known to the obscure. At least three companies were selling rock T-shirts for toddlers – two had Ramones offerings. Maybe the bands who turned CBGB into the birthplace of American punk did not sell branded merch at the time, but thirty years later, Ramones T-shirts have outsold Ramones albums ten to one. And CB's itself had a sizable Magic booth; in fact, its clothing line grossed $2 million in 2004, double the revenue of the actual music club, which later shut down.

Of course, music-related T-shirts were only one category. A sizable percentage of the apparel on sale at Magic really exists solely as a carrier for symbolic meanings developed elsewhere in the marketplace. *Playboy* had a huge display of its branded apparel, and *Hustler* was there, too. *American Chopper,* the television show, had a big space, as did Fender guitars and *Lowrider* magazine – one of several brands that offered a working bar, live events, and DJs. *Lowrider,* as far as I knew, was just some specialty publication for fanatics of a particular style of car, but now sold apparel as well.

Kung Fu Inc. had shirts promoting the scabrous antiauthority clip-art comic *Get Your War On* and the indie-chick pornography brand SuicideGirls. Old Varsity sold college-wear. An endless number of television shows and movie properties were represented, from Adult Swim to ESPN to *Redneck Comedy Roundup.* One of the biggest booths was stuffed with T-shirts and other apparel carrying the symbol of John Deere, the maker of heavy farm equipment. Then there was X-Lab, distributor of shirts that say things like "Fuck the Fucking Fucks." Now *that's* purple.

Finally, there were T-shirts that simply advertised consumer products. Coastal Concepts had Burger King and Reese's Cup shirts. Logotel had shirts for Kellogg's, Hostess, M&M's. There were Moon Pie shirts. Others had Ford, Dodge, and Chevy shirts. And if you are still imagining that you are thirsty, there were shirts for 7UP, Mountain Dew, RC, Dr Pepper, A&W root beer, Miller High Life, Corona, Guinness, Budweiser, even Hamm's and Mickey's. A company called Brew City offered up the "subversive" versions that assumed brand literacy in order to mock it, by way of emblems like Schitt, in the style of the Schlitz logo.

Eventually, I turned a corner and was confronted with the Che booth. Here, in a fairly large and lavish display, a company called Fashion Victim was peddling to interested retailers a huge array of shirts, banners, and other items featuring the iconic image of Che Guevara. It also offered Lenin shirts, Mao shirts, Pancho Villa, Emiliano Zapata, and Geronimo shirts. Fashion

Victim's website explained: "Join the revolution with us here at Fashion Victim! These are revolutionary times, so where better to get the gear you need. We have all the latest designs in the world of propaganda and revolution, not to mention we are the only licensed retailers of Che Guevara shirts in the US of A."

Even this brief tour of the Magic trade show suggests that those four and a half rational factors aren't going to be quite enough to steer Consumer Economicus to a decision. We say we make choices based on factors like value and comfort – but what happens when we face a nearly infinite variety of things that are close to identical on a functional level? Perhaps, like Miuccia Prada, Consumer Economicus thinks that buying a "symbol" is a sign of "weakness." But in the real world of the Pretty Good Problem, symbols are more important than ever.

ecko unltd.'s cul-de-sac cred

The knee-jerk bias against logos that consumers display when quizzed by pollsters should be no surprise. Even if we concede that, yes, some symbols and objects really are important to us after all, we remain suspicious that symbolic meaning can be invented – by, for example, professional branders and logo makers. Valuing an object just because it's a symbol – of status or anything else – sounds fake, contrived, phony. This is why most descriptions of the new consumer emphasize our demand for *authenticity*.

While evoked constantly, the word is seldom defined. But one can presume that the *authentic* symbol is grounded in some kind of empirical, provable reality – that if you burrow down behind it, you will find exactly the things that the symbol purports to represent. Think of it as the difference between a trophy obtained by winning a race and an identical trophy obtained by forking over a few bucks at a pawnshop: One is clearly authentic in the way that the other is not.

So maybe the Apple brand connects with consumers because

its products really are innovative and different, and Nike's brand is authentic because it can be tied directly to the company's roots as an enabler of athletic achievement. Any symbol that fails this basic authenticity test, according to this line of thought, will fail with the new Consumer Economicus.

But who *really* decides what's authentic and what isn't? Just across the street from the Las Vegas Convention Center, in a temporary building that was the size of a house, I found an interesting case study in how complicated the answer to that question can be. The structure was emblazoned with the stark silhouette of a rhinoceros: the logo of apparel brand Ecko Unltd. The Ecko rhino, on T-shirts, baggy jeans, and other garments, has become a widely recognized symbol, familiar in dozens of rap videos and on streets (and cul-de-sacs) all over America, and in five thousand retail locations, from specialty shops to malls. Its most explosive growth has occurred in the years since the turn of the twenty-first century – right alongside the growing rhetoric about logoproof consumers.

American hip-hop culture, with its roots dating back to the gritty realities of the Bronx in the late 1970s, provides a particularly interesting backdrop for discussing authenticity. Clearly, hip-hop has long since gone mainstream, and as both a musical genre and a recognizable visual style is widely consumed outside of the tough urban environments where it first flourished. Even so, as anyone with passing familiarity with contemporary hip-hop knows, it's a culture that remains positively obsessed with authenticity – almost every top-selling rapper makes his or her own street cred (maybe a past dealing drugs, maybe direct experience with violence, maybe just an autobiography tied up in big-city poverty) a primary lyrical subject. In the early 2000s, as hip-hop evolved into an aesthetic available in suburban department stores under the rubric of "urban" apparel, connections to the authentic street remained important. Urban apparel redefined the young men's clothing business, and most of the successful brands had some direct link to hip-hop – Rocawear through Jay-Z and Damon Dash; Sean John through P. Diddy; Phat Fashions through Russell Simmons.

Ecko was as big as, or bigger than, any of the hip-hop-associated brands just mentioned. Many people would likely have recognized that rhino symbol on Ecko's freestanding building at Magic, but few would have been able to tell you much about the man behind it: a white, baby-faced thirty-three-year-old from the Jersey suburbs. Marc Milecofsky grew up in Lakewood, about an hour and a half south of Manhattan, and spent more time in malls than in the streets. His father was a pharmacist, his mother a real estate agent. He had two sisters, one of whom was his twin, Marci. (The name Ecko is derived from a family story: When his mother was pregnant with Marci, the doctor informed her of an "echo," which turned out to be Marc.) In about the fifth grade, he started to think about the relationship between style and social groups. He also figured out that not every place was as ethnically and culturally diverse as Lakewood's public schools: At extended family get-togethers, it was a source of amusement that young Marc was into this exotic thing called break dancing. Not that he could do it very well – "too fat," he told me. He couldn't rap, either; but he could draw.

He learned about graffiti culture through photography books by Martha Cooper and Henry Chalfant. Visiting a cousin in Trenton, he told me, he would see "all the freight trains that I guess had run in New York, bombed with graffiti." Graffiti characters replaced comic books as his primary visual influence. He raked leaves to raise the money for a pair of Adidas shell toes, like Run-D.M.C. had. He learned about Polo through a reference in "La Di La Di," by Doug E. Fresh and Slick Rick. Style was cultural expression, and customizing clothes was "a big part of the urban dialect," he explained, so he took up the airbrush. By his early teens, he was charging classmates to make designs on their jeans or shirts, in his parents' garage. "I was waitressing at a pizza shop, and I was counting my singles," Marci told me. "Marc was counting off twenties."

As a student at Rutgers in 1992, he dreamed up six designs and screen-printed them on T-shirts that he sold. Soon he changed his name (first to Echo and later, after a trademark dispute with another company, to Ecko), teamed up with his sister and another Rutgers student who wrangled financial backing, and started coming to trade shows like Magic to sell his designs under the banner of what would become Ecko Unltd. A lot of new brands, including his, were writing their names out in graffiti-style lettering, so he wanted a symbol instead. The obvious thing to do was lift some icon of the rising new hip-hop culture that so entranced him, like a turntable or a spray can. Instead he found his inspiration in his parents' Lakewood den, where his father kept a collection of kitschy little rhino statues. He didn't think about it so much then, but he has thought about it a lot since.

The first brand logo worn on the outside of a garment is believed to be the Lacoste crocodile: 1920s French tennis star René Lacoste, playing off a nickname given to him by the press, had one embroidered on a jacket he wore and then tennis shirts he designed and sold after retiring. We've seen plenty of logos come and go since then, and of course they all start out with no particular meaning. A logo can acquire its meaning from the product it is attached to or the people who use the product – in ads, in the real world, or in the gray area in between, such as pictures of celebrities in magazines. Ecko's ads, in *The Source* and *Vibe*, had high production values and put the rhino on a surprising range of maverick recording artists who were not mainstream stars at the time – Talib Kweli, Beatnuts. Lucian James, whose branding agency, Agenda Inc., did some consulting projects for Ecko, points out that the rhino also referenced the symbol language most familiar to the then emerging youth culture: the language of the Polo pony and the Lacoste crocodile. The language of brands. The rhino both participates in this language and subtly satirizes it. "Rhinos are not exactly aspirational," James notes.

Sales went from $15 million in 1998 to $96 million by 2000, then rocketed to more than $400 million today. "I think it's like something sublime," Ecko said to me, speaking about successful logo icons in general. "When something is aesthetically beautiful, people react. And when you can assign a meaning and value to something and summarize or capture all of that instantly, that's something that I think human nature just gloms on to."

If it's true that symbolic meaning cannot be invented – that a symbol must tie back to an empirical reality to qualify as authentic and thus be embraced by consumers – then Ecko's success seems curious indeed. Here, after all, is an outsider suburbanite who created a logo that became synonymous with hip-hop culture and urban style.

But symbolic meaning *can* be invented. After all, think about Ralph Lifshitz. He grew up in a Bronx apartment, far from the milieu of the patrician upper class. He saw the swells in the movies and during the summers that he worked as a waiter in the Catskills, in the 1950s. He wanted to be like them, so he dressed like them, even in high school. Eventually his father, a Russian immigrant, changed the family surname to Lauren.

Ralph Lauren dropped out of city college, got a job as a seller of suits at Brooks Brothers, and toiled away in the nether regions of the rag trade until he designed a line of fancy neckties that was picked up by Bloomingdale's in 1967. They were sold as emblems of status, under his new brand name, Polo. In her book *The End of Fashion*, journalist Teri Agins credits Lauren with going on to invent "lifestyle merchandising," building what looked like exclusive little boutiques, replicated in countless department stores. A working-class Jewish kid from the Bronx defined WASP status in a way that was accessible on a mass scale. He made it acceptable for the skeptical sixteen-year-old Jersey mall rat who would become Marc Ecko and who never gave a thought to whether the relationship between that Polo symbol and the man who created it was an "authentic" one or not.

the "projectability" of hello kitty

Logos, then, like any other kind of symbol, can have real meaning, and that meaning can be created. This is true even if the resulting symbol lacks "authenticity" in the sense of a direct, demonstrable link to a factual backstory. But there is one more aspect to this first step in cracking the Desire Code. It's the thing that turned Sanrio into a billion-dollar company.

A Japanese firm, Sanrio has been in the "character goods" business since the 1960s. By one count, its artists have dreamed up more than 450 cute little creatures. The word *character* is a little misleading. The characters created by, for example, the Walt Disney Company or Marvel Entertainment first reach the world through a comic book or a movie or television show. They have attributes, personalities, and backstories. Sanrio's characters (often animals) do not. They first reach the world by being emblazoned on products. Although they might be aesthetically charming, they are empty of specific meaning.

One of Sanrio's creations is probably familiar to you; certainly it's familiar to young women all over the world and has been for decades. In 1974, Yuko Shimizu was a young designer on the staff of Sanrio. She had created several characters for the company, but none had caught on. Over time, she later explained, "I realized simplicity was what was important." She was given the assignment of dreaming up some more characters to adorn small vinyl purses. She came up with six designs, only one of which did particularly well. That design was quite simple: a cat with a bow on its head and no mouth. ("I couldn't express the mouth in a cute way," Shimizu said, "so I decided not to use it.") After some debate, her managing director gave it the name

Hello Kitty and started putting the character on stationery, handkerchiefs, aprons, and so on. Before long, Shimizu was receiving fairly extraordinary fan mail. "I felt the power of Hello Kitty," she later recalled somewhat cryptically. "And felt that it could be used as a tool for communication between people."

Sales of items bearing Hello Kitty's elusively inexpressive but undeniably cute likeness climbed through the 1970s, stalled briefly, rose again in the 1980s, and after another dip experienced tremendous growth again starting in the mid-1990s. In their book, *Hello Kitty*, business journalists Ken Belson and Brian Bremner say that by the cat's thirtieth anniversary, Sanrio was making around six thousand Hello Kitty products a year, granting paid licenses to others who made sixteen thousand more, and selling them in forty countries. (About ten thousand Hello Kitty items are generally available in North America.) The ever rotating product line has included all manner of toys, clothing, stationery, and the like, but also appliances, toothbrushes, golf bags, spatulas, bikes, computers, mobile phones, and, in one instance, a $30,000 diamond-encrusted wristwatch. Although Hello Kitty was seen strictly as a young girls' phenomenon in the United States for many years, that had changed by 2004, when Sanrio research found that a third of the customers in its U.S. stores were people over eighteen, shopping for themselves. This epiphany was followed by the release of Hello Kitty lingerie and jewelry. In 2007, MBNA was offering a Hello Kitty Platinum Plus Visa card. Sanrio's licensees have included not simply anonymous commodity makers, but acclaimed designers like Richie Rich and Traver Rains, whose Kitty-emblazoned Heatherette dresses sold for $1,000 and were worn by the likes of Paris and Nicky Hilton. And, of course, Hello Kitty appears on a great variety of T-shirts, from the most basic to more rarefied options, like a collaboration with designer Paul Frank that sold at Bloomingdale's and other department stores.

The astonishing success of Hello Kitty has been the subject

of much speculation. Some aspects of that success seem straightforward enough. For starters, Hello Kitty is adorable. And celebrities in Japan, and later in the United States, have embraced the icon in one media-saturated setting or another, presumably inspiring some copycat consumption. But there must be more to it than that.

While Sanrio has made certain "biographical" information about her known, if you feel like tracking it down (she lives in London, she has a sister who bakes cookies, and so on), she is not, like Snoopy or Mickey Mouse, a character who has engaged in memorable adventures or has developed a personality of any kind. This is intentional. "We work very hard to avoid things that would define the character," a Sanrio executive has explained. Similarly, the company also does very little advertising on behalf of this, its most profitable emblem. Nor can the mouthless cat be said to "stand for" some social or cultural idea – like the Polo emblem's supposed connotation of upper-class leisure or the Ecko rhino's (possibly debatable) links to urban culture. Hello Kitty stands for nothing.

Or, perhaps, for anything. Yuko Shimizu has said that she was never thinking about anything other than making an image that would appeal to little girls. "The simplicity is what made people understand Hello Kitty," she concluded. A perceptive study of the Hello Kitty phenomenon by Tokyo-based cultural scholar Brian J. McVeigh suggests an interesting theory that is implied by his paper's title: "How Hello Kitty Commodifies the Cute, Cool and Camp." While he notes factors like "accessibility" and consistency, the most compelling factor he isolates is "projectability." Hello Kitty's blank, "cryptic" simplicity, he argues, is among her great strengths; standing for nothing, she is "waiting to be interpreted," and this is precisely how an "ambiguous" – and let's be frank: meaningless – symbol comes to stand for nostalgia to one person, fashionability to another, camp to a third, vague subversiveness to a fourth. "Without the mouth, it is easier for the person looking at Hello Kitty to project their feelings onto the character," explains a Sanrio spokesman McVeigh quotes. "The person can be happy or sad together with Hello Kitty." Hello Kitty, is a "mirror that reflects whatever image, desire, or fantasy an individual brings to it." Belson and Bremner return to this theme repeatedly in their book on the business of Hello Kitty. "What makes Kitty so intriguing is that she projects entirely different meanings depending on the consumer," they write. The cat is "an icon that allows viewers to assign whatever meaning to her that they want."

Many of the consumers that McVeigh interviewed about Hello Kitty complained about corporations targeting them, making them buy things – things like more Hello Kitty products. But as he pointed out, "Capitalist forces do not simply foist knickknacks on the masses, and we must give credit to the individual consumer who, after all, chooses to purchase certain incarnations of Hello Kitty but not others (or chooses not to buy Hello Kitty at all)." After all, if Sanrio's managers could create dozens of Hello Kittys, they most certainly would – and they are trying all the time. In more than three decades of effort, they have never come close.

Not only can logos have meaning, and not only can that meaning be manufactured – it can be manufactured *by consumers*. Ultimately, a cultural symbol that catches on is almost never simply imposed, but rather is created and then tacitly agreed upon by those who choose to accept its meaning, wherever that meaning may have originated. That's what Hello Kitty is: a cultural symbol. And a successful brand.

the hundreds

Bobby Hundreds, needless to say, is not particularly impressed by the likes of Hello Kitty, or Marc Ecko, or any of the brands at Magic.

Well, that's not completely true. There's at least *one* brand that Bobby Hundreds believes in. It's called the Hundreds. This is the brand that he and his business partner, known as Ben Hundreds, founded in 2003. The Hundreds came about when Ben and Bobby met not while skateboarding, but at Loyola Law School in Los Angeles, where they had some first-year classes together. They bonded over their mutual interests in art, music, and design – and their mutual horror of becoming the respectable suit-wearing drones their parents wanted them to be. Seeking a more fulfilling alternative, they decided to start something of their own: a brand. The Hundreds sold T-shirts, with designs created by Bobby. Ben runs the business side. And that's why they were at Magic. They had a booth, and they were selling their shirts to retailers, meeting with magazine editors and trend consultants, and networking.

They had created their first line of shirts less than two years earlier. Department store chains were too mainstream for the Hundreds; instead, they wanted to get their T-shirts into certain skateboard shops or independent "streetwear" stores. Their bête noir was Urban Outfitters, which they saw as the ultimate corporate vulture. The first store they set their sights on was Fred Segal, a trendsetting boutique in Santa Monica. They showed up one day in 2003 and "ambushed" the buyer. "There are fifty new T-shirt lines that come out every day," Bobby explained to me, so they knew that theirs would rise or fall on the strength of the Hundreds as a brand. "We really emphasized that we weren't just a T-shirt line – we were more of a lifestyle" that aimed to "bring this subculture out," he said. "And I guess we sold him on that."

The Fred Segal deal helped them persuade other retail buyers to give the Hundreds a try. By the time we met up at Magic, the Hundreds had distribution in scores of stores, in eight states and fifteen countries. I'd noticed that their website included what was essentially a fan club section – you could join the

Hundreds "bomb squad" and get stickers to put up around your city. I assumed this was bravado. Bobby told me I was wrong. "We get so many e-mails every day from kids, not just in America, but around the world, who want to be somehow involved in the Hundreds," he said. Just like Ecko or Polo or Hello Kitty, or any other brand that finds an audience, the Hundreds meant something to its fledgling – but surprisingly enthusiastic – consumer base. People were starting to glom on to it. The Hundreds had created a symbol that had meaning, and that was cracking the Desire Code.

Surveying the sea of brands at Magic, I found it tempting at first to conclude that consumers reach for these commercial symbols because we live in a world riddled with logos. But eventually I realized that maybe I had the cause and effect backward. Maybe we live in a world riddled with logos because symbols are something that we enjoy, desire, and even need.

chapter two

the straw man
in the gray flannel suit

THE FUNDAMENTAL TENSION OF MODERN LIFE . . . OUTLAWS
AND OUTCASTS . . . JOINING IS OVER . . . OH, DOTAGE–UP
YOURS! . . . IDENTITY LEISURE

the fundamental tension of modern life

Accepting that symbols, brands, and logos can acquire meaning
– especially in the age of the Pretty Good Problem – is the first
step of understanding the Desire Code. The second step is
understanding what those symbolic meanings do for us. There
are many answers: Consumers of the Ecko rhino, the Polo logo,
the Hundreds brand, and Hello Kitty are clearly different sorts
of people, with different stories. Let's start with one story that's
not connected to any of those symbols: Ed Templeton's.

Templeton was born in 1973, in the suburbs of Orange County.
He was raised there, and he lives there today. When he was in
grade school, his father left home, leaving his mother with kids
she could not really control. "There was a broken-home situation,"
he told me somewhat blandly. Growing up, he was "a nerd," he
continued. "I didn't know any of the cool kids." He could not
figure out how to fit in; he was not a joiner. "I wanted to be a
ninja," he added.

Apart from the ninja bit, I think Templeton's basic dilemma is an easy one to understand. Here's one way to think about it. When I was in grade school, we watched a lot of films. Perhaps they were a relatively easy way to quiet the children down for a while. But remembering this period as an adult, I'm struck by the realization that those films all had one of two themes.

One was: Deep down, each of us is different, unique, and special.

The other was: Deep down, we are all just the same.

For years I shared this observation, for laughs, before it finally occurred to me that this was no joke. In fact, it articulated what is more or less the fundamental tension of modern life.

We all want to feel like individuals.

We all we want to feel like a part of something bigger than ourselves.

And resolving that tension is what the Desire Code is all about.

outlaws and outcasts

So back to Ed Templeton. Templeton took up the skateboard in middle school, in the mid-1980s, largely because "I didn't have this father figure around who was going to kick my ass if I did something wrong," he explained. "I noticed early on that a lot of kids who were into skateboarding were from broken homes." His fellow skaters were "outcast kids," he continued, and there was an "outlaw aspect" to what they were doing. Skateboarding was illegal in many of Orange County's public spaces, and Templeton was arrested several times.

Many of the skater kids that he hung out with overlapped with the Los Angeles punk scene of the 1980s. If a band could not get a show in a cool club, it would put on a show in a park; if skaters were not likely to be featured in a magazine, they would make their own zines. And if you couldn't find (or afford) a skateboard with cool enough graphics, you made your own. The stickers and designs created by underground skateboard artists, reprinted in skate magazines, became potent symbols to many kids like Templeton. "I found out some of the guys that I really looked up to as skateboarders did their own graphics. And I thought that was the coolest thing ever." Templeton decided he would do his own graphics, too.

From that outcast loneliness, from something close to nothing, Templeton had begun to forge an identity and become an individual. He started looking at art books in mall bookstores. He went pro as a skater in 1990, which gave him the chance to go to Europe, where he actually spent some time in museums. And he started to paint. Today he is an underground skate legend, founder of his own board company, and a painter and photographer whose work sells in galleries in the United States and Europe.

Skateboards or devices quite like them date back to the early 1900s, but the "outlaw aspect" of skateboarding can be traced to the 1970s, fifty miles up the California coast from Orange County, to a section of Venice Beach. In a neighborhood that was in terrible disrepair – an amusement park called Pacific Ocean Park had failed in 1967 and been demolished in 1973 – assorted locals from hardscrabble backgrounds surfed and skated the urban ruins. Some, who would later become the subject of the 2001 documentary *Dogtown and Z-Boys*, formed a group that competed as a kind of team on behalf of a local skate and surf shop called Zephyr. The reverence accorded the members of this group today is suggested by the alternative newspaper *L.A. Weekly*'s judgment that the Zephyr skaters "defined the language, made the idols, built the myths, established the canon, bled and bruised the sacraments, and in the end forged the aesthetic that skateboarding, and by extension modern youth culture, adheres to still."

The details are not particularly important here – and inevitably there are alternative accounts arguing that the whole Zephyr thing is overrated – but the poetry of this particular creation myth is unbeatable: Literally beyond the end of the American frontier, in the ruins of a failed amusement park that jutted several hundred feet into the ocean, in an era when the whole American idea seemed vulnerable, something brand new was invented. "One of the reasons we're attracted to these guys, I think, is because they lived authentically," commented Catherine Hardwicke, director of *Lords of Dogtown,* a wide-release 2005 Hollywood film about this group. "They rode their skateboards, and their jeans were fucked up because they could only afford one pair. They weren't sitting there watching TV, they were doing shit they loved, you know, and they cared about it and felt it vibrantly. . . . You can't help but be attracted to them because they lived by their instincts."

All of which is a major reason why young guys on skateboards have been so thoroughly absorbed into the iconography of marketing and in recent years have been used to sell everything from cell phone service to soft drinks. These days, talented young skaters send "sponsor me" videos to equipment makers, hoping to get "on flow" (meaning that they get free, branded, product). A skater named Skyler Siljeg was on flow by the age of ten, with almost twenty sponsors, including Jones Soda (which got its name onto Siljeg's helmet when he was five years old) and Black Flys sunglasses, along with various equipment and apparel makers like Quiksilver. A marketing research firm called Label Networks (specializing in "youth culture marketing intelligence") was among those attempting to decode skateboarders with a 2005 "consumer research study" of "thousands" of examples of the species and their "influence . . . on youth markets in general," which it offered for $1,250 a pop to brand managers in the skateboarding and "related lifestyle industries."

The skateboarder resonates as a true individual of a particular type. In a book called *The Hero and the Outlaw,* two scholars, Margaret Mark and Carol S. Pearson, offered a theory (extrapolated from the work of Carl Jung and others) that revolves around twelve archetypes, explained in a manner that supposedly provides a blueprint to corporate brand managers for understanding and shaping cultural meaning in ways that benefit their products. Among these are several that could be applied to the skateboarder: the Explorer (who is engaged in a journey to discover a better world); the Hero (who "takes great risks in order to contribute to society"); and the Outlaw. The Outlaw seems like the most obvious bet – since the archetype is estranged from the community, flourishing in "hidden and shadowy" places. Mark and Pearson wrote: "While the Explorer also stands at the edges of society, Explorers just want to be free. By contrast, the Outlaw actually wants to disrupt things, shock people, [foment] a revolution, get away with something."

Pretty cool, right? But it's important to add the other piece of Mark and Pearson's sketch of the Outlaw archetype: "The Outlaw feels helpless and seeks the experience of power even if only in the ability to shock or defy others." Helpless? That isn't usually part of the equation when we think of our individualistic outlaw heroes. But think again about those Zephyr outlaws: a downtrodden neighborhood in the era of Vietnam, race riots, Watergate, stagflation, and oil shocks was a good place and time to feel helpless. The 1970s are often thought of today as a time of bad disco and worse haircuts, but it was also the moment when the Sex Pistols found an audience that responded to the concise howl *No future.* "We surfed," one Zephyr original later said, "while America went down the tubes." But, of course, one can feel helpless in a middle-class suburb, too – just as Templeton and his broken-home outcast friends might have.

The real attraction of the Outlaw isn't just individualism, it's defeating helplessness with self-reliance. In addition to serving as an exemplar of authentic living, the skater is depicted as a person who makes something out of nothing – and expects help from no one in doing it. The skater outlaw personifies the sense that deep down, each one of us is unique.

joining is over

But you will recall that this is only half of the fundamental tension of modern life. The other half is feeling like part of something bigger. Most discussions of the skater outlaw don't dwell on that side of what seems like such an individualistic pursuit, but it's there, and it's crucial.

When marketers talk about the desire for the modern consumer to express his or her individuality, they flatter us and pander to us – and they frighten us. Because we know what lies on the wrong side of individuality: *conformity*. It is the dread thing. Nobody wants to be like the vacant man in the gray flannel suit of Sloan Wilson's famous 1950s novel or one of the real-life conformists whom William Whyte fretted were being created by the "pressures of society against the individual" during the same period in his book *The Organization Man*.

What's odd about the ongoing resistance to gray flannel culture is that, as a practical matter, it disappeared long ago. As writer Alan Ehrenhalt has noted, *The Organization Man* "mistook the end of something for the beginning of something" and documented what was, in effect, "the last act in a long period of national cohesion." And indeed, decades of the apparently societywide "togetherness" that Whyte described, from the Depression through World War II and into the 1950s, have been followed by decades of not-so-togetherness. In the influential 2000 book *Bowling Alone,* sociologist Robert Putnam made the case that since the late 1960s there has been a marked decline of "social capital," which he defined this way: "connections among individuals – social networks and the norms of reciprocity and trustworthiness that arise from them." He argued that useful sites of social capital, such as civic groups and other forms of traditional community that were central to American life for much of the twentieth century – from Parent – Teacher Associations to casual card games among neighbors – have gradually and steadily withered away. On the very first page of *Bowling Alone,* the national membership director of one service organization sums it all up concisely: "Kids today," he states, "just aren't joiners."

Meanwhile, the veneration of the individual has been a major theme of the 1960s, 1970s, 1980s, 1990s, and, still, today. Each era makes the case in a slightly different way, while the more substantial manifestations of that long-ago age of togetherness – things like lifetime employment and pensions and company health care – quietly fade. We're now told we can expect to change not just jobs, but careers, several times. Most of us couldn't find a way to be the man in the gray flannel suit even if we wanted to.

This brings us back to Ed Templeton. Not long after I first spoke with him in 2005, I went to see some of his artwork and photography at the Orange County Museum of Art in Costa Mesa, California, about forty-five minutes south of Los Angeles. The roads that led to it were superclean and orderly: the controlled environment of suburbia. When I arrived at the museum, it was hard to miss the visual incongruity of this reassuring neatness, and the huge, confrontational mural on the building's facade, in the unmistakably propaganda-meets-pop-culture style of the legendary street artist Shepard Fairey. It was about 8:30 p.m., and the sprawling parking lot was almost completely full. It was the opening party for an exhibition called "Beautiful Losers," and the main hall of the museum was packed.

"Beautiful Losers" was a monument to the rejection of mainstream commercial conformity. The front gallery was lined with the album covers of bands like the 1980s American hardcore heroes Black Flag; glass cases displayed dozens of homemade zines. Farther back in the gallery were skateboard decks, easily a hundred, arranged in rows that reached all the way to the thirty-foot ceiling and decorated not just with the work of artists like Fairey, but also the wildcat skateboard companies founded by members of this outsider subculture, from Zoo York to Toy Machine. The fifty or so artists in the show, whose works were produced mostly in the 1990s and early 2000s, are part of a generation of creative people whose primary influences have been, according to the catalog, "skateboarding, graffiti, street fashion, and independent music."

Clearly, this was no gathering of drones in gray flannel suits. On the other hand, it was certainly a gathering. You could call it a subculture. Or a scene. Or perhaps you could even call it a community. Because here is what the individualistic stereotype misses about skateboarding: It is not only an individual sport, it is also something that people do together. Even the outlaw Zephyr crowd drew tremendous strength from a collective identity.

Ed Templeton didn't sign up with a corporation or a neighborhood improvement association. But he did become part of something larger than himself. "Somehow the punker kids were the only ones who accepted me into their group," he recalled. "These outcast kids. And they skated. They had their skateboards, and they were the only ones who would say, 'What's up?' to me. And the next thing you know, I'm a punker, out of nowhere."

Skate culture is not an isolated case of individuals who, as a result of feeling marginalized by mainstream culture, form a new social group, bound together in part through recognizable visual symbols. The influential 1979 book *Subculture: The Meaning of Style,* by Dick Hebdige, deconstructed punks, mods, teddy boys, and others. Hebdige called them "spectacular subcultures," and his observations apply to any number of subsequently studied groups, from Goths to b-boys to riot grrrls. Communicating "significant *difference,*" as well as group identity, Hebdige wrote, "is the 'point' behind the style of all spectacular subcultures."

Templeton continued: "I started skateboarding, and that in essence was the saving thing. Had I not found that and took that step to hang with those kids, would I have ever found out what my life could become? So I look back on that very fondly, finding skateboarding. Finding a group of kids who were into skateboarding completely saved me." Deep down, they were all the same. So Ed Templeton took a look at those skaters, and he did what millions of kids have done since the days of the Zephyr skaters: He joined.

oh, dotage – up yours!

Most of these groups Hebdige wrote about, and their modern descendant groups, were and are made up of young people. In fact, youth culture hardly seems like a site of marginalization from mainstream society lately – American pop culture generally, and particularly the commercial persuasion business, is obsessed with youth. But people search for ways to resolve that tension between feeling unique and feeling like part of a community whether there is a marketing research firm there to document it or not.

Consider, for example, the Red Hat Society, notable for bright costumes, exuberant group behavior, and the fact that it is made up of women age fifty and over. Here the subculture motive is to challenge the way that society expects older women to behave. "It's a very genuine feeling – 'You need to get off the stage now and go sit somewhere in the back,'" Sue Ellen Cooper, the sixty-year-old "founder and Queen Mother" of the society, told me. "Well, no, I'll tell you when I'm ready to do that." This is not exactly the same as punk's generalized middle finger to society, but there is an element of refusal to go along with mainstream values – a bit of an "up yours" to assigned social roles.

Founded in 1998, the society had within seven years signed up about 850,000 members worldwide. It also operated a three-thousand-square-foot retail shop, had twenty-six licensing deals, and sold hundreds of products through department and specialty stores as well as its website, including at least thirty varieties of actual red hats. Cooper told me that this is not what she expected to happen. The story goes that she bought a red fedora in a Tucson, Arizona, thrift store in 1997, on a whim. Later she came upon a poem by Jenny Joseph, called "Warning," about an older woman who wore red hats and purple clothes. She gave red hats to a few friends as birthday gifts and rounded up a group to wear the hats, along with purple dresses, to a tearoom. Subsequent gatherings followed, a handful of articles sparked the formation of more chapters, which led to more media stories and more chapters – thirty-five thousand of them, in fact.

What these women do when they meet is, basically, goof off. Fred Cohen of the film production company Creative Presentations has, while working on a Red Hat documentary, recorded Red Hatters engaged in everything from drum circles to fashion shows to dance parties to huge conventions where they gather in the thousands. He has also interviewed health care experts on the benefits of all this open-ended fun and belonging. "Something about being in a purple dress and red hat makes them free," he told me.

Early on, Cooper recalled, members wanted T-shirts and sweatshirts – as well as help finding suitable hats. When third-party companies started to pop up to meet those needs, Cooper figured it was time for the Red Hat Society to start making its own official products. It may seem odd that a social group would require a commodity element. But as Hebdige pointed out back in the 1970s, even the most rebellious subcultures are on some level consumption based, grounded in the world of leisure rather than work.

One of the original Zephyr crew has said that their objects – surfboards, then skateboards – always had symbolic power: They were "totems. Functional artifacts." Such an object, wrote

Hebdige, becomes a means of communicating meaning, even (or maybe especially) if that meaning is a variation on or subversion of the object's original, intended purpose. The "most mundane objects" can be subverted and "take on a symbolic dimension" – like a safety pin or a skateboard. Or a red hat. And thus the extensive line of Red Hat stuff, from Keds-made shoes to pricey jewelry to a best-selling book and even a lifestyle magazine.

There are many ways to resolve that tension between wanting to feel like an individual and like a member of a group. Religion, the military, work, and even politics offer such opportunities. But the "Beautiful Losers" crowd and the Red Hat Society offer examples of very different ways to do something that appears quite similar – using symbols of leisure activities and material culture to help us feel as if we have resolved the tension between individuality and belonging.

identity leisure

In the marketing world, the idea that shared consumer tastes add up to something like community is a pervasive one. Brands like Apple and Harley-Davidson are forever being deconstructed and picked over to try to figure out what it is that gives them such a loyal, cult-like following – what it is that makes their consumption bleed over into something that, at least, resembles community. "The time has arrived for brands to take their place among others as new iterations of community in contemporary society," argued Douglas Atkin of the ad agency Merkley + Partners, in a book called *The Culting of Brands*.

Albert Muniz, an assistant marketing professor at DePaul University, has been studying "brand communities" for years. "I had an old Saab in grad school," he explained to me. "It was beaten up, and people would stop me and have thirty-five-minute conversations in parking lots about my car. I got intrigued about what was going on and started interviewing people and going to Saab dealerships and observing people." He was studying "the community around Saab."

Muniz argued in an early paper on the subject (co-written with Thomas C. O'Guinn of the University of Illinois at Champaign-Urbana) that brand communities *are* real communities. When I asked him about this, he acknowledged that it's more typical to cite the culture of consumption as something that undermines social togetherness, not creates it. But he countered that groups of Saab, Bronco, and Apple admirers – all studied by Muniz and O'Guinn – even possessed "a sense of moral responsibility." That responsibility is rather limited: The examples tend toward things like Apple users giving one another free technical and troubleshooting advice. But his point is that they do it selflessly, out of a sense of community. "Our point of view is: This is a human phenomenon, we are social beings," Muniz told me. "If community gets lopped off over here, it will emerge somewhere else."

I doubt that Muniz's idea of community would pass muster with Robert Putnam, who underscored the importance of creating social capital that extends beyond a group and to a larger vision of society. But it's easy to see why equating mutual fandom with community would appeal to marketers: Because we all feel that need to resolve individuality with belonging, brand makers are more than willing to sell us something that feels like a solution.

No wonder, then, that it's so easy to draw a straight line from the do-it-yourself spirit embodied by "Beautiful Losers" to the "mass customization" strategies of megabrands like Nike that make it possible for you to pick and choose among colors and styles to design any unique sneaker you want (as long as it has a Nike swoosh on it). This sounds like a typical story of co-optation – like fancy designers cribbing grunge looks from young people and selling it back to them as fashion. And sure, there's some of that going on.

But the truth is more complicated, for two reasons. The first is that even in the days of Dogtown, skateboarding had a partly commercial agenda. Back then it was a fairly straightforward one: Teams and riders and competitions were underwritten by makers of skateboards and skateboard wheels and so on, who obviously hoped to popularize the sport itself. Several of the original Zephyr skaters formed partnerships that put their names on skateboard brands. One, Stacey Peralta, teamed up with an entrepreneur named George Powell in 1978 to form Powell Peralta.

This happened at the height of the mass-media, mass-culture era, a time when small companies could hardly afford to, say, make a prime-time television commercial. So there was no major ad campaign promoting the skater way of life. Instead – long before a thousand advertising gurus had added the words *viral* and *meme* to their PowerPoint shticks – it was a phenomenon that moved in a truly underground, below-the-radar, alternative-to-the-mainstream way. Among other things, Powell Peralta formed a team it called the Bones Brigade, and in 1982 Peralta released a video of his riders doing tricks and behaving like outlaws and having a great time. Sold through skate shops, such videos became a standard tactic of board companies and created an aesthetic that influenced everyone from critically revered filmmaker Spike Jonze to the creators of *Jackass*. Powell Peralta was also known for excellent graphics and memorable ads in a handful of skateboarding magazines. (While Stacey Peralta directed *Dogtown and Z-Boys*, the documentary was funded by Vans, the shoe company.) In 1993, Ed Templeton, like Peralta and others before him, started a company – it had the appealing name Toy Machine Bloodsucking Skateboard Company – basically planning ahead to have a way to make a living when he eventually got too old to skate professionally.

So that's the first reason that it's not quite right to suggest that the DIY skate scene was a purely uncommercial thing before the big companies came along and capitalized on it. The second is that by the time the "Beautiful Losers" show opened in Orange County, a funny thing had happened within the outlaw culture of skateboarding. Sales of skateboarding "hard goods" – helmets and wheels and actual skate decks – totaled around $809 million. But sales for T-shirts and shoes and other "soft goods" brought in much more, around $4.4 billion. Skate shoe sales, in fact, were growing faster than any other category of athletic shoes, according to NPD Group, the retail-data monitor. Of course, just because you own a pair of skate shoes doesn't mean you have to skate. Which is precisely what has happened to the skateboarding culture over the past decade: It has become possible to participate in the *idea* of skateboarding without actually skateboarding.

To someone like Ed Templeton, this is absurd. And that should matter. Even professional marketers who pay lip service to the idea that marketing departments do not have full control over a particular brand's core meaning still believe that someone does control it – the early adopters or alpha consumers or thought leaders. But it turns out that having the first say does not mean you get the final say.

That's why Tony Hawk is the most famous skateboarder of all time. He is about five years older than Templeton. Like Templeton, he is a skateboarder who went pro (joining Peralta's Bones Brigade at the age of twelve, in fact). But unlike Templeton – and, more to the point, unlike some early adopters of skateboarding's outlaw culture – he has not spurned the mainstream's attention. He has done his spectacular skate tricks on every talk show you can think of and has endorsed dozens of products that have no particular link to skateboarding. He has a clothing line, and has been the star of a series of skateboard video games that were such an enormous success that they made him one of the best-paid athletes in the world.

"There's a fan base now that doesn't necessarily want to

participate," Hawk has said. By that he means they don't want to participate by actually skateboarding; they clearly *do* want to participate in the broader idea of this form of leisure and the group identity it seems to represent. They clearly want, in other words, to join the "community."

That isn't a mistake or a fluke. It's a key to understanding how symbols help us solve the problem of balancing individuality and belonging. Often they do so precisely because they have some version of the "projectability" that helped convert Hello Kitty from a meaningless drawing into a global icon. Every member of the community helps define the community. That is to say, these symbols aren't defined by rational rules; they're flexible and open to individual interpretation. Seeing how those interpretations happen is the next step in cracking the Desire Code.

chapter three

rationale thinking

where to find the desire code

Symbols can have meaning that transcends rational consumption factors, partly because they help us solve the problem of balancing individuality and belonging. Those are the first two layers of the Desire Code. The last steps are understanding how this plays out in the individual – and, of course, in the marketplace. Why does a particular product or brand connect with huge swathes of individuals who seem to have nothing in common? And even more mysterious, why does this happen even now, when the traditional version of "mass marketing" (that is, simply repeating a commercial message until a majority of the American public can't avoid it) is a strategy that gets less practical every day?

Brand managers and commercial persuaders tend to look for answers in whatever it is they are trying to sell. How, they ask, can we make this thing more innovative or that brand more remarkable (or, frequently, more "cool")? I don't mean to suggest that they ignore the consumer. They don't. Scrutinizing the consumer went hand in hand with mass marketing's rise. As early as 1920, one research firm interviewed almost all the families in the town of Sabetha, Kansas, and a few years later, as historian Daniel J. Boorstin related in *The Americans: The Democratic Experience*, "took the first national pantry survey, based on inventories in 3,123 homes in eighty-five neighborhoods in sixteen states." Studies of consumer preferences in the late 1920s guided the Western Clock Company to make a "smaller, thinner" clock that was "an immediate commercial success." (Proving, as one research guru of that era observed, that "the consumer is king.") And so on.

Today, companies spend hundreds of millions of dollars studying our behavior – asking us questions, dispatching corporate ethnographers to scrutinize us in our kitchens. In recent years, they have offered to "collaborate" or "co-create" with us – by, say, letting us make design suggestions, or send in ideas for product names, or provide instant online feedback about their wares. Within the commercial persuasion industry, this sort of customer interaction is seen as a sea change, on the theory that it's the opposite of the one-way communication of a traditional thirty-second ad.

And yet, much of this really amounts to saying: "But enough about me. What do *you* think of me?" That's not much of a dialogue. In the end, even today's product makers and brand owners must – understandably, really – filter their view of the consumer through the things they still control, like form and function and image. If you're a clock maker, then what you have the power to change is your clocks and possibly how your clocks are perceived. So the producer of clocks, or most anything else, must inevitably behave as if the key to cracking the Desire Code lay in the object: To attract Consumer Economicus, build something that helps people solve a problem, or do a job, better than before.

Some of the examples I've offered so far – skateboards, red hats, Hello Kitty – have already shown that the interaction between consumer and consumed is more subtle and unpredictable than simply figuring out consumer problems and dreaming up ways to solve them. Perhaps the most important reason for this is that we don't always know, and could never really articulate even if we did, what problems we're trying to solve until we encounter the solution. In the next chapter, I'll get back to things consumed – and consumed on a mass scale. But to make clear what I mean when I say the dialogue between consumer and consumed is a secret one, this chapter deals not with specific brands and objects, but with us.

A useful starting point can be found in a book called *How Customers Think,* by Gerald Zaltman, a fellow at Harvard University's interdisciplinary Mind, Brain, Behavior Institute. Borrowing a concept from social psychology, Zaltman dwells on the human tendency to rely on stories as a way of understanding and explaining the world – and ourselves. Naturally, we want to tell (and think) interesting and meaningful stories about ourselves – stories that are coherent, that add up. Zaltman argues that brands and logos and products have a place among the symbolic tools we use in telling those stories.

Needless to say, we also reach for symbols that have nothing to do with commercial culture or brands: a wedding ring, a crucifix, a patch referring to a particular division of the army, a bumper sticker praising one's home state, and so on. But as the title of his book indicates, Zaltman is addressing an audience that's interested in people as customers – and in addition to his Harvard credentials, he's the cofounder of a research firm called Olson Zaltman Associates. This chapter draws mostly on work from researchers who study human behavior, as opposed to consumer behavior. But it also draws on the work of others who, like Zaltman, have a particular focus on commercial persuasion and on why we buy what we buy. Given the effort they are putting into figuring us out, we may as well try to figure us out, too.

the interpreter

In the 1950s, a suburban housewife named Marian Keech made a bold prediction: An enormous flood was going to destroy the world. She named a specific date, and she named her source: aliens from the planet Clarion. These aliens had also informed her, she said, that she and her followers would be rescued from this calamity and spirited away in flying saucers. Keech was not a publicity seeker. She and her followers were secretive. They were not recruiting, perhaps because it would have been bad form to show up for the saucer escape with too many people. In any case, she believed what she believed.

But she was wrong. There was no flood. There were no flying saucers.

Keech did not, however, simply admit that she was wrong. Instead, she and her followers offered a face-saving explanation, the details of which are not particularly compelling. What *is* compelling is the changed nature of the way that Keech interacted with the rest of the world: For the first time, she called the press. In fact, she had all her followers calling the press now, too. Faced with what to most of us would seem like indisputable evidence that they were completely wrong, they had the exact opposite reaction: They *insisted* they were right. They were no longer content to keep their important insights to themselves. They told everyone they could. They became evangelistic.

All of this was studied very closely, and in real time, by social psychologist Leon Festinger. He had, in fact, predicted that this was what Keech and her followers would do. Essentially, they had invented, on a nonconscious level, a rationale for their behavior that justified it despite clearly contradictory evidence – much the way a smoker who knows cigarettes are dangerous invents rationales for having another one just the same. Festinger labeled this phenomenon "cognitive dissonance." Moreover, his argument was that Keech and her followers did not become more publicly insistent that they were right *despite* overwhelming evidence to the contrary, but *because of* the overwhelming evidence to the contrary. "If more converts could be found, then the dissonance between their belief and the knowledge that the prediction hadn't been correct could be reduced," Festinger wrote. Elliot Aronson, another social psychologist, built on Festinger's work in arguing that we regularly adjust our beliefs to make sense of the facts in a way that allows us to tell ourselves, "I am nice and in control." In his book *The Mind's Past*, Dartmouth professor Michael S. Gazzaniga surveys these insights, adds findings from his field of neuroscience, and introduces a useful concept: "the interpreter."

The interpreter is Gazzaniga's name for the functions of the mind that enable us to make sense of the world and construct a coherent narrative of our lives much like the one Zaltman proposes – even if doing so sometimes involves errors of judgment and perception and memory. The casual student of psychology will be familiar with the sources of these errors. There's "the confirmation bias" that makes us give greater weight to messages and perceptions that confirm our preexisting beliefs and less weight to those that don't. There's our tendency to overestimate our control over the fortunate events in our lives and deemphasize our responsibility for the unfortunate ones. People are more likely to get angry when it's hot, focusing that anger on whatever "intentional object" the conscious mind is trained upon and not the completely unrelated factor (weather) that's exerting a nonconscious influence. And so on. Keech's story is an extreme, and obviously quite rare, example of just how much power the interpreter can exert.

The interpreter is a thing bent not on manipulation, but rather on seeking "to understand the world," as Gazzaniga writes. It is with us as we experience day-to-day life and as we remember those experiences. It's almost certainly impossible – and probably not even a good idea – to control the interpreter. But it's worth understanding something of how it does its job.

eat popcorn

Critics of consumer culture often talk about our materialistic obsessions, but the truth is closer to the opposite: Much of our consumer decision making plays out somewhere below the level of explicit, conscious thought. This may conjure up corny theories of subliminal marketing, exemplified by "the popcorn hoax." This notorious incident from the 1950s involved a man named James Vicary claiming to have boosted popcorn sales at a Fort Lee, New Jersey, theater by flashing the words *Eat Popcorn* for one three-hundredth of a second during the showing of a film. Under challenge to replicate this extraordinary claim, he eventually admitted that he had trumped up the data. Scary stories about subliminal marketing have continued to pop up over the years, but they are invariably debunked. Any number of articles mocking subliminal advertising and those who believe it works have said, in so many (or in one case these exact) words: "People don't walk around in a semitrance; buying is a rational, cognitive process."

That's a comforting thought, but, in truth, debunking silly hoaxes proves no such thing. The vast majority of our brain's activity – 98 percent of it, by one estimation – happens outside of conscious awareness. This is a theme of behavioral economics, a field that has gotten quite a bit of attention in the past few years. A good deal of the breakthrough research in the field was conducted by Daniel Kahneman and Amos Tversky, who in the late 1970s and early 1980s basically applied cognitive science to a new realm. For example, they published work indicating that people make decisions about risk partly in reaction to how a problem is framed – their risk tolerance changes depending on the wording of the question they are asked, even if the issue described is, in reality, identical. Other research has dealt with a variety of human foibles: Most people think they are better-looking, smarter, more talented, even that they are better drivers, than most other people, and so on. Kahneman was eventually awarded a Nobel Prize in economics.

The lessons of behavioral economics are often applied to stock market investing and the like, but the field offers a challenge to Consumer Economicus as well: While the rational factors that we think of as guiding our purchase behavior – price, quality, and so forth – all involve conscious decision making, what we buy is affected by a host of nonconscious factors. This is why the study of nonconscious effects on consumer behavior did not disappear in the 1950s. Today, however, such research is carried out not in the theaters of New Jersey, but at top universities, by way of peer-reviewed research papers or even taking high-tech pictures of neurons firing in the human brain.

remember the magic?

The Yale Center for Customer Insights, for example, was founded in 2005 and is overseen by an affable and lively-minded man named Ravi Dhar; its "corporate affiliates" include IBM, Samsung, Pepsi, and Procter & Gamble. And it has conducted a number of research projects that suggest a few ways the interpreter works in real time. One such experiment examined how "nonconscious priming" can affect consumer choices. It built on several earlier strains of research showing, for example, that "priming," in the form of subtly exposing subjects to particular words, can make people in certain situations more polite, or hostile, or cooperative – and that people generally failed to link the priming and the change in their behavior. The Yale researchers decided to look at whether "priming for sophistication" would make people buy a more expensive variety of chocolate.

One of the experiments involved 105 undergraduates, divided into two groups. All completed a six-question form, which included a self-sophistication rating on a 1–7 scale. All were also asked to unscramble twelve sentences. Then, in what the subjects were told was an unrelated task, they read some information about two candy bars and answered another questionnaire. One of the candies, Aero bars, cost $1.09. The other was called Valrhona, a fancier-looking, $1.69 bar.

For the first subjects, there was indeed no relation between the sentence unscrambling and their choice of candy bar. And when asked to choose which of the bars they would prefer to buy, 73 percent chose the cheaper Aero, often saying they had based their decision – quite rationally! – on price. For the other half of the subjects, however, most of the scrambled sentences contained words like "opera," "champagne," and "sophisticated." The subjects in this group, then, had been primed for sophistication. And 80 percent of them picked the Valrhona.

Those who picked the more upscale bar were asked specific questions about their choices, and of course they tended to mention rational things like quality. A handful of subjects, when questioned, guessed that the unscrambling exercise may have affected their choice, but none correctly surmised how. In other, similar experiments, involving whether to see a highbrow or lowbrow movie or what to order at a restaurant, subjects were consistently unable to draw a link between the subtle priming and their choices. The interpreter was at work.

In addition to processing what's happening right now, the interpreter helps us sift through all the information that is not necessarily reaching us instantly or directly, but is lurking in our memories, maybe having gotten there gradually without us ever really thinking about it. The academic research on false memories is extensive. Elizabeth Loftus, a psychology professor at the University of Washington, has done groundbreaking work on varieties of false memory, some of it involving eyewitnesses in legal trials who are shown to have remembered things wrongly. Other research has demonstrated instances of a "memory shift" (remembering having held a particular opinion you didn't have, when subsequent events have made your original point of view look bad) that happens without our knowing it. One overview across eight studies found that on average, 31 percent of participants produced false memories. And there's plenty of anecdotal evidence to support that conclusion. People even "remembered" seeing the first plane striking the World Trade Center on live television, when of course it was not broadcast live.

The relationship between commercial persuasion and memory has been a theme in the work of Kathy Braun-LaTour, an assistant professor at the University of Nevada at Las Vegas. Her dissertation at the University of Iowa concerned how advertising affects memory, and some of that research (later published in the *Journal of Consumer Research*) revolved around a series of tests involving subjects tasting different sorts of orange juice and then sharing their memories about it later. The taste of the different juices was altered by, for example, spiking them with some vinegar. Subjects each tasted one of the juices, which they were told was a new brand called Orange Grove. Later, half of the subjects were shown advertising material suggesting that Orange Grove tasted great. (This was presented as a slightly different task, in which they were supposed to offer Orange Grove's nonexistent brand managers feedback about ad campaign possibilities.) Then – in an interesting variation on the Pepsi Challenge – they were given several juice samples and asked to identify which was the one they had tried earlier. Finally, they were asked to describe the taste of Orange Grove.

Among those not exposed to advertising, about half were able to correctly identify which juice they had tried earlier. Those who had been exposed to ads turned out to be a good deal less reliable – only about a quarter of them picked right. More striking is the *way* in which most of them were wrong: After seeing the ad materials, they frequently picked out a juice that was better than the one they'd actually tried. That is, their memory of their sensual experience was, evidently, shaped by advertising. One participant who had tasted "the vinegar-tinged salty orange water," and was in the group that did not look at ads, called the stuff "terrible ... bitter and watered-down." Another subject, who drank the same liquid but *did* see the ad material, recalled it this way: "It tasted real sweet. It quenched my thirst. Refreshing."

Braun-LaTour later teamed up with Loftus and a third researcher, Rhiannon Ellis, to take this a step further. At the time, Disney World was running an advertising campaign encouraging Baby Boomers to bring their children to the park, with the general theme "Remember the Magic." The study asked, What if such a campaign "implanted memories into consumers of things that never happened?"

Participants were given lists of twenty typical childhood events and asked to indicate which ones they remembered having happened to them, rating their certainty on a 0–100 scale. One of the items was "Met and shook hands with a favorite TV character at a theme resort." A week later they came back, and were shown a (fake) print ad for the theme park, making the "Remember the Magic" case in autobiographical terms – "remember the characters of your youth," Mickey, Goofy, and so on. Moments later, the experiment leader from the first week announced that the childhood experience data had been coded wrong and that everyone would have to fill out their forms again.

After seeing the ad, about 90 percent of these subjects reported a greater likelihood of having shaken hands with a cartoon character at a theme park than they had beforehand. Asked whether the ad might have had an effect on their memories, almost all said no.

Finally, the researchers repeated the experiment, with a twist. This time, the ads and ad evaluation questions were tweaked to include Bugs Bunny, who (you might recall) is not a Disney character at all. About 16 percent of subjects subsequently claimed that, as a child, they had shaken hands with Bugs Bunny at a Disney theme park. Subsequent research found that repeated fake-ad exposure led to higher false memory rates – 25 percent in one study and 36 percent in another. In one of those studies, subjects who had indicated they remembered meeting Bugs were asked point-blank what exactly they recalled about this incident; 62 percent remembered shaking Bugs's hand, and more than a quarter specifically recalled him saying, "What's up, Doc?"

More recently, neuroscientists working with functional magnetic resonance imaging machines to take pictures of neurons firing in a particular section of the brain have suggested that brain activity among those recalling "true" and "false" memories appears to be quite similar. It's all the same, apparently, to the interpreter, as it helps us keep "our" stories straight.

pattern invention

Now, there are several caveats to all of this. Those false memory rates, for example, are well below 100 percent. Merely seeing an ad is obviously not going to make you rewrite your entire life experience. And although such "source memories" are not always reliable, they are easier to distort if the scenario seems likely – for example, few if any would be misled into remembering meeting the president, or Elvis, or an alien from the planet Clarion, at Disneyland, no matter what ads they saw. As for the "priming" effects studied at Yale and elsewhere, they would be extraordinarily difficult to duplicate in the real world on behalf of a specific product.

These caveats are important, because you should not come away from learning about the interpreter by concluding: Wow, people are idiots. That's not the point. And behavioral science researchers (Gazzaniga emphatically included) will tell you that it's not even close to true. While nonconscious thinking has, in the past, been linked to ideas about repression and so on, the more recent view is that it is simply a matter of efficiency. In his thoughtful and impressive book *Strangers to Ourselves,* Timothy

D. Wilson, a professor of psychology at the University of Virginia, notes that at "any given moment our five senses are taking in more than 11,000,000 pieces of information." That's simply a lot more than the conscious mind can deal with. Relying on nonconscious thought, then, is "vital to our survival," Wilson suggests. Gazzaniga strikes a similar theme and points out that all in all, the brain does a pretty amazing job. Most of the time, he writes, "our interpreter works beautifully to help us understand the world."

The lesson is simply that we can be affected by influences that we are not directly aware of; this is not a wild-eyed argument, but a central theme of much cognitive study. Where the interpreter can fail us is when it is confronted with "giant data sets or meaningless ones," Gazzaniga explains. "When the variables are enormous, or when we insist on imposing logical structure on nonsense. We see connections where there are none." Although our brains are good at processing a lot of information, they are not perfect. As Wilson put it, "We often unconsciously bend new information to fit our preconceptions." When that happens, *rational* thinking gets replaced by *rationale* thinking. And rationale thinking is, quite often, precisely the thing that, without our ever quite knowing it, unlocks the Desire Code.

To illustrate his point about the interpreter's insistence on what I'm calling rationale thinking – finding patterns and meanings where they do not exist – Gazzaniga suggests a rather crushing party game. You set up your victim by claiming that you have in mind a particular sequence of numbers, arranged in a particular pattern; you want to see if he can figure it out. He should start guessing numbers, and you'll guide him toward the proper "rule" you have in mind by saying "yes" or "no." So the poor sap starts guessing. But in fact you have no set of numbers in mind, and you simply answer randomly until, at the end, you say "yes" to four guesses in a row. Then you ask the now triumphant subject to explain the system or theory he followed to crack your secret code. At this point, the victim will invariably advance some theory that purports to explain the pattern. "Everyone has one!" Gazzaniga marvels.

After you've revealed that the secret is there is no secret, he adds, "The guest, usually mortified, will not talk to you for a month."

No surprise! Who wants to be outed as a rationale thinker, inventing patterns where none exist? Nobody, of course – even though we're all susceptible to such thinking.

And one of the reasons that we're particularly susceptible to rationale thinking when we buy is something pretty obvious: Getting new stuff can feel pretty good. This is something that commercial persuasion professionals don't talk about all that much when discussing how difficult their jobs have supposedly become. You would think that they are stuck addressing a public of devout monks who transcended material temptation long ago.

Maybe you don't need anybody to tell you that this is not so, but there's plenty of research to back it up. Part of the pleasure of getting stuff is actually rooted in something not unlike the purple cow factor that Seth Godin talked about: Novelty that breaks a familiar pattern (like the same old herd of brown cows or the same old T-shirt designs at the mall) can suggest potential reward – inspiring anticipatory spikes of dopamine, a chemical in the brain that is often associated with sensations of pleasure. Gregory Berns, a professor in the department of psychiatry and behavioral sciences at Emory University, has argued that the real key to dopamine release (which can also happen in reaction to unpleasant things, like a loud noise) isn't in the reward – it's in the potential. "I have come to understand novelty as the one thing that we all want," he wrote in his book *Satisfaction: The Science of Finding True Fulfillment*. Any perceived source of surprising pleasure can activate the part of the brain that is equipped with dopamine receptors – making money, eating something delicious, or owning that incredibly beautiful pair of shoes.

Berns and a colleague once conducted an experiment exploring how unexpected or unpredictable encounters with the potentially pleasurable can affect our feelings. It involved two groups of subjects, each receiving alternating drips of water and Kool-Aid into their mouths. For one group, the liquids alternated in a recognizable pattern; for the other, water and Kool-Aid switched off randomly. Based on brain scans made during the study, Berns and his fellow researchers concluded that subjects in the group that experienced the sweeter stuff unpredictably were experiencing greater pleasure, as the uncertain anticipation gave them a dopamine boost. A British firm called Neuroco studied the similar high that shopping can provide more directly, rigging up shoppers with portable brain monitors. "Shopping is enormously rewarding to us," neuroscientist David Lewis, the firm's director of research and development, told *The Wall Street Journal.*

A traditional account of how we make decisions about whether to go ahead and buy whatever it is that's giving us a dopamine rush would have Consumer Economicus weighing the pleasure of a purchase now versus other, future uses of that purchase cost for different, utility-maximizing options. Again, behavioral research challenges this scenario. Stanford neuroscientist Brian Knutson and colleagues looked at brain activity of subjects who were asked to make consumption decisions and suggested that what really happens is more of a battle between the pleasure of getting and the "pain of paying." Another part of the brain, the insula, is activated by anticipation or experiences of something bad or disgusting or painful – including, researchers say, a whoppingly high price tag.

As Carnegie Mellon's George Loewenstein has noted, credit cards are one effective shortcut around the buzz-kill of the insula, letting dopamine rule the day. In the context of Gerald Zaltman's storytelling theory, rationale thinking can be another shortcut: We're buying not out of the simple anticipation of pleasure, but rather for some more rational-feeling reason that fits a personal narrative. As Zaltman writes, it doesn't actually matter whether those personal stories are objectively true; what matters is that they're consistent. We can recognize patterns, but we can also invent them.

Here is an example of how rationale thinking might play out in the consumer mind. The Viking Range Corporation happens to be a frequently cited example of the sort of thing that satisfies the demanding new consumer. Its story has been told often: The company made available professional-quality stoves to everyday people (or at least to those who could afford them; they cost about $4,000) and built a $400 million business. If you're curious, Viking's products got a "very good" rating from *Consumer Reports,* but they weren't named as the best buy, even in the high-end category. It hardly matters: Viking is *the* top-end range brand and could probably launch a T-shirt and apparel line if its owners wanted to. (Actually, after I wrote that sentence I checked, and it turned out they were already selling $20 T-shirts and other apparel; the company also attracts Viking pilgrims – members of the Viking community? – to a special cooking demonstration center at its Greenwood, Mississippi, headquarters.)

In their book *Trading Up,* about the "better-educated, more sophisticated," and "more discerning" modern consumer, Michael J. Silverstein and Neil Fiske contend that buyers of Viking Range products are expressing their "Individual Style" as well as their interest in adventurous seeking of new experiences – presumably culinary ones, in this case. Then they add this observation: "Some 75 percent of Viking cooktops installed are never used." Clearly, there's some dissonance involved in proudly owning an object that expresses your interest in fine cooking – and not cooking with it.

Or consider the sport utility vehicle. One reason SUVs became so popular is that they felt so safe: all that metal surrounding you as you towered over the punier cars all around. But of course, the data show rather convincingly that SUVs are far less safe than smaller cars. (And in fact, the feeling of safety may contribute to this, by lulling drivers into carelessness.) Before you blame this on big companies victimizing helpless, passive consumers from the old days before the recent revolution that gave us the power to hold them accountable, it's worth noting that journalist Keith Bradsher tells a somewhat different story in his definitive book on the SUV phenomenon, *High and Mighty*. The SUV evolved largely in response to research into what consumers wanted and to what succeeded in the market. Carmakers conducted massive and detailed surveys, involving tens of thousands of consumers and research efforts "backed up by many interviews with consumers in focus groups," on a scale that dwarfed such efforts by politicians or media outlets. Consumers wanted four-wheel drive even though hardly any used it; they wanted to sit high in the vehicle because it felt safe, even though it wasn't. Auto executives seem to have been perplexed by and the engineers almost contemptuous of what consumers wanted – but of course, they sold it to them anyway and in fact crafted advertising that played directly to consumers' dissonant desires.

None of this means that faulty interpretation or delusion explains everything we buy. But it does suggest the complexity of individual-level consumer decisions. This complexity has always presented a challenge to commercial persuaders. And as the more recent changes in media and technology in the twenty-first century have made it harder to reach a huge audience with short, simple, and endlessly repeated messages, their task seems nearly impossible. In fact, it seems hard to believe that any single product or brand can catch on with a mass audience anymore. But it still happens – not just despite our rationale thinking, but because of it.

chapter four

ignoring the joneses

rational success

One of the most successful and high-profile new-product launches of the new century has been, of course, the iPod. People tend to forget that when the now celebrated device made its debut in late 2001, the initial reaction was mixed. Apple was not, as you might assume, ahead of the curve in recognizing the power of music in digital form. It was practically the last computer maker to equip its machines with CD burners. It trailed others in creating jukebox software for storing and organizing music collections. And various portable digital music players were already on the market and finding early-adopter audiences before the iPod was even an idea. The first version of Apple's device weighed 6.5 ounces and held about one thousand songs – which was a lot more than most popular MP3 players at the time. But it was also quite pricey: about $400, so much more than existing digital players that it prompted one online skeptic to suggest that the name might be an acronym for "Idiots Price Our Devices."

In rational terms, the object seemed to deliver on quality and perhaps would deliver on pleasure – but the cost looked like a big problem. So at first, sales weren't all that impressive. According to *Advertising Age,* Apple spent $28 million advertising the iPod in the United States in its first few months on the market, and consumers bought just sixty-nine thousand of them – meaning the company was actually spending a little more than $400 for every device it sold on marketing alone. This called to mind the Newton, Apple's pen-based personal organizer that was ahead of its time but carried a bloated price tag to its doom. Yet within a year or two, it was clear that the iPod was not another Newton. And in fact, by 2007 Apple had sold upwards of one hundred million of its music players world-wide.

One of the initial skeptics whom the iPod later won over was, actually, me. While I'm a devoted music fan, and I was immediately attracted to the idea of one thousand songs in my pocket, I was also put off by the price. Couldn't I really get by with a less powerful but much cheaper digital music player – if I felt I had to have such a device at all? I remember going into an Apple store during this period, handling one of the first-generation iPods, and telling the clerk it was simply too expensive. A few months later (in the summer of 2002), I bought one, full price. By then I had worked out my rationales: It would make airplane trips for work more bearable; I've been an Apple customer since college and believed they made good products; and really, a serious music fan like me would use the thing to its full potential and get my money's worth.

Not long after that, I happened to go to a retreat for the online magazine *Slate,* which was then owned by Microsoft. This was still early enough in the life of the iPod that pretty much nobody else at the retreat had really handled one yet. I'm generally not an early adopter of gizmos (at that time, I still hadn't gotten around to buying a cell phone), and there was something oddly pleasing about watching a bunch of people – Microsoft employees, no less! – pass around my Apple purchase, clearly impressed, if not by the music I'd stuffed it with, then with the device itself. I remember having the vague hunch that this object could become a hit, the way these people pawed it. But another part of me suspected that, in the end, it would be a profitable niche product, like Apple's computers, that appealed to a particular segment of the consumer population, but not to the masses.

I was wrong. So what was it about the iPod that made it such a success? Well, that's not quite the right question. The key is in the secret dialogue between the iPod and those of us who bought it.

the object

In late 2003, when the iPod was in its third generation and pretty clearly on its road to being not just a hit, but a consumer-culture icon and a mass-market phenomenon, I shifted from my role as someone who had bought something to my role as someone who tries to figure out why other people buy things.

The best starting point seemed to be the technological underpinnings of the device – its guts, as it were. I spoke to David Carey, founder of a company called Portelligent, which tears apart electronic devices and does what might be called "guts checks." He performed his first iPod autopsy in early 2002, months after its release; he helped me understand the impressive internal design, built around a tiny hard disk. The most popular digital music players before the iPod came along did not use hard disks. Rather, they used another type of storage technology, referred to as a "flash chip." These took up less space – which meant the device could be smaller – but held less data (in this case, fewer songs). If the crucial equation was "largest number of songs" divided by "smallest physical space," Apple seemed to have broken from the pack by coming up with a physical configuration that included a hard drive.

But in truth, the iPod wasn't the first MP3 player to use a

hard disk. That honor goes to a different device, released around two years before Apple's product hit the market, by a Singapore-based company called Creative. (Apple allegedly even approached Creative in early 2001 about ways the companies might work together, but Creative wasn't interested. That didn't come out until some years later, after Apple paid Creative $100 million to settle legal wrangles that arose after Creative sued for patent infringement in 2006.) Clearly, the technical innovation of using a tiny hard drive was not enough, by itself, to crack the Desire Code on a mass scale.

The iPod differed from Creative's product in several ways. For one thing, the iPod was aggressively advertised and marketed, something Creative hardly bothered with. And then there was the form factor. Many of the experts I spoke with felt the key to the success of Apple's device lay in how easy and intuitive it was to use, with as few buttons as possible and its now famous "scroll wheel." Others pointed to more explicitly aesthetic considerations: The iPod just looked gorgeous. Still others argued that the secret to its success was its integration with Apple's jukebox software, iTunes, which in turn was linked to an online store with a wide selection of music that could be bought and used seamlessly with the device. After hearing all these theories, I decided I needed to go to the source.

Apple's Cupertino, California, headquarters is a series of connected buildings arranged in a circle, and behind this surface is a kind of enclosed park. It looks like public space, but of course it isn't: You can't get to it unless you're an Apple employee or are accompanied by one. When I interviewed people at Apple, they were curiously vague. I asked about the technical specs of the device, for instance, and I was told that the answers amounted to so much "esoterica" that consumers don't care about.

Jonathan Ive, Apple's friendly and soft-spoken vice president of industrial design, spent about ten minutes telling me about the iPod's packaging – the way the box opens, how the foam is cut – before I could even ask him a question. He talked about the unusually thin and flexible FireWire cable, about the "taut, crisp" cradle that the iPod rests in. He talked about the white headphones (or "ear buds"). "I remember," he said, "there was a discussion: 'Headphones can't be white; headphones are black or dark gray.'" But uniform whiteness seemed too important to the product to break the pattern. So they made the headphones white. Okay, fine, but cool packaging and white headphones couldn't be what made the object a hit, right? Ive ventured that perhaps the key was the iPod's "overt simplicity." This was about as specific as the conversation ever got.

I didn't feel any closer to an answer when I was led farther into the Apple complex, to that parklike area within the ring of office buildings. Along one side of this hermetic oasis are a bunch of tables, set just outside the company cafeteria, and a sign that reads "Cafe Macs." I sat with my PR minder in this pleasant spot and watched Steve Jobs, in shorts and a turtleneck, approach in long, energetic strides.

My visit happened to coincide with the publication of a pessimistic installment of *The Wall Street Journal*'s "Heard on the Street" column, which noted that some on Wall Street were waiting to see what would happen to the iPod once Dell came out with its combination of music store and music player, the Dell DJ. Was this the moment when history repeated itself and the innovations of Apple were aped by a competitor and taken mass in a somewhat dumbed-down iteration? One investor quoted in the *Journal* article implied as much, saying that this was the rival with the greatest chance of success: "No one markets as well as Dell does." This was causing some eye rolling in Cupertino. Dell, to the Apple insiders, was a mere merchandiser, a shill of gigs per dollar. A *follower*. Dell had not released its product when I met Jobs, but he still dismissed it as "not any good."

Actually, Jobs seemed a little annoyed in general. Looking back at my notes, I found it remarkable how many of his answers began with some variation of "No," as if my questions were out of sync with what he wanted to say. After half an hour of this, my inquiries really did start to fall apart, so I didn't expect much when I resorted to asking, in so many words, whether he thinks consciously about innovation. "No," he said peevishly. "We consciously think about making great products. We don't think, 'Let's be innovative!'" He waved his hands for effect. " 'Let's take a class! Here are the five rules of innovation, let's put them up all over the company!'"

Well, I said defensively, there are people who do just that.

"*Of course* they do." I felt his annoyance shift elsewhere. "And it's like . . . somebody who's not cool trying to be cool. It's painful to watch. You know what I mean?" He looked at me for a while, and I started to think he was trying to tell me something. Then he said, "It's like . . . watching Michael Dell try to dance." The PR minder guffawed. "Painful," Jobs summarized.

Jobs had heard the predictions that history would repeat, and his innovative device would end up a niche product, and he had no patience for any of it. And indeed, the Dell MP3 player and any number of others that have come and gone since 2001 have hardly dented the iPod's dominance. In fact, its share of the MP3 player market has actually grown – from about 60 percent in 2003 to 75 percent in 2006.

"We don't underestimate people," Jobs told me. "We really did believe that people would want something this good, that they'd see the value in it. And that rather than making a far inferior product for a hundred dollars less, we're giving people the product that they want and that will serve them for years, even though it's a little pricier. People are smart; they figure these things out." The point that companies – like Dell – may have no great reputation as innovators but have a track record of winning by playing a price-driven, low-margin volume game was dismissed. "For whatever reason," he said with finality, "the superior product has the largest share. Sometimes the best product does win. This may be one of those times."

Maybe so. But I departed Cupertino with a distinct sense that I had not isolated the precise nature of the iPod's bestness – let alone figured out why it had cracked the Desire Code of disparate millions of consumers. I had talked to the people who dreamed up and made the iPod and an assortment of design experts and the technology pros and the professors and the gurus. Finally, I talked to Andrew Andrew.

Andrew Andrew is a "highly diversified company" made up of two personable young men, each named Andrew. They dress identically and seem to agree on everything; they say, among other things, that they have traveled from the future "to set things on the right course for tomorrow." They require interviewers to sign a form agreeing not to reveal any differences between Andrew and Andrew, because to do so might undermine the Andrew Andrew brand – and since this request is more interesting than whatever those differences might be, interviewers sign it.

Among other things, Andrew Andrew were working as DJs who would "spin" on iPods, setting up participatory events called iParties. Thus they had probably seen more people interact with the player than anyone who doesn't work for Apple. More important, they put an incredible amount of thought into what they buy and why, so Andrew remembered exactly where he was when he first encountered the iPod: 14th Street near Ninth Avenue in New York City. He was with Andrew, of course. A friend showed it to them. Andrew held the device in his hand. "We knew," he says. "We had to have one." (Well, two.)

One night, I went to an Andrew Andrew iParty at a club called APT on the spooky, far western end of 13th Street in Manhattan. They showed up at about 10:00 in matching sweat jackets and sneakers, matching eyeglasses, matching haircuts. They connected their matching iPods to a modest Gemini mixer that they had fitted with a white front panel to make it look more iPod-ish. The iPods sat on either side of the mixer, on their backs, so they looked like tiny turntables. Between songs, each

Andrew analyzed the iPod for me. They talked about how hard it was, at first, to believe that so much music could be crammed into such a tiny object. They talked about using the scroll wheel to zip through those endless lists of songs. "It really bridged the gap," Andrew finally observed, "between fantasy and reality."

This enigmatic-sounding statement hints at an important point: As impressive as the iPod's technical specs and design elements are, these rational factors alone were not quite enough to explain its success.

salience and relevance

Two basic conditions must be met for any dialogue to occur between consumer and consumed. The first is salience. This simply means we have to know about something, be familiar with it, have it easily accessible in our mind. Most early advertising – prior to 1920, say, and certainly prior to 1900 – consisted largely of simple announcements that a particular good or service that people probably wanted was, in fact, available.

Even today, salience matters: You are in no position to desire an iPod if you have no idea what it is. The more you see something, the more familiar it becomes – not as a result of the thing changing, but as a result of your brain changing through repeated exposure. A variety of studies have demonstrated our comfort with the familiar – even when choosing among sequences of random shapes, people tend (without realizing it) to start choosing the ones that recur. Not so long ago, a neuroscientist using MRI scans flashed the logos of two car brands at a group of test subjects: the familiar Volkswagen and a rather obscure European car brand called SEAT (which is actually owned by VW). The SEAT logo sparked MRI patterns that suggested the brain was working away trying to remember or place what the thing was; the VW logo, meanwhile, "produced a strong pattern of activity in the part of the brain associated with positive emotions, self-identification and rewards," according to *The Wall Street Journal.*

This is why salience – the mere awareness that a thing exists in the world – is such a big part of what the commercial persuasion industry aims to achieve. As an example of the difference that salience can make, look at the pharmaceutical industry, which has seen its sales and profits rise massively since a 1997 change that loosened rules on drug advertising, which the industry now funds to the tune of $5.3 billion a year. One interesting success story is a drug called Requip, launched with an advertising blitz in 2005 by GlaxoSmithKline and zooming toward sales of $500 million the following year. Requip treats "restless legs syndrome," a malady that previously "few people had heard of," *The Wall Street Journal* noted, and that some doctors weren't even sure was real.

This brings us to the second condition: relevance. The number of things that are familiar to us obviously goes up each year, but only a small number are relevant. In some circumstances, it's what's relevant to us that *becomes* salient to us: If you're in the market for a car, you notice car ads; if not, you probably don't. (Indeed, the advertising we are most likely to notice and remember is advertising for the things we have already bought.) Another road to relevance is problem-solving innovation – if you need to get from one place to another, and all you have is a horse and buggy, then the moment the Model A becomes salient, its relevance will likely be immediately self-evident.

But relevance can also be, for lack of a better word, invented. A famous example is Listerine. A disinfectant, it had been sold and advertised since the 1870s. If you needed disinfectant, maybe this was the brand you'd choose. But in the 1920s, the Lambert Pharmacal Company, the makers of Listerine, wanted to increase sales, which was unlikely to happen by way of a sudden spike in demand for disinfectant. So in what was considered an unorthodox and risky move at the time, their advertising began to describe a new problem that Listerine solved: "halitosis." This was a term, historian Vincent Vinikas relates in his book *Soft Soap, Hard Sell,* that someone at Lambert "discovered" in a British periodical and that "the company decided that Listerine could cure." Its advertising underscored that the "invisible Judas" halitosis, or bad breath, was an awful problem that many people had (and didn't know they had because not even their friends would tell them) and that Listerine could solve.

What's important about this example is that it involves no innovation in the product itself: The exact same stuff had become relevant in whole new ways – it could help you avoid social scorn or a ruined romance. There had been no change in what was inside a bottle of Listerine. There had been a change in the people who bought it.

a not-so-rational success story

Before I return to the iPod, consider another object that went mass not long after the famous music player did – but for reasons that, at first, seem much more mysterious. In May 2004, round hunks of yellow, synthetic silicon rubber stamped with the phrase LIVESTRONG went on sale at Niketown outlets, Foot Locker stores, and various independent retailers around the country. These bracelets cost $1 each, and proceeds were earmarked for the Lance Armstrong Foundation, a nonprofit charitable organization associated with the champion cyclist, who is famously a cancer survivor. "Live Strong" is the foundation's motto; yellow echoes the color of the lead rider's jersey in the Tour de France. Sales really took off when the Tour de France got under way that summer. Armstrong wore the wristband, and so did his whole team, including mechanics; as the race wore on, competitors and even officials starting wearing it. As Armstrong cruised to a record-setting victory, celebrities started wearing the bracelets, and soon they were everywhere – a charitable must-have. John Kerry wore one while making his speech to accept the Democratic nomination in the presidential election.

Demand outran supply, and a secondary market popped up on eBay. Eventually, more than forty-five million LiveStrong bracelets were sold, in more than sixty countries. A host of imitators followed. They came in every color and pushed every message – Tsunami Relief (charitable), Support Our Troops (patriotic), Chosen (Jewish), Choose Hope (um, optimism?), and, inevitably, LiveWrong (opposition to the wristband trend). A category of good, the rubber wristband, went from nonexistent to mainstream, wearable trope.

There is, really, no rational reason to buy such a thing. It doesn't help you do a job you are trying to get done, it does not solve any problem, and it serves no practical function. It does not improve the buyer's quality of life. It is not beautiful. No one needs it. Sure, roughly 70 cents of the $1 retail price of the original LiveStrong bracelet went to the Lance Armstrong Foundation, and buying one might make you feel good about supporting a fine charity – but if your goal is to help fund cancer research and you have $1 to spend, why not give the whole thing to the foundation? Indeed, before production of LiveStrong bracelets was ramped up, buyers on eBay were paying $8, $10, or more for them – many times the retail cost, and with no money going to cancer research at all.

Look around on the Internet, David Hessekiel of the Cause Marketing Forum suggested to me at the height of the rubber bracelet fad, and you'll find all manner of items one can buy to support various causes. Most are obscure and have little meaning in the culture at large. Yet the yellow bracelet became salient to the masses and relevant to millions. Somehow it brimmed with meaning.

In comparison with the widely scrutinized iPod, the reasons for the success of the LiveStrong bracelet have received relatively little analysis. After all, there really wasn't all that much to say about its form and even less about its functionality. The path of its salience seems clear: It was worn by celebrities and public figures on television, then it was worn by other people on the subway, at the mall, and so on. But why did so many find it relevant?

Obviously, few if any of those who bought the LiveStrong bracelet did so because they had been consciously seeking a brightly colored accessory and concluded that this was the top-quality choice for the price. Nor is it likely that many consumers encountered the bracelet while in the course of shopping around for a way to support cancer research, or form a symbolic bond with Lance Armstrong, or participate in a trend, or pay tribute to a loved one.

Yet the answer is suggested by this very variety of meanings and uses. As the LiveStrong bracelet became more and more salient, it benefited from the "projectability" that helped make Hello Kitty a multigenerational, global icon. One person wore the bracelet in tribute to or in support of an individual known to the wearer. Another liked the idea that it was bright yellow, attracting attention and theoretically inviting questions (yet remaining totally uncontroversial, unlike red AIDS awareness ribbons). Another was attracted not just by a good cause, but by association with a heroic athlete at the peak of his popularity. Another might simply like being part of a large effort to change the world for the better. More of us found reasons the object was relevant to our own stories; more of us found rationales to buy it. This array of ways to be relevant, from the intensely personal to the blatantly public, is what made the bracelet a champion of the goodwill game and an indisputably meaningful thing. It had little to do with any particular property of the object; it had everything to do with us.

multiple choice

And this brings us back to the iPod. In contrast with the LiveStrong bracelet, the iPod is wildly functional. This is certainly one reason that it, too, was able to cobble together a mass consumer audience from disparate niches: music fans, gizmo addicts, Apple loyalists. *Newsweek* declared America an "iPod

Nation" in the summer of 2004, stressing the way the device worked as an individuality tool. For instance, the article reported on the work of a University of Sussex professor who was at the time engaged in a study that involved interviewing thousands of iPod users and who argued that the ability to haul around our personal sound tracks, thousands of songs of our own choosing, was empowering. "People define their own narrative through their music collection," the professor asserted, adding that the random-play shuffle feature particularly beguiled the iPod owner with a continuing audio museum of his or her own good taste.

But if ability and power in managing awesome amounts of music was enough to make a mass hit MP3 player, then Creative would be a well-known brand name today. Moreover, most of us don't really need all the functionality the iPod offers, yet it also pulled in niches to whom that functionality was, at best, a rather abstract attraction. For instance, some users complained to *The New York Times* in 2004 that their iPods favored certain songs while in random-play shuffle mode. The paper of record quoted an Apple executive assuring an anxious iPod nation that the device cannot become a "fan" of any artist – and pointing out that such problems can be managed away by using the Smart Playlist feature. "Most people interviewed for this article had never heard of Smart Playlists, let alone used them," the *Times* noted. Most people interviewed did not even understand all the functions that they paid a premium to obtain.

Around this same time, *The Village Voice* pointed out one attraction that had nothing to do with the device's functionality: the white headphones. After all, the music on *any* MP3 player reflects the individual taste of its owner, wrote Izzy Grinspan. But "no other gadget has been so successful at developing a certain kind of image." It's the headphones that "identify a user at 30 yards, so that it's possible to scan a subway car and instantly know who's in the club." Indeed, references to a quasi-tribal "iPod nod" were soon in circulation – and there was a minor backlash against it among some consumers, who decided to wear black headphones.

It's impossible to know if Jonathan Ive's story of the white headphones coming about almost as an afterthought is fully accurate or perhaps shaded by either modesty or mythmaking. Either way, they certainly became the device's defining visual element, its most powerful source of salience, whether in the company's dancing silhouette ads, on the guy next to you at the gym, or on the girl two tables over in some café. Taken together, it added up to the sense of implied togetherness that Grinspan wrote about.

If the key to the iPod had been individuality *or* togetherness, technology *or* style, form *or* function, it would not have been as successful as it has been. The more salient the iPod became, the more consumers discovered ways that it was relevant – but not because of any single specific property of the device. The key wasn't in a single answer; it was in the variety of answers. And this is what connects it to the LiveStrong bracelet. The iPod succeeded not because of any specificity, but because of multiplicity. It fit into many disparate personal narratives, by way of many disparate rationales.

to whom we're telling stories

There's one last point about the stories that symbols and objects help us tell and that unlock the Desire Code in the process. Cultural critics often say that telling stories through objects is precisely what's wrong with contemporary consumers. Virginia Postrel, in her book *The Substance of Style,* correctly summarizes that critique concisely: "It's all about status." That is, these critics say we glom on to symbols and objects as a means of impressing, or even competing with, an audience. It's a never-ending game of "status-oriented oneupmanship," in which we "just want to stand out, or at least not look bad, compared with [sic] other people," Postrel wrote.

In challenging this view, she considers restaurant-quality

kitchen stoves – the Viking range, in fact. Do people who spend thousands on such items, yet rarely use them, do so merely to outstatus their neighbors? Postrel countered that this is simpleminded. Her theory is that even seldom-used Viking stoves offer an aesthetic reward: Consumer Economicus acquiring utility in the form of pleasure. That sounds to me like more of a rationale than an economically rational way to acquire thousands of dollars' worth of aesthetic pleasure, but Postrel has a point about the inadequacy of status seeking as an all-purpose explanation for consumer behavior that seems illogical to third-party observers.

As a critique, status theory is really just a variation on a complaint that dates back more than a century. Thorstein Veblen introduced the idea of "conspicuous consumption" in his book *The Theory of the Leisure Class,* in 1899. He applied it to examples like the man who parades about in "stainless" linen, with a "lustrous" hat and superfluous walking stick. This man, Veblen argued, is sending a message to an audience: that he clearly cannot be involved in "any employment that is directly and immediately of any human use." He is making the objects serve as visible "evidence of leisure," in a story he is telling about himself, to whomever he may encounter. In other words, it's all about status and other people. It's about – to use the familiar cliché – keeping up with (or outdoing) the Joneses.

Curiously, many marketers to this day rely on a very similar theory. In the lexicon of the trade, conspicuous consumption is revised into the more upbeat notion of "the badge." When marketers talk about the badge, they mean broadcasting through some kind of symbol or object a statement about our selves. Like Veblen's ornery concept, badge theory suggests that what we buy has more to do with communicating to an audience than it does with satisfying our selves. Couldn't this same basic idea, whether coming from an enthusiastic marketer or a cynical culture critic, also explain the iPod and the LiveStrong bracelet? I don't think it can, or at least that it can't explain their success in full.

But I am certain that badge theory can't explain a brand like Method. Founded in 2001, Method – a maker of dish soap, spray cleaners, hand wash, and so on – has gone from one shop in San Francisco to its current availability in thousands of stores from coast to coast, including the chains Target and Linens 'n Things; by 2006, Method's annual sales were reported at around $60 million.

The most noticeable thing about Method products, and their chief selling point, is that they look really cool. But dish soap is not something we parade around town with, like Veblen's conspicuous walking-stick owner. So who cares what the bottle looks like?

That, actually, is just the sort of attitude that Method founders Eric Ryan and Adam Lowry set out to change, preferably on a mass level. Ryan, a former marketer who had done work for the Gap, Saturn, and other brands, found himself appalled at the mundane state of home care products. Consumers have a high interest in the places they live, he explained to me, yet "when you walk down the aisle dedicated to products to take care of your home, it's one of the most low-interest categories in the world."

True enough, and perhaps a cue to change the subject for most people, but Ryan saw an opportunity: What if you could do something different with home care products? Soon he was working with his friend Lowry, a chemical engineer, creating sprays and soaps that were meant to be environmentally safe, smell good, and – crucially – come in packaging that looked sensational.

Before making the leap to national stores, they approached the celebrated designer Karim Rashid, who among other things had created a hit trash can for Target and thus presumably knew how to make design "add value," as the ad pros say, to the most utilitarian objects. A pitch e-mail Ryan sent to him fills out what he had in mind:

The design goal is to reinvent the banal dish soap that looks like a relic of the 1950s and sits on every sink across the landscape of America. We want you to approach it not as a packaging assignment but from a product perspective to create an object for the kitchen that is as iconic as a salt and pepper shaker . . . We will bring fashion and function to a tired category that almost every American interacts with on a daily basis. Anybody can make perfume look good, but it takes a real design genius to find a way to reinvent soap. Are you our design genius?

Yes, Rashid said, he was their design genius. He came up with a unique design for a dishwashing liquid container that had a spout located on the bottom rather than the top. Clear, filled with colorful soap, and shaped like an hourglass with a rounded top, it looked like a sculpture; it would later win a design distinction award from the magazine *I.D.* It was also disconcertingly large, underscoring its role as a proud object that need not be shamefully squirreled away. This particular design actually failed in the marketplace, because it was "too progressive for the mass audience," Ryan later said. (I owned one of these, and I think it might have failed because it didn't work very well.) But that was a rare misstep, and in any case the "good design" had gotten the company a lot of attention on the selling point that was consistent with its overall approach: Form preceded function throughout the Method line.

Form turned out to be a good hook, Ryan told me, for his target audience of "progressive domestics." Curiously, it seems that for many of these people, the quality of the soap itself was not a very important factor in their decision to buy Ryan's product. Ryan said much of the company's feedback from enthusiastic customers boiled down to "I kind of thought it wouldn't work, but at least I'll have this cool container left over. Then I got it home and used it, and I'm shocked at how well it actually works." As for environmental safety, that was "a goal" that Ryan sounded almost surprised to have achieved. (Method products do contain small amounts of petroleum-derived ingredients in combination with vegetable-derived ones, in what even hard-core greenies seem to believe is a reasonable compromise; according to an editor of *The Green Guide*, they also use some synthetic dyes and fragrances that some environmentally correct types tend to frown on.)

To the extent that the company could afford to advertise, it tended toward quirky ploys like "pop up" stores (which would exist for only a month or two, as a publicity stunt) or booklets bound into magazines like *Real Simple* and *Organic Style* that expressed the full point of view of the brand, which Ryan considered "launching a philosophy, not a product."

It's not easy to come up with a purely rational defense for buying a cool-looking bottle of dishwashing liquid that you don't even think will work. On the other hand, theories of conspicuous consumption don't really explain such a purchase, either. This is not an elaborately carved walking stick used on a busy promenade. The only thing less plausible than paying a premium for a high-design dish liquid simply because you want to clean dishes is to do so because you think that any more than a tiny handful of people will ever see, notice, and be impressed by that bottle.

But those people are not the real audience for your story. What the Joneses might think is, really, little more than a rationale, at best. Because what you are really doing is telling that story *to yourself*. That's who the interpreter is working for.

"we want actions"

There's nothing intrinsically wrong with buying Method cleaning products, LiveStrong bracelets, or iPods. But understanding how your interpreter might affect your decisions – understanding the difference between rational thinking and rationale thinking – matters. Recall what Gazzaniga said about the conditions in which our interpreter can fail us: when it faces gigantic or meaningless sets of data; that's "when we insist on imposing logical structure on nonsense" and "see connections where there are none."

It's not hard to see how this applies to our consumer lives. Every day we deal with a massive data set called the marketplace, and there's much to it that could be characterized as meaningless or misleading. To wade into it believing that you are Consumer Economicus, that every pattern you spot is real, and that there's no need to think twice is to completely miss the lessons of the interpreter. As Timothy Wilson observes in *Strangers to Ourselves,* it's precisely because we don't tend to think of regular advertising as something we have to be on guard against, or even take seriously, that it works on us in much the way we imagine subliminal advertising might. "The failure to recognize the power of advertising," he wrote, "makes us more susceptible to it." Considering yourself immune to advertising and branding is not a solution; it's part of the problem.

The quest to interpret the interpreter is not limited to academia. A variety of companies are actively looking for ways to decode our responses to varieties of commercial persuasion. Some major advertising agencies have even hired cognitive scientists to help tweak ad imagery – to figure out, say, what brain scans of male whiskey drinkers aged twenty-five to thirty-four tell us about their reactions to pictures of spring break partying or of friends bonding around a campfire.

I once listened to representatives of nine firms that specialize in this sort of thing, participating in a presentation and panel discussion for the marketing trade in an auditorium in lower Manhattan. Some measured facial movements, others used "skin conductance" gizmos. In all cases, the goal was to uncover the way the nonconscious mind works and how such knowledge might be useful to brand owners who were willing to pay for it.

This particular conference happened to occur right around the time that Malcolm Gladwell, whose best seller *The Tipping Point* had been a sensation among marketers, published his second book, *Blink: The Power of Thinking Without Thinking.* The newer book had been released perhaps a week beforehand, but three of the speakers managed to reference it. One of them had already worked a slide into his PowerPoint presentation showing the inside of the book's jacket, which read, "Don't think – blink!"

Most of us hardly need to be told to go with our gut instinct: We do it all the time. In *Strangers to Ourselves,* Wilson relates an anecdote about a reporter saying to him: "I gather you are saying that people should never think about why they feel the way they do and should simply act on their first impulses?" Wilson was "horrified" and had "images of people following the reporter's conclusions about my research, leading to increases in teen pregnancy, drug relapses, and fistfights," he writes. "It would be odd for a psychologist to tell people never to think about themselves, and this is not my message." It's really not Gladwell's message, either, but you can see why that version of it appeals to marketers and the research companies that work for them. Rational thinking, one speaker noted that morning, leads to conclusions, whereas emotional thinking, based not on deliberation but on following impulsive gut instincts, leads to actions. "We want actions," he summarized.

The business of the commercial persuasion industry is not to trick us, but to give us a rationale, something that will inspire Consumer Economicus to take "actions." And the patterns and data sets that confront us have been getting bigger, more unwieldy, and much harder to avoid. It's unlikely that the basic human cognitive behaviors that make up the Desire Code have changed in recent years or can change very much in the years to come. But lots of other things are changing, very quickly and quite a bit. Your interpreter will have plenty to do in the new era of murketing.

part two
murketing

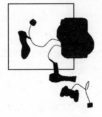

In April 2002, Jamie Kellner, the chairman and CEO of Turner Broadcasting, had something to say about the revolutionary technology of the digital video recorders, such as TiVo, that were just starting to gain national consumer attention. These devices (as is now well-known) are a bit like souped-up VCRs, allowing you to, among other things, click right past the advertising in shows you have recorded. "Because of the ad skips," Kellner declared, "it's theft. Your contract with the network when you get the show is you're going to watch the spots. Otherwise you couldn't get the show on an ad-supported basis. Anytime you skip a commercial . . . you're actually stealing the programming."

Not surprisingly, Kellner was ridiculed. Aside from the apparent absurdity of anyone even wanting to "steal" the junk on commercial television (his critics laughed), this hapless flunky for the infotainment complex was clearly sputtering and flailing because a killer app was taking control away from him and his dinosaur industry. He was obviously in denial about the complete transformation of traditional, ad-supported network broadcasting. Of course, back in 2002, as one observer pointed out, there were actually more outhouses than digital video recorders in U.S. homes. But as early as 1999, when TiVo barely existed, *The New York Times* passed along the assertion of a Forrester Research analyst that this device presaged "the end of network television." Within ten years, the analyst declared, 80 percent of American homes would have one, and the "viewing of commercials" would be halved.

In the years since, TiVo became just one entry on a list of potentially revolutionary innovations tied to television, the Internet, or both: Google and YouTube, MySpace and Facebook, on-demand audio and video for the iPod and other devices, and so on. Everything was bad news for old media – like network TV – and thus good news for everybody else. "The fundamental premise of traditional broadcasting is its ability to control the viewer," *Wired* magazine later chimed in, asserting that this control is "being blasted away entirely" by the technologies of freedom. Meanwhile, *Time* magazine declared that the Person of the Year for 2006 was none other than You. ("You control the information age. Welcome to your world.")

"This scenario," *Advertising Age* columnist and media observer Bob Garfield told one interviewer, "is potentially the most wonderful thing imaginable for media consumers in a democracy." Unless, he added, you happen to be a marketing industry veteran. "Then you're fucked big-time."

If you had to reduce this new technological freedom to a single gesture, that gesture would be the click. The roots of the click can be traced all the way back to the 1950s, when the Zenith Corporation began experimenting with small wireless units that used ultrasound waves to control television sets from across the room. (A magazine ad for one of these early remotes, the Flash-Matic, noted that not only could it turn the set on and off and change the channels, but it had a mute feature that allowed you to "shut off annoying commercials.")

Eventually the click became the core gesture not just of remote controls, but of the personal computer, wireless communication devices, and the video game console. The click changed everything, doing away with that old scenario of "millions of people sitting in their shuttered homes at night, bathed in that ghostly blue television aura," as the business best seller *The Cluetrain Manifesto* described preclick consumers: the "passive couch-potato target demographic." The click is our escape route and a divining rod – this song is boring (click), this show is a rerun (click), this link looks interesting (click), this commercial is long and annoying (click).

The click does not mediate experience; it mediates media. It makes the clicker feel unpassive and free from control. To find the "just right" stimulus or diversion or information among dozens of DVD bonus features, the hundreds of cable channels, the thousands of songs on your iPod, the millions and millions of websites, to navigate the infinite possibilities of virtual worlds offered through the PlayStation and the Xbox, or the Internet-enabled terrains of Second Life or World of Warcraft, is to exercise the freedom from being trapped in a subpar media experience for even one second longer than is necessary: click.

Although most of human history has been click-free, practically any resident of the industrialized world born after 1980 has never known a world without a pervasive click presence. And it so happens that these technologies dovetail with certain attitudes among contemporary youth. The market research firm Yankelovich touted a report on the generation growing up with TiVo, instant messaging, wireless homes. It found that 78 percent of twelve-to-seventeen-year-olds feel "being in control" is important and a sign of success. "This generation is about authenticity, authorship, and autonomy," summarized Ann Clurman, senior partner at Yankelovich. "They want to customize and to have a nonpassive media experience."

And there is now a click for their every desire. TiVo gives us freedom from network ideas of "prime time" as well as advertising. YouTube frees us from the notion of the show itself (just click to see the highlight your friend sent or to watch some new creation she spliced together from existing sources or digital-videoed in a friend's bedroom). Wireless communication adds freedom of movement, among other things, to the equation. The iPod gives us freedom to program our own daily sound track. Podcasting and the Web give us freedom to seek out information and even become a producer or disseminator, rather than simply a consumer. Computer and video games free us from one-way, passive entertainment: The gamer does not watch the action, but rather controls it, shapes it.

The conventional wisdom about all this can be broken into two parts. The first is simply that a big change is under way and will keep getting bigger and, you know, changier. That seems true enough. In fact, hardly anybody denies it.

The second part of the conventional wisdom is basically that what's bad for television executives is good for America – and indeed the world. Big changes enabled by technology and led by youth will result in a previously unimagined empowerment. Those changes allow us to "collaborate" with, or exercise control over, big media, big brands, and big everything else. Gone are the days when the big guys could shove lowest-common-denominator fare down our throats, ordering consumers around and forcing us to buy their products and content. All the big experts say so.

The mass market – indeed, massness itself – is dead. No longer must we accept the stultifying, homogenized monoculture of decades past, as niche expression is made available to us at last. Companies must, as more than one guru has put it, provide "personalization."

Thanks to all of this, rationality will triumph in the marketplace of ideas and the marketplace itself.

Free at last, we can all be individuals in ways that were never possible.

And this is what we want: the custom, the personal, the individual.

The rational dominates; freedom wins.

Thanks to the click, the consumer is in control.

What, then, might the future look like?

murketing

At Alberta Park in northeast Portland, Oregon, about a hundred serious bicyclists, most of them young men, many tattooed and pierced, and at least one wearing striped tights and a floral thrift shop dress, arrived en masse on a Saturday evening. They gathered near a fenced-off hardtop court and, in teams of three, began a "bike polo" tournament. Almost all were bike messengers, about a third of them local (the rest came from Seattle, San Francisco, and elsewhere), and they lived up to the image of couriers as marginal, testosterone-charged troublemakers. They drank beer, smoked cigarettes (among other things), and yelled profane insults at one another.

On a broad stretch of Miami Beach shorefront, on a morning so perfect that it looked just like a commercial, three guys fussed with kiteboards – contraptions that consist of large, crescent-shaped parachutes rigged atop miniature surfboards. They were preparing themselves for an outrageous stunt: They planned to kiteboard to Cuba.

Inside an unmarked club in downtown Manhattan called Sixes and Eights, a young and distinctly multicultural crowd awaited the start of a DJ show featuring up-and-comer PF Cuttin, New York legend Qool DJ Marv, and headliner DJ Jazzy Jeff. At about 10:30, there was no dancing but a lot of networking and cell phone checking; people were pacing themselves, since the party was meant to go until 4:00 a.m.

Somewhere in Los Angeles, a couple of teenagers did skateboard tricks for a few friends, laughing and joking and killing time.

And at July 4 weekend cookouts up and down the East Coast and into the Midwest, guests arrived with packages of chicken sausage for their hosts, friends, and family members, to throw on the grill.

The people in these various scenes from the four corners of

the United States – each of which I'll bring you back to in the chapters ahead – have something in common. It's not just that many of them are members of the media-savvy, hard-to-market-to demographics that companies covet. What these scenes have in common is that each was made possible by some kind of brand sponsor – a relationship that was not only tolerated, but welcomed. These are all scenes from communities, and from a culture, now taking shape right alongside – and arguably because of – the mighty click. This is the new world of murketing.

Murketing, you will recall, is a word that I made up. And to be perfectly honest, I originally meant it at least partly as a joke, a satire of the annoying tendency of branding wizards to clutter the language with endless streams of silly neologisms. But there was a serious intent as well: I started using the word around the time that TiVo was beginning to get widespread notice, and by then I had been paying professional attention to commercial persuasion and the culture of consumption for a couple of years. Like many others, I believed that a significant shift of some sort was under way. "Murketing" served as my shorthand description of the practices of certain brand managers who aimed to blur the rules of the traditional sales pitch – to make marketing more murky.

But as I spent time dwelling on, and in, the borders between producers and consumers, I began to see murketing not just as a name for a set of tactics used by one side in a kind of struggle, but as a description of a relationship that was strangely interconnected, even reinforcing. And in time, I also found the phenomenon a little less amusing.

The dominant theories of consumer empowerment I sketched earlier have a surface logic and an undeniable appeal. But I often found that they did not line up with what I was seeing and hearing in the real world. Trying to reconcile this disconnect guided my reporting and research over the next several years. That period turned out to be the formative one for our current era of murketing.

chapter five

chuck taylor was a salesman

OFFICIAL MEANINGS . . . WHERE TIMBS COME FROM . . . ROOTS
OF MURKETING: THE 1980s . . . PINK BOOTS . . . OWNING
CONVERSE . . . CHUCKS FOR THE MASSES

official meanings

When marketing gurus talk about corporate brand managers
needing to "collaborate" with consumers, what they mean is that
those marketers no longer have as much control over the
"meaning" of a brand. Brand meaning has long been considered
a thing that is carefully built, shaped, managed, maintained, and
owned by the brand's corporate creators: Picture a bunch of suits
in a conference room, hashing out what exactly they are selling,
not just in terms of the product, but in terms of a kind of cultural
message to send or emotional promise to make. Perhaps they
consult the results of focus groups or other research that has
identified a consumer need or other market opportunity. Once
their idea is finalized, it is pushed on the masses by way of ads,
packaging design, and so on. If the idea changes, they're the
ones who change it. The process is a top-down one, and they
are on top.

The masses do not always acquiesce – and they never did.
Product and brand failures are as old as products and brands.

For instance: New Coke, introduced with the full might of traditional branding power in the still mass America of 1985 (slightly more than half of all television viewers were watching *The Cosby Show* that season), was roundly rejected by consumers in one of the most spectacular marketing flops of all time. This despite millions of dollars' worth of prelaunch research that included extensive taste-test data and interviews with around two hundred thousand consumers. The whole point of New Coke had been to give consumers what the company had concluded they wanted and would prefer. It turned out they didn't. And New Coke failed.

The mass-marketing era has been filled with brand and product failures large and small. The Ford Motor Company poured massive resources into consumer research for the marketing of the new car model it introduced in 1957 – but the Edsel tanked just the same. Although Procter & Gamble is widely recognized as a branding giant that used mass-media heft to build some of the best-known products of the twentieth century (Tide, Scope, Crest, and so on), it also launched plenty of products that aren't so well-known today, because they failed, too: bathroom-tissue brands Banner and Summit; Fling, a paper towel; toothpaste Pace; an aspirin called Encaprin; a bleach named Vibrant; liquid detergents Solo and Vizir; a tablet-style detergent called Salvo; and a "soft" cookie launched under its well-known Duncan Hines brand that, despite aggressive and expensive mass advertising, fizzled out.

So it's not quite right to say that everybody used to be perfectly passive couch-potato "androids" who did whatever advertising told them to do. The simple act of *not buying something* has always been – and remains – the form of consumer power that brand managers fear most.

But is it even true that those who *did* choose to consume a particular brand or product also consumed its "official" meaning?

where timbs come from

The makers of Timberland boots know exactly what their brand is all about. They have known it for years, and they have not come to it as a result of sniffing and focus grouping around popular culture looking for the Next Big Trend to align with. Timberland is not a trivial company; its 2006 global revenue was more than $1.6 billion, almost half of that from international markets. Jeffrey Swartz, the company's CEO, spoke with me about Timberland on a sunny fall morning in a park in Lawrence, Massachusetts. A boyish forty-two, with a wave of brown hair and glasses, Swartz clearly enjoyed talking about Timberland and what it stands for. He spoke quickly, with few pauses, in an almost excitable free-form flow that always seemed to bend back around to a particular set of answers, no matter the question. I started out by asking something about consumer segmentation, and his reply began with how the company came into being.

The company that became Timberland was run by Swartz's grandfather Nathan Swartz. The Abington Shoe Company, as it was called back in 1950, had a factory in northern New Hampshire run by a Camel-smoking ex-marine named Joe Butler. Butler, a difficult man to satisfy, told Sidney Swartz (Nathan's son and Jeffrey's father) that if he was so clever, he ought to make a shoe that would keep his feet from being cold and wet all the time. Motivated largely by a desire to show Joe Butler a thing or two, Sidney Swartz began to experiment with various waterproofing processes, and after a number of attempts came up with a waterproof boot. Butler was impressed and suggested that maybe the foreman of the stitching room could use a pair, too. Following the enthusiastic response of these first two users, in 1973 Abington released to the market what it called the Timberland boot. It was such a success that five years later the company was renamed. With a few modifications, this six-inch leather work boot with padding at the ankle – known among consumers as the

Construction Timb and in the footwear business by its production number, the 10061 – remains Timberland's biggest seller to this day.

So that's the story. Very simple: It's about a crusty, no-nonsense New England factory man, indifferent to anything but pure functionality. If his father had given any thought to aesthetics, fashion, or marketing, Swartz assured me, the boot would have matched the fashion of the time and been a rustic, earthy color – not something close to yellow. Swartz did not tell the colorful Timberland creation story because it is entertaining; he told it because Timberland has a clearly defined self-image, a top-down meaning strictly adhered to in every communication with the marketplace. One magazine spread from the late 1990s, for instance, paired an image of the company's Weather Trekker model with a miniessay about potential. A black-and-white photograph of the muddy, well-used shoes was captioned with a brief recapitulation of Timberland heritage, the functional attributes of the product, and the statement "We are proud of these boots." This official meaning came straight from headquarters, presented to the consumer. But I've picked an image from the late 1990s because by then Timberland had acquired a different meaning to a segment of consumers in the real-world marketplace.

Swartz took over day-to-day operations of the company in 1991, and even by that time, Timberland remained essentially a regional company. But a funny thing was happening to the brand: It was being embraced by a group of consumers that the company had not targeted and frankly did not understand: the "urban" consumer.

Timberland boots "stood up beautifully to urban elements like concrete, barbed wire, and broken glass," the hip-hop lifestyle magazine *Vibe* observed in an ode to the boots in its September 2005 issue. By the early 1990s, hip-hop and R&B artists were "bringing Timbs to the forefront of urban fashion. Soon everyone from thugs to step teams were stalking, walking in their six-inch construction boot," the magazine continued. A theme of the *Vibe* piece was the boots' surprising durability in "the fickle urban market," where fifteen years later they remained "an oft-referenced staple in hip-hop and R&B." And indeed, when the Museum of the City of New York presented an exhibition titled "Black Style Now" in late 2006 and early 2007, it included the Timberland boot (with baggy jeans, a New Era baseball cap, and an oversize white T) as part of what it labeled "the global hip-hop uniform." That durability has been a surprise, but maybe it shouldn't be, because really urban consumers did more than embrace Timberland. To a significant degree, they *defined* Timberland. They did it without being invited to "collaborate." And if they hadn't done it, it's hard to believe that Timberland would have gone from a $200 million company in the early 1990s to a $1.6 billion global brand of today.

The legend goes that the first "urban" buyers of Timberland boots were New York City drug dealers – guys who had to stand on the street all night and needed the best possible footwear to keep them warm and dry. (Just like Joe Butler! Sort of.) Perhaps a legend is all that is, but by the 1980s, Timberland boots were popular at Michael Persaud's New York high school. "We were that group, that generation that really grew up with hip-hop," said Persaud, who went on to cofound Persaud Brothers, a marketing and promotion firm that specializes in the urban/hip-hop market. "Especially in the eighties, we were all about the next hot thing, discovering these things and making them our own," Persaud continued. He remembered Gucci and other luxury brands catching on. "I *had* to have that Gucci watch," he told me, looking back with a mixture of puzzlement and amusement at what motivated his teenage self. He chalked it up to a mix of product quality and aspiration – wanting what was perceived as the best. Persaud and his contemporaries tried Caterpillar boots, they tried other brands, and they settled on Timberland. They certainly didn't know anything about the folksy, workingman creation story that Swartz would later tell me. They knew that the boots were made with nice leather, held up well in the elements, and were expensive. They weren't sold in African American neighborhoods, but that was okay: Seeking the boots out, traveling to the Timberland store in midtown – this was all part of the experience, part of the attraction.

By the early 1990s, Timberland's new fans were gaining mainstream attention. *The New York Times* observed that Timberland had, "in the parlance of the street, become 'dope' and 'phat.'" Apart from making itself sound silly, the *Times* made it clear that no one at Timberland had seen this coming. And even when it came, the company *still* couldn't see the turn of events for what it really was. "Timberland is being adopted by a consumer that we didn't know existed relative to our target audience," Swartz told the *Times* back then, adding that his brand was all function, not fashion. Not only had the company not intended to expand its audience in quite this way, from Swartz's comments, it sounded an awful lot as though its intention had been the opposite: "If you want to buy us and you are not our target customer, we don't have a point of distribution that speaks to your lifestyle." Using words that he either chose very poorly or the *Times* selected in an unfortunate way, Swartz (who was thirty-three at the time) said that while the hip-hop consumer's "money spends good," the fact remained that his brand was aimed primarily at "honest working people."

This interview became a bit of a legend; a segment of the burgeoning hip-hop consumption audience slammed Timberland as an exploitative company that refused to support a culture that was supporting it – for example, by taking out ads in magazines like *Vibe*. Boycotts were discussed. But ultimately, the complaints did little to Timberland's actual sales; some consumers complained about Timberland ideology while wearing Timberland boots.

It's pretty clear, revisiting the article, that Swartz was more careless than calculating in his thinking about what was happening to his brand; he was a well-intentioned, slightly clueless New England businessman, not a predatory corporate bigot. One of the few times he has ever gotten directly involved in writing advertising copy for Timberland was his authorship of the slogan "Give Racism the Boot," one of many cause-marketing initiatives that predated his dustup with the hip-hop nation.

Still, Swartz *had* made a fundamental mistake. This wasn't that he seemed to think hip-hop was just an ephemeral trend. It was that he quite clearly believed he could have the last say on what his brand really stood for – on what Timberland really *means*.

roots of murketing: the 1980s

If do-it-yourself, skateboard, punk-influenced, "Beautiful Losers" culture is one key precedent for the murketing era, then hip-hop culture is the other. In *Can't Stop Won't Stop: A History of the Hip-Hop Generation*, Jeff Chang casts this culture as a thing happening "in the shadows of the baby boom," a "revolutionary aesthetic" that was "about unleashing youth style as an expression of the soul, unmediated by corporate money, unauthorized by the powerful, protected and enclosed by almost monastic rites, codes, and orders." There's a bit of that Outlaw archetype again, and Chang often sinks into romanticism, insisting on evaluating hip-hop as a fundamentally progressive and political movement, an argument that often proves strained.

But his history is thorough and insightful, and he identifies the key cultural, and economic, moments. "If blues culture had developed under the conditions of oppressive, forced labor," he writes, "hip-hop culture would arise from the conditions of no work." In a parallel to the Zephyr skaters scene, early hip-hop was a DIY affair; its birthplace, the South Bronx of the 1970s, seemed a hopeless wasteland, a zone of such squalor and disrepair that Mother Teresa visited. The symbols of self-made community mattered, even if here they took the form of street gang emblems. Chang quotes a Bronx gang leader of the time: "We were living our lifestyle. Back in England every family had their coat of arms. This is our family coat of arms."

It's not uncommon today to hear aficionados of the culture tell the story of hip-hop as a kind of fall from grace – from expressive purity to excessive materialism. "Hip-hop music made something out of what was considered nothing," Chuck D, front man of the seminal rap group Public Enemy, lamented to one twenty-first-century interviewer. "I mean, one of my main reasons for jumping onto hip-hop was because I liked the idea of defying the odds, being the underdogs. We ain't got no money, but we're happy with what we do. It was *you* that was important, and everything else would define you *after* you defined yourself. It wasn't like a brand defined you, *you* defined the brand."

In a clear and literal example, when Chuck D wore Philadelphia Phillies or Pittsburgh Pirates baseball caps in music videos, he transformed the "meaning" of the symbol simply by wearing it: It was understood implicitly that the "P" didn't stand for a sports team anymore – it stood for Public Enemy.

An even more compelling, and crucial, instance involves rap pioneers Eric B. and Rakim. Look at the cover of their 1987 album, *Paid in Full*. It is a famous image in certain circles, not because the artists are clutching fistfuls of cash and standing before a backdrop constructed of money (including hip-hop's favorite unit of currency, the $100 bill). And not because of their blingy-before-there-was-a-name-for-it gold chains. It's famous because of the custom tracksuits worn by the artists, distinguished primarily by enormous Gucci logos. It seems surprising that the owners of this luxury brand, whose clientele presumably prefers subtlety, would make such a thing, and in fact they did not. The suits were instead the creation of a Harlem resident named Dapper Dan.

Dapper Dan was (and is) a legendary customizer – his clients in the 1980s included Biz Markie, Big Daddy Kane, LL Cool J, and Salt-N-Pepa. He frequently used luxury brand logos as elements in a custom pastiche, in much the same way that a rap producer might lift a groove from Parliament or a beat from a James Brown record. As Persaud suggested, the Gucci logo certainly had currency in Harlem street style by the early 1980s; if you look at photos from that era, you may wonder where these garments positively *covered* with the logos of Gucci and other luxury brands came from. They came from Dapper Dan and other customizers, who seized these symbols that were loaded with top-down meaning from the world of haute couture and essentially used them to create something new, from the bottom up. The "Black Style Now" exhibit I mentioned earlier – the one that included Timberland boots as part of the global uniform of hip-hop – also included several Dapper Dan pieces, including a 1982 glazed calfskin jacket all-over-screened with Louis Vuitton logos and a jacket featuring Nike logos that apparently predates any actual Nike clothing.

Dapper Dan was not the only figure "collaborating" with corporate symbol makers long before marketing experts started talking about giving potential customers "permission" to do such things. In June 1986, a group of young graduates of New York's High School of Art and Design set up shop at the Coliseum Mall in Jamaica, Queens. Calling themselves the Shirt Kings, they sold that familiar commodity the T-shirt, given fresh value by way of custom designs – for example, the Tasmanian Devil of Looney Tunes fame, holding an Amstel Light. "A large part of their success was due to their use of childhood cartoon characters emblazoned on their merchandise in urban contexts," explained the curators' notes at the "Black Style Now" exhibition. Although the shirts took about half an hour to make, they cost $50. Needless to say, the Shirt Kings weren't clearing any of this with the trademark holders.

Both the making and the buying of such garments stand as a vivid example of a bottom-up seizing of absolute control of a logo, a brand, and its meaning. Through Dapper Dan's creations, luxury brands were given, against their will, a fresh significance to a new consumer who had never been those brands' intended target.

One of the founders of *Paper* magazine, a downtown New York fashion publication that started in 1984, has referred to the adoption of high-luxury logos by early hip-hop consumers as both the birth of the knockoff and a "brilliantly subversive political style movement." These emblems of "conservative" upper-class brands like Gucci and Vuitton were turning up "on the streets and at rap concerts," where urban kids "plastered these all over their casual sports clothes, as if to say, 'You think I can't afford to buy into your world? Look, I can put Gucci logos all over my tracksuit or baseball cap if I want!' And so the bootleg was born."

Actually, these clearly were not "bootlegs," since the whole point was not to re-create or knock off or otherwise counterfeit an actual Gucci product, but rather to create a *new* product Gucci-ed up by Dapper Dan or another customizer. And there's not much evidence to support the idea of politically subversive intent. The seizing of luxury logos was a fascinating turn of events, but not because it was intended as a rebuke. Indeed, the "Black Style Now" curators' notes say that customers "embraced Dapper Dan's aesthetic of outspoken, brazen clothes of instantly identifiable style and cost."

It's not just that hip-hop's creators were – like many of the DIY pioneers of "Beautiful Losers" culture – scrappy entrepreneurs whose underground-by-necessity promotional strategies were eventually hijacked by megabrands. That's true, of course. But hip-hop's hustling entrepreneurialism never really had any built-in qualms about material culture. Indeed, it's hard to think of another spectacular subculture that has emerged in the past fifty years that has so exuberantly venerated the leveraging of nonmainstream authenticity into entrepreneurial and material success.

Despite the revisionist history of many observers, what is now called bling was crucial to hip-hop long before P. Diddy was seen Jet Skiing in his bathrobe on the French Riviera or demanding that all the guests at his latest after-party have fresh manicures. The quasi-superhero costumes and space suits of early rap acts rather quickly gave way to a style more grounded in earthly material power – from the brand-dropping lyrics of the rapper Slick Rick that impressed Marc Ecko in his tween years to the enormous gold necklaces worn in the early 1980s by Kurtis Blow, Run-D.M.C., and many others. "For generations, black people were economically disadvantaged," Cheryl "Salt" James of Salt-N-Pepa later said. "So bling is a way for us to say, 'We're making it too!' It makes you feel good about yourself. Those shackles are platinum now."

Hip-hop was always grounded in the "authenticity" that the trend industry has lately found so important. But that authenticity wasn't just about being from the ghetto – it was about getting out of the ghetto. Certain influential hip-hop artists and their fans are "the best brand-building community in the world," the trailblazing rapentrepreneur-turned-lifestyle-mogul Russell Simmons has said. And this is particularly true for high-end products, he explained to me in an interview. "The reason they're good at luxury products," Simmons told me, "is because they've come out of so much struggle. They've looked around and studied, and when they get their first dollar they know exactly where it goes." Hip-hop rebellion was not against capitalist, material culture. Its rebellion was against *exclusion from* capitalist, material culture. Its rebellion was the rebellion of inclusion.

And it has succeeded. Today, Simmons argued, it's the hip-hop consumers who decide "if the Phantom Rolls-Royce or the Maybach is the coolest on the street – and they do it in the way that the rest of the world follows."

pink boots

Timberland reached a turning point in the late 1990s. Basically, Swartz told me, it started with retailers questioning whether he was "aware" of the boot's fashion status. Clearly Timberland was aware but had more or less ignored what seemed like a deviation from the brand's core meaning – it still offered boots only in basic colors because there was no *functional* reason to make, for example, a pink one. Swartz resisted such things, not because he had a problem with who his consumers were, but because he believed that functionality was the essence of his brand, and pinkness did not contribute to that. But his managers kept pushing him. "It was like 'If you want to have a conversation, a relationship, it can't be all about you,'" he recalled. "'Are you willing to listen?'"

He saw their point, but he still wasn't sure. He continued: "I asked my dad: 'What do you think Grandfather would say about the pink boot?' And my father says, 'Your grandfather would ask you how many pairs did you sell?' Okay. So that's one test, the commercial test. 'What do you think he would ask about the integrity of the brand?' And my father said, the questions he'd ask aren't about what it looks like; he'd ask if it was guaranteed, he'd ask the craftsmanship questions. He doesn't care pink or green or blue or brown." And thus: the construction Timb in pink, in blue, in a variety of colors that had offered nothing new other than fashionability.

In a way, Swartz told me, he is still not certain that he really understands the pink boot, and he worries on occasion about the test of time. But the proof is in the product line: Timberland's basic waterproof promise has been applied to a vast and ever changing array of styles. The company hired the marketing firm run by Michael Persaud – the guy who grew up as part of the Timbs consumer base in New York City. Persaud Brothers helped get the product to, for example, Big Boi of OutKast. The firm gave him the pair he is wearing on the cover of the massively successful album *Speakerboxxx* and gave Alicia Keys the pair that she wore in a hit Usher video. Later, Timberland brought a full-time urban marketing director on staff and launched promotional projects such as hiring artists to decorate unique leather billboards in spots like 188th Street and Fordham Road in the Bronx – and of course has been taking out ads in *Vibe* for years.

owning converse

While Dapper Dan and his contemporaries were reinventing the consumer-brand relationship in New York City in the 1980s, I was a teenager in a small Texas town, working out that fundamental tension between individuality and belonging. Certainly logos had some kind of meaning back then, but somehow it didn't seem as complex or pervasive. The Future Farmers of America kids wore Wranglers, the preppy kids wore Polo shirts, and as a result, I avoided both those brands. Like Ed Templeton, I had aligned myself with a smaller group that might have been considered "outcasts." The setting was a little too rural for skateboarding, but thanks to MTV and certain independent record stores in nearbyish Houston, we were more or less up on some version of the punk – or maybe "new wave" – subculture style. I suppose we considered the things we wore as emblems of rebellion: safety pins, self-bleached jeans, thrift store shirts, army surplus jackets. And Converse Chuck Taylor sneakers.

As I mentioned in the introduction, it was my realization – many years after high school – that I was bothered by Nike's purchase of Converse that made me understand I was not as immune to brand meaning as I had always thought I was. And it's safe to say that I'm not the only person who thought of himself as being above, and perhaps resistant to, the whole marketing thing, but who nevertheless saw Chucks as something different.

After the sale in 2003, Nike jacked up the marketing budget for its new brand. The managers of Converse hired the advertising agency Butler, Shine, Stern & Partners, of Sausalito, California, to handle the $10 million account. Butler, Shine came up with a quintessential click-era strategy, and one that was at the time quite novel: It would invite Converse fans to make ads. "Converse is a brand that is uniquely qualified to rely on its consumers to express themselves creatively," Greg Stern, president of the agency, explained to me. "It's always been worn by creative people; the brand itself is a symbol of creative expression."

Some sample ads made by Converse-wearing friends of the agency were posted to a site called ConverseGallery.com (along with one hundred cleared music tracks that potential ad makers could use), and then the agency "seeded" blogs and chat groups with an invitation to brand fans to "express yourself" by making a spot. People submitted more than 1,200 films, according to agency creative director John Butler. At least 41 of these became bona fide Converse ads. "We've given [our customers] the biggest canvas we have to express themselves – our advertising," Erick Soderstrom, Converse's global marketing chief, told *BusinessWeek*.

One expects that people working on behalf of a brand would talk up its authenticity and so on. But Kalle Lasn? He's the editor of *Adbusters* magazine, one of the noisiest and least compromising contemporary critics of the commercial persuasion industry. In 1999, he published *Culture Jam*, a book that railed against the "mental pollution" of marketing, blaming a culture of media images and endless sales pitches for rising rates of depression, alcoholism, even suicide. *Silent Spring* and other totems of ecological awareness "shocked us into realizing our natural environment was dying, and catalyzed a wave of activism that changed the world," he wrote. "Now it's time to do the same for our mental environment." Proposed solutions involved "demarketing," "subvertising," and a "guerrilla information war."

Given all of this, it was a surprise when, in October 2003, *Adbusters* announced that it planned to sell a sneaker. The controversy over the working conditions at factories in Asia where much sneaker making has been outsourced had quieted since the 1990s, but part of the point seemed to be to find a new way to apply pressure – and to offer consumers a chance to express their opinions through shopping. Instead of a traditional logo, the shoe featured a roughly circular smudge – a black spot meant to serve as visual representation of the antibrand. Made with environmentally friendly materials and ethical labor, the Blackspot would be designed to stand for big ideas: in this case, socially minded entrepreneurialism and grassroots capitalism. Lasn described the sneaker, straightforwardly, as "a kind of loose Converse knockoff."

This was not long after Nike had acquired Converse. Lasn contended that his sneaker's black-spot antilogo would spike his product with greater meaning. But to riff off the Converse look was to concede that, somehow, the Chuck Taylor All Star was not considered simply a commodity, but had a kind of integrity and meaning that had been besmirched by new corporate owners.

What is it about Converse, anyway?

chucks for the masses

The coolness of Chucks is, at this point, so legendary that it is taken for granted. Everybody knows it's the ultimate rebel sneaker, worn by a generation (or two) of fashion-rejecting punks. Stern had given me more examples of Converse wearers: Jackson Pollock, John Belushi, and John F. Kennedy. A famous *New Yorker* article that introduced the idea of the "coolhunter" into the national vocabulary actually opened with a Converse anecdote: Working for Converse, one of the coolhunters in the piece had deduced that "the cool kids had decided they didn't want the hundred-and-twenty-five-dollar basketball sneaker with seventeen different kinds of high-technology materials and colors and air-cushioned heels anymore," the 1997 article explained. "They wanted simplicity and authenticity."

Converse was actually on the verge of coming unraveled in 1997, in a culmination of a variety of problems (including the fact that whatever the cool kids thought, the expensive, high-tech shoes were slaughtering Converse in the marketplace). "In the 1990s, Converse couldn't keep up with Nike's high-performance shoe innovations," *The Washington Post* later summarized. In addition, the company still produced its sneakers in the United States rather than the low-wage sites used by its competitors, and its acquisition of sports apparel company Apex had caused problems. By 1999, the Converse had about a 2 percent share of the athletic footwear market; it lost $43.6 million, on revenues of $231.8 million; the following year, sales collapsed to $145 million, and in 2001 Converse declared bankruptcy. In reorganizing, the company shuttered its U.S. factories and moved production to Asia. It had about two hundred employees left when Nike bought the brand in 2003.

If you pick and choose carefully, you can find things here that bolster the idea of Converse's "authenticity": It held out longer than most shoe makers in caving to the controversial business of sourcing production overseas, for instance, and its low market share made the brand a de facto underdog.

All of this overlooks the fact that once upon a time, Converse had been the Nike of its era – dominant, endorsed by major athletes and popular nonathlete "lifestyle" consumers. Marquis Mills Converse founded the Converse Rubber Shoe Company in 1908; its first sneaker designed for basketball – a very young sport at the time – was the Converse All Star. Released in 1917, it was apparently quite innovative. A year later, a seventeen-year-old named Charles "Chuck" Taylor bought a pair. Taylor, the story goes, loved basketball (having been captain of his high school team in Columbus, Ohio) and loved the All Star. He even suggested possible improvements (involving better traction and an ankle patch for better support) at a company sales office in Chicago. Converse brought Taylor on board, and by 1923, his signature was right there on the patch of the Converse Company's flagship product.

Taylor played for a variety of pro teams while working with Converse, making him arguably the first player-endorser ever. And for the next forty years, he traveled around the country putting on basketball clinics – and promoting Converse shoes. "Chuck Taylor was considered a missionary for the game, traveling and preaching the basketball gospel to all who would listen," a tribute to the sneaker in the alternative-culture magazine *Mass Appeal* explained. "His sermons involved showing up to nameless gyms in a suit and some All Stars and spending the afternoon making baskets blindfolded or backwards, sometimes dropkicking the ball into the basket from 50 feet away." Instead of advertising, Converse hired any number of former ballplayers to give such clinics and handed out free pairs of All Stars to coaches. Taylor was the MVP of the sales team, racking up three hundred thousand miles a year and going through at least thirty Cadillacs.

Looking beyond athletes, the company also catered to what marketers today would call "lifestyle" consumers, introducing low-top shoes in the 1960s, along with a range of new colors (green, indigo, orange, and so on). At one point, it has been estimated, 90 percent of athletic shoes were Converse. Magic Johnson and Larry Bird endorsed Converse shoes, and the brand remained a force in pro basketball through the 1980s. When Michael Jordan's North Carolina team won the NCAA championship in 1982, he was wearing Converse. Nike's revolution in shoe technology and shoe marketing (aided, of course, by its paid endorser Jordan, the Chuck Taylor of his era) basically beat Converse by playing a better version of a game that Converse invented. Converse was a quintessential mass brand – that failed.

Who, then, bequeathed it its rebel cachet? It wasn't a meaning that came from the top. Chuck Taylor wasn't a counterculture icon; he was a salesman. Most of the company's official marketing had revolved around endorsements from athletes. When JFK and Pollock wore Converse, they were wearing some of the *least* individualistic sneakers around. Can we trace it all back to, say, the Ramones? The main problem with that theory comes into focus if you actually look at the cover of the first, groundbreaking Ramones album, from 1976: The four original members are all on the cover, in their leather jackets and unkempt hair and ripped jeans and filthy . . . Keds lace-ups and Sperry slip-ons. Marky Ramone has said that Dee Dee later was known to wear Chucks, but he, Johnny, and Joey all favored Keds.

It hardly matters. Because it wasn't any brand campaign or any indie-rock celebrity that gave Converse the meaning we're all so familiar with today. It was consumers who wore the sneakers. Long before Converse and its ad agency got around to giving consumers permission to make thirty-second spots on its behalf, those consumers had owned the brand's meaning. They didn't collaborate on it or co-create it – they created it.

And as with Timberland, it also hardly matters whether those consumers were what the brand owners had in mind. Whether back in the 1980s or today, consumers can give a brand a whole new set of meanings, whether they are granted official permission to "collaborate" or not. What's new is not that this is something that became possible only recently, thanks to technology or the new youth culture. What's new is that marketers have figured it out.

rebellion, unsold

THE MILITANT CONSUMER . . . BIKE MESSENGER POLO . . . THE
MYSTERIOUS RETURN OF PBR . . . NEWFANGLED YOUTH . . .
THE PROTEST BRAND . . . ROOTS OF MURKETING: THE 1940S
. . . SEE THROUGH THIS . . . MAKING THINGS UP

the militant consumer

The dimensions of the latest trends in consumer behavior were
outlined in an overview in the *Harvard Business Review*. This new
zeitgeist, the august publication explained, is being fueled by
"the efforts of consumers themselves," who have lately "become
articulate." One of the defining features of this fresh paradigm
is the new consumer's "demand for information." They are
banding together, becoming "better educated and better
organized," with a "growing familiarity with the mechanics of
advertising" and the endless range of gimmicky sales tactics.
They have "suffered from deceptive and stupid advertising" long
enough, and it is only inevitable that power should shift to them
in an economy that has moved from scarcity to abundance. "These
changes," the article summarized, "have tended to make
consumers more critical and to enhance their importance." Such
was the state of things . . . in 1939.

The *Harvard Business Review* was not the only observer to

essay the power and savvy of the newfangled consumer of that era. (Nor would this be *HBR*'s last word on the subject of consumer-centricity. In 1960, it published Theodore Levitt's "Marketing Myopia," a widely praised article pointing to the importance of a "thoroughly customer-oriented" business model. The products successful companies sell are "determined not by the seller but by the buyer. The seller takes cues from the buyer so that the product becomes a consequence of the marketing effort, not vice versa." He pointed to the U.S. auto industry's struggles at the time as an example of how to do it wrong.)

In 1939, *Business Week*, in a lengthy report, advised its executive readership about new forms of consumer skepticism and organization and argued that this "discontent" was something "businesses cannot afford to overlook because it has already assumed the proportions of a real threat to producers and distributors of advertised brands." The magazine suggested that *listening to consumers* was one way to solve the problem, noting with some optimism an upcoming conference bringing together various business and advertising experts, among others, to explore the theme "What Consumers Want." (Such efforts, the magazine stressed, cannot be faked; "if it is lacking in a sincere desire to do something for the consumer, that worthy will be quick to see through the disguise.") *Advertising Age,* in 1940, declared that the "militant consumer" is "THE major problem facing business – and particularly advertising" in the decade to come. *Ad Age* indicated that "to most advertising and merchandising men" this new consumer was "an incomprehensible ogre."

Apparent similarities to our own era notwithstanding, that earlier "consumer movement" was quite distinct in its way. It was founded on collective action and included proposed solutions like cooperatives. There was also a lot of interest among some groups in labeling schemes involving grading systems and quality seals. *Business Week* noted the "fear that if the program should succeed the consumer would be tempted to buy solely on the basis of price and grade comparison and would not therefore be as responsive as at present to other product virtues detailed in advertising – unmeasurable virtues like style and flavor, for example."

In any case, ours is clearly not the first era in which commercial persuaders have felt threatened by a bosslike – or, perhaps, ogre-like – consumer. But consumer resistance takes distinctly different forms these days.

bike messenger polo

The rowdy bike messengers at that park in Portland, Oregon – yelling, slugging beer from forty-ounce bottles, and smashing into one another in their "bike polo" matches – did not seem the sorts to play any kind of role in the creation of brand meaning. They seemed like another variation of the Outlaw archetype: Willful outsiders, indifferent to rules and norms, with the creatively reconfigured and customized bikes, they were authentic and alive and as far removed from the rigid world of commercial persuasion as it is possible to be. They seemed not just indifferent to the culture of branded materialism, but hostile to it.

But what appeared to be a slightly unlawful party in the park was in fact part of the West Side Invite, prizes for which were underwritten by a $1,750 contribution from the Pabst Brewing Company. Curiously, there were no banners or signs announcing the beer maker's role in their fun, and no one from Pabst was on-site to glad-hand the bikers. Pabst Blue Ribbon – PBR, as fans call it – was in the midst of a highly unlikely comeback, and the unruly bike messenger subculture had something to do with that. If the stories of Timberland and Converse show us that it was possible for consumers to "collaborate" in, or simply invent, brand meaning long before corporations started talking about letting them do so, PBR's story adds a new wrinkle. Unlike the owners of the Timberland brand, PBR's marketers did not flinch at the sight of an accidental consumer base. And unlike the Converse team, they didn't belatedly convert consumer-made meaning into a showy ad gimmick. What they did do is a key chapter in the new culture of murketing.

the mysterious return of pbr

In 2001, sales of PBR declined – just as they had been doing steadily for a quarter of a century – and dipped to less than a million barrels a year. This was the brand's lowest sales figure in decades, a dizzying 90 percent below its 1975 peak. Then, in 2002, sales rose, 5.3 percent. The momentum picked up the following year. Soon the brand was endorsed in *The Hipster Handbook,* a paperback dissection of cool, and popping up in trendy bars from the Mission District to the Lower East Side. Sales in Chicago alone popped 134 percent. Some observers suggested that trendiness would quickly reverse into a backlash, but sales grew steadily each year, and in 2006 the brand's volume was more than 1.6 million barrels, according to trade publication *Beer Marketer's Insights.*

The growth started and was most pronounced in Portland – a city best known in the cosmology of beer as a haven for fancy "craft" offerings. There, the lowbrow brew had risen to the number five-ranked beer in town and the fastest-growing of the top fifty domestic beer brands. In local supermarket sales, it trailed only Coors Light, Budweiser, Bud Light, and Corona.

At first, even the people at Pabst – which had barely advertised for more than twenty years – were at a loss. The trend-explaining industry framed the rise of PBR as part of an alleged "retro-chic" movement. A subset "white trash" theory linked PBR to Levi's (whose sales had actually fallen) and trucker hats (a fad that was revealed and snuffed out almost simultaneously, when Ashton Kutcher wore one on his MTV show, *Punk'd*). One zeitgeistmeister even suggested that PBR drinkers were inspired by the blue-collar heroes of 9/11. Some cited the famous scene in *Blue Velvet,* when the character named Frank Booth, played by Dennis Hopper, reacts to another character's preference for Heineken by saying: "Heineken? Fuck that shit! *Pabst Blue Ribbon!*"

None of this was particularly convincing. *Blue Velvet,* for example, came out in 1986, and it seems odd to overlook fifteen years of falling sales in all demographics in all parts of the country and credit the movie with an eventual resurgence. It surely doesn't hurt to have a connection to Dennis Hopper and David Lynch, and the movie is an important part of the PBR mystique, but it hardly explained the brand's resurgence.

The job of finding a less ethereal explanation – one that the Pabst Brewing Company could actually *do* something about – fell to Neal Stewart. Stewart was a baby-faced twenty-seven-year-old when he joined Pabst as a divisional marketing manager in the summer of 2000. PBR was anything but hot. For the most part, the company was still focused on its stalwart forty-five-to-sixty demographic. Stewart mentions low-grade car-racing sponsorships, country music events, and "fishing promotions." But a sales rep in Portland had noticed that "these alternative people" were "starting to get into the brand," Stewart, who had blond-streaked hair and a snowboard on his office wall, told me. The rep, Stewart said, "was as straitlaced as could be. He wasn't someone who really understood the culture." Pabst had not been targeting these drinkers, he added: "It was just a group of people who embraced the brand."

So Stewart went to Portland to visit bars where PBR was selling. He dropped into the Lutz Tavern near Reed College. Slumming students here used to drink Blitz, a low-priced, locally brewed brand that went out of business in 1999. That year, the owner of the Lutz Tavern decided to start selling cans of Pabst for $1 (they cost the bar about 35 cents each) as a summer special. Years later, the sale still hadn't ended, and PBR was the bar's top seller. Stewart then braved the Ash Street Saloon, a bike-messenger hangout downtown. Portland bike messengers had also favored Blitz, again because it was cheap. They had switched to PBR, too. Those bar visits were startling. Stewart would walk in – wearing street clothes, never a Pabst logo – tell the bartender who he was, and "really just sit there," he recalled. "The word would leak out – 'Hey, the Pabst guy is here.'" He carried a bag of PBR key chains and T-shirts; Stewart had once been a cog in the gigantic Anheuser-Busch marketing machine in St. Louis and had firsthand experience with barging up to drinkers and foisting trinkets on them. For the Pabst guy in Portland, that wasn't necessary: "I was mobbed."

The interesting thing about this was that the common theme among those who "embraced the brand" seemed to be that they were young, smart, often skeptical types – the kinds of people who can't be fooled by marketing and in fact tend to detest it.

newfangled youth

The early twenty-first century was, it would seem, a uniquely trying time to sell anything at all to young people. In early 2006, *Forbes* ran an article about teenagers that stands as a typical model of the way contemporary youth – the seventy million or so Americans born between 1979 and 1994, often referred to as "Generation Y" or "the Millennials" – are written about in the context of commercial persuasion. Like other such articles, it asserted that selling to these exotic creatures is harder than ever. "For retailers catering to the teenage market, life used to be a lot simpler. Develop a product most of them wanted, market the heck out of it, then sit back and watch the group mentality kick in, assuring big sales of the latest trendy sneaker or clothing item." This era was declared to have ended – just recently. "Homogeny and old group stereotypes are out, individualism and authenticity are in," the magazine announced.

Earlier, *The Wall Street Journal* published a series of articles about marketing to young people. "They can tell when they're being marketed to," the producer of a teen-oriented movie lamented to the *Journal*, which asserted that "the ability to decode marketing messages is like a birthright" to this generation. "The same formulas that resonated with earlier generations no longer work," summarized a report on a panel discussion by teen-focused marketers. "Generation Y doesn't trust the traditional news media as much as earlier generations . . . Youth in this group . . . hate being ad targets." According to another study from a marketing firm, two-thirds of teens say there is "too much marketing and advertising in the world." An earnest PBS documentary confirmed for its viewers that teenagers "don't operate the same way as the rest of us. They're a stubborn demographic, unresponsive to brands and traditional marketing messages."

What's with these newfangled young people? One expert contends that they are so "sophisticated" because "they've lived through wars, they've lived through a lot of instability." Another agrees that members of this age group, having grown up in a fast-changing and even chaotic world, are "very pragmatic" about money and the importance of planning for the future: "They don't want to be as stressed as their parents, they want to be able to relax. And many of them say that being in control of their lives is a sign of success in adults."

Most of all, they are individuals, not followers. That's why they supposedly don't shop at the Gap or listen to popular music, like those old robotically conformist teenagers. And what do they consume instead? According to the *Forbes* article: Abercrombie & Fitch and sneakers that Nike "lets you customize" online. "The teen preference for individualism can also be summed up by today's hottest product – Apple Computer's iPod. While it may have achieved 'gotta have it' status, Apple got it there by equipping it with the capability to allow for individual preferences – kids can load it with whatever music suits their tastes." An accompanying sidebar claimed that in the past, "buying the latest CD kept you from feeling left out," but now it's all about "filling your iPod with your own tunes, with little mind as to who else might have them."

Okay. Now take another look at the allegedly "easy" method of selling to young people in the good old days: "Develop a product most of them wanted." Oh, is that all? Just develop a product most youth want? Sure, *anybody* could do that. (And if you develop a product "most of them want" today, won't most of them, um, want it?)

As for the iPod: *Every* MP3 player, including all the various models that predated Apple's famous device, has the "capability to allow for individual preferences." Likewise, the Walkman, a CD player, and even a record player not only can be, but almost always is, loaded with music that suits the taste of whoever owns it. If you have a teenager who wants an iPod, buy him or her a lower-priced knockoff. Explain that having the same stuff everybody else has is *out* and that this will make him or her more of an individual. See how that goes over.

Besides, how do we square this marketing-resistant generation with another point that the experts always make: that many members of Generation Y demand the toniest designer clothes, the best cell phones, the most complex lattes? *The Washington Post* strolled high school halls filled with Louis Vuitton and other luxury brands and pointed out that teenagers buy designer labels at double the rate of the population at large, and that a typical college sophomore carries a $2,000 credit card balance. A study by the Keller Fay Group, released in 2007, claimed that teenagers have roughly 145 conversations about brands *a week*.

It makes you wonder what it means to "see through" the tactics of marketers and brand makers.

the protest brand

The early adopters of PBR tended to be just the sort of clever young people who can easily decode the commercial pitches swirling around them (or at least the subset of that group that's old enough to buy beer). This was the conclusion of Alex Wipperfürth, founder of a San Francisco marketing boutique now known as Dial House. His firm did a little consulting work for Pabst, and Wipperfürth later wrote a book that drew on his work for PBR and other brands; it's called *Brand Hijack,* and a hijack is exactly what he saw in the story of PBR. Although he mentioned *Blue Velvet,* the heart of his analysis turned on a slightly different axis, one that pulled everything from vague identification with the working class to the no-future ennui of staring down a winner-take-all economy. The most interesting aspect of his theory, however, was that PBR's fan base grew not despite the lack of marketing support, but *because* of the lack of marketing support.

The beer industry as a whole spends about $1 billion a year to pitch its product. Most of this advertising, through huge TV campaigns and relentless logo slathering, is devoted to image building (not surprising, since *Consumer Reports* concluded a few years ago that even devoted fans of the megasellers Budweiser and Miller Genuine Draft could rarely tell them apart by taste). Long-neglected PBR had no image. It was just there. Scarce and cheap, it had few negative connotations, and a rumor that Pabst was about to go out of business (untrue) worked for some as a "rallying cry," helping make it an "underground darling." Beyond that, it was a kind of blank canvas, where brand meaning could be filled in by consumers. And that's pretty much what happened.

The single key text in Pabst marketer Neal Stewart's codification of the meaning of PBR was, of all things, the book *No Logo,* by the journalist and commentator Naomi Klein. Published in 2000, *No Logo* presented an argument about branding and marketing overload, the bullying and rapacious mind-set that this trend represented, and evidence of a grassroots backlash against it, especially among young people. Klein's view was that this would feed a new wave of activists who targeted corporations. Stewart's view was that the book contained "many good marketing ideas." He said it "really articulated the feelings, the coming feelings, of the consumer out there: Eventually people are gonna get sick of all this stuff" – all this marketing – "and say enough is enough."

Under these circumstances, the thinking went, PBR needed to stay neutral, "always look and act the underdog," and not worry about those who look down on the beer (they could be dismissed as snobs whose negative opinion only boosts PBR's street cred). The analysis that Wipperfürth put together even said that PBR's embrace by punks, skaters, and bike messengers made it a political, "social protest" brand. These "lifestyle as dissent" or "consumption as protest" constituencies are about freedom and rejecting middle-class mores, and "PBR is seen as a symbol and fellow dissenter."

To me, this line of thought sounded fairly close to satire. But it guided the way Stewart proceeded. A traditional response to the discovery that "alternative people" were buying the beer in Portland – taking out ads on local alt-rock stations – was nixed. Partly because it seemed crucial to at least appear to be doing as little as possible, when Kid Rock's lawyer came sniffing around to work an endorsement deal, Pabst said no. The company also passed on the chance to back a major snowboarding event or to sponsor an extreme athlete. Even upbeat five-year plans for where the brand could go envisioned no television advertising at all. So what does that leave? It leaves things like cash payments to rowdy bike messengers who want to screw around in the park but don't want to deal with banners or company reps getting in the way.

It's striking how many of PBR's minirelationships were initiated by the representative of some subculture approaching

Pabst. Stewart didn't court the bike messengers of Portland; one of them approached him. Later, he started hearing from messenger groups in New York and elsewhere. Other sponsorship requests were relayed to him through contacts at undergroundish magazines like *Vice* and *Arthur*. Each little sponsorship effort – skateboard movie screenings, art galleries, independent publishers – expanded the network.

Of course, another reason for this approach was that Pabst really was a bit player in its industry, and the PBR marketing budget was measly. Stewart reckoned that a deal with Kid Rock – maybe half a million to sign him up and another million promoting the association – would have emptied his coffers for the year. Still, PBR was starting to sound like some kind of small-scale National Endowment for the Arts for young American outsider culture, which seemed sort of cool, although not quite a marketing strategy. And more to the point, sales growth continued apace.

A year or so after Stewart took his trip to Portland, I took one. I was met there by Scott Proctor, who a few months earlier had joined Pabst as its Oregon sales manager. A beer business veteran – he referred to bars as "accounts" – he had spent years working for Blitz-Weinhard before its brands were sold or discontinued and its brewery shut down. He remembered Pabst having "a minute base" in Portland: In 1999, the company had just forty-one bar accounts there. Five years later, the number was more than ten times that. Proctor, forty-eight, was affable – and openly baffled by the "weird" PBR base. "I've seen some different accounts than I would normally see, if I was gonna go have a beverage myself," he remarked. "I had to open my mind a little bit."

Just before my visit, a Portland alternative paper, *Willamette Week*, had run a big picture of a guy drinking PBR at the Lutz Tavern, with a blurb that mocked "middle-class, college-educated, salaried Portland hipsters" for drinking PBR. "It's totally not indie rock! So there!" Was a backlash under way, then?

We visited the Lutz Tavern, a homey place with a pool table and an apple green linoleum bar top. As "Planet Claire" played on the jukebox, the bartender and a few postcollege-age patrons, all of them young women drinking cans of PBR, mulled the state of the brand. They promptly brought up the no-advertising thing, and while the subject of poseurs treating the beer as a fashion accessory came up, it didn't seem like much of a problem. They encouraged us to eat down the block at the Delta Café, which sold southern-style food and, for $3, forty-ounce PBRs served in a small bucket of ice. When we drove through the vaguely bohemian Hawthorne neighborhood, every bar seemed to have a PBR sign. In the Fred Meyer grocery store, there was more shelf space in the cooler for PBR than for Budweiser. It was like a parallel universe.

Later (without Proctor) I went to Alberta Park to check out the bike polo shenanigans. Ryan Kelley, a comparatively mild-mannered messenger who actually arranged the first PBR sponsorship, allowed that the beer's newfound popularity was slightly annoying. "But basically," he said, "we're going to drink whatever beer costs a dollar." (That's Pabst.) Another rider, Tad Bamford, sweaty, with big hoop earrings and an open cut on his elbow, looked at me as if I were a fool when I asked him whether PBR's trendiness might cause him to abandon the drink. "Yeah, I know all about that." He paused. "And I couldn't care less." He seemed to be finished with me at that point, so I moved on.

Eventually, I ended up at the dank and scruffy Ash Street Saloon, where I met a twenty-eight-year-old named Phil Barnes, who had recently gone through four tattoo sessions to get a Pabst logo about a foot square burned into his back, which he showed me. "Pabst is part of my subculture," he said emphatically. "It's the only beer I think about." He was a skateboarder, worked as a cook, and described his peer group as "scumbag punk rockers." Barnes was a little cagey about talking to me at first – his friends worried that somehow a picture of his tattoo would get used to promote Pabst and he wouldn't be compensated. Later, however, he noted that he had never seen a Pabst ad of any sort, which he liked because it showed that "they're not insulting you." Barnes had seen that *Willamette Week* item making fun of PBR drinkers, and he had given it a lot of thought. He had concluded that he did not care. "The only thing that's going to stop me from drinking Pabst is when I die," he said, lighting a cigarette.

roots of murketing: the 1940s

Youth-culture consumer behavior really is worth understanding, but clearly the dominant theories of the brandproof young person don't seem to square with the story of PBR, let alone with the almost alarming brand loyalty of a guy like Phil Barnes.

Much of today's rhetoric about young people is not as new as it sounds. As Thomas Hine explained in *The Rise and Fall of the American Teenager*, the earliest iteration of what we today recognize as youth culture arose in the 1920s and became a fully realized "social invention" in the 1940s. Through the nineteenth century, most young people simply transitioned into the adult work world as soon as they were able, because families needed the money; "there were probably more teenagers working in mines than attending high school. There were certainly many more teenagers working in factories." The fourteen-year-olds of the time were "viewed as inexperienced adults."

But a couple of decades into the twentieth century, the influence that young people can have over their elders – frequently discussed as a new development by trend watchers today – was already in place. "Immigrants' children taught their parents how to behave in America and thus acquired a measure of authority we still accord to our youth," Hine writes. The boomy 1920s were "the first great era of youth fads," many of which (like Valentino pants and the Joan Crawford flapper look) came from the movies. It was also in this era that young men and boys introduced their parents to a cool new device called the radio. People began to worry that perhaps children were (to use a popular recent phrase) getting older younger. "The Modern Youth Is Far Different from the Youth of Yesterday," advertising trade magazine *Printer's Ink* advised its readers in 1922: The "boy of today" is " 'wise' beyond belief . . . [H]e analyzes. His mind really thinks, quickly." The old stories of his parents don't interest him, as he focuses on the new world ahead and how he will shape it and "bust" the "older folks' . . . suppression of youth." (Meanwhile, Dorothy Parker was poking fun at the packaging of youth difference, or "Younger Generation Inc.," as she called it, as early as 1923: "The incoming fashions helped the young people's cause along," she wrote in *The Saturday Evening Post* that year. "Bobbed hair and short skirts were news items. . . . Women's clubs all over the country passed resolutions stating that they never in all their lives had seen anything like it.")

While the Depression put the youth-culture trend on hold, the New Deal did much to cement it as part of the basic fabric of society. In particular, new laws were designed to keep teenagers out of the workforce, basically to protect job opportunities for men with families to support. "The enforced separation of young people from the economic mainstream," Hine writes, sparked "the emergence of high school as the common experience of young Americans," which "led directly to the emergence of teenagers as we know them today." High school enrollment in the Depression increased by 50 percent, from 4.43 million to 6.5 million. These developments "bureaucratized" teenagerness, as he puts it, and teens occupied a new social role, "whether they liked it or not."

By the 1940s, teens in particular were "seen as style setters," and clothing manufacturers were already targeting them with teen-specific labels. In about 1944, a coolhunter prototype named Eugene Gilbert emerged as perhaps the first guru of the youth market. His insights included pointing out that "teenagers would respond to retailers who cared about what they wanted" and that "the best way to find out what young people really wanted was to get other teenagers to ask them." He even had a network of five thousand "teenage pollsters." (He also later figured out that his "young poll takers could themselves influence their subjects to buy his clients' products and make them fashionable," an insight that "increased [Gilbert's] profits.") Gilbert estimated 1958 teen purchasing power was $9.5 billion, or about $68 billion in 2007 dollars. Plus, as he pointed out at that time, teens could and did influence their parents into buying "new, more stylish furniture or clothing, or a new car."

It was by way of 1940s youth culture that the notion of identity leisure was created, right along with the various youth-culture stereotypes that have been repeated ever since. Baby Boomer youth culture, and a good deal of the rock music that served as its sound track, was supposedly about (at least in part) challenging bourgeois materialism and a vacant consumer culture. In *The Conquest of Cool,* writer Thomas Frank describes how starting in the late 1950s, leading ad makers like Bill Bernbach crafted their work for a generation that was "smart and extremely skeptical toward conventional advertising." A commentator on the advertising business, listing the reasons that it had trouble in the 1970s, started with: "You had a baby boom generation that was cynical about the American dream, at least the way Madison Avenue portrayed it." Much of the subculture expression on view at that "Beautiful Losers" show was created by members of the next inhabitants of this social category – Generation X – who decoded supposedly youth-friendly products like OK Soda as attempts to commoditize the so-called slacker aesthetic and were appalled. As Frank pointed out, commentators of that era "almost mechanically" repeated the youth market conventional wisdom of the 1960s. ("Consumers, especially young consumers, have learned to tune out conventional ads," *Business Week* revealed in 1996.)

The reality of youth in each of these generations was the same as today: It is an age for resolving the fundamental tension of modern life. "Despite the mythology of youth as a revolutionary and utopian time," Hine points out, "study after study suggests that teenagers' principal preoccupation is to adapt, to find a place in life." Here Hine hits upon a psychological truth: Even childhood games, tied up as they are in pretending and role-playing, are emotion-laden exercises in trying on identities. The most obvious sources of a tension-resolving identity – the family you have built, the work that you do, the religious or perhaps national community that you belong to – gained a new rival, which was how you spend your leisure time. For a young person, leisure and consumption were – and remain – a good deal more salient than any of those other concepts, for reasons that are self-evident. Leisure decisions are the easiest way to reconcile the tension between fitting in and standing out. This does not make modern youth different from all who came before. It makes them just like you, or me, or anyone who is reading this book and has been, or is, young: that is, everybody.

see through this

Here, then, is the real problem with the argument that this new generation sees right through traditional advertising and therefore is not fooled by its messages: *Everybody* sees right through traditional advertising. You'd have to be an idiot not to recognize that you're being pitched to when watching a thirty-second commercial.

But recognition is not the same thing as immunity. And what's striking about contemporary youth is not that they are somehow brandproof, but that they take for granted the idea that a brand is as good a piece of raw identity material as anything else. These are the consumers, in fact, who are most amenable to using brands to fashion meaning for themselves – to define themselves, to announce who they are and what they stand for.

As it happens, I have never heard anyone make the case for generational difference better than Jeri Yoshizu. She's a key player in the marketing of a new Toyota automobile, which I'll say more about in a little while. We once had a conversation about Generation Y, and particularly about how it differed from the previous youth market, which had been labeled Generation X – of which both she and I were a part. In general, she said, "X is a lot more pessimistic." She told an anecdote about a friend from her college days, an alt-rock type, who has ended up driving a shuttle bus for a university and refused to sell ad space on it; apparently, he didn't want students to think he was selling them out in some way. Yoshizu sounded impatient with her friend's attitude. "Those kids don't care," she said. "They understand. Y accepts advertising and marketing." They are not, she argued, hung up on the notion of "selling out."

This was essentially the opposite of what I had been hearing and reading about the new youth culture. But it squared more easily with the notion that, as some have argued, this is arguably the *least* rebellious generation since the youth concept was invented. "They adore their parents, they want to succeed, they're optimistic, trusting, cooperative, dutiful, and civic-minded," a writer in the conservative *City Journal* enthused. "If Millennials have a problem with authority, it's that they wish they had *more* of it." *American Demographics* reported that its polling found that 67 percent of teenagers "give Mom an A." In another poll, about 74 percent of college students said succeeding financially was an important life goal, compared with 40 percent who said so in the late 1960s. Yoshizu's theory also made more sense out of why, say, self-styled ad-hating consumers would take on a sponsor to fund their art shows or bike polo matches. It's not that contemporary youth are somehow more crass or materialistic than anybody else, let alone the Generation X or even Baby Boomer iterations of youth culture. "They're just smarter," she said.

making things up

The Blackspot sneaker that I mentioned earlier – the creation of the antibrander, Kalle Lasn, and his *Adbusters* crew – is premised on the belief that a logo (or antilogo) product can have real meaning for people who are sick of logos; it is premised on the belief that the marketplace of goods is a marketplace of ideas. The "hijacking" of PBR shows how this really can happen, although it's different from the Blackspot idea in two important ways.

The first is that while the meaning of the Blackspot as a sort of protest brand was created by *Adbusters* and announced to potential consumers, the meaning of PBR as a kind of protest brand did not come from its owners; it came from the grass roots, from consumers, from the bottom up.

And here is the second difference: On the side of every can of Pabst Blue Ribbon is a P.O. box in Milwaukee. Pabst does trace its roots to a brewery founded there in 1844. These days, however, Pabst Brewing Company is based in San Antonio. In 1985, the brewery was bought by Paul Kalmanovitz, a self-made beer and real estate baron. While other big brewers were spending to build national, image-based brands, Kalmanovitz's idea, apparently, was to buy up ailing ales, slash all associated costs, and let them "decline profitably." Kalmanovitz died in 1987 (Pabst is owned by the charitable foundation he left behind), and his lieutenants ran the show for the next dozen or so years along the same lines. The current Pabst Brewing portfolio includes Schlitz, Carling Black Label, Falstaff, Olympia, and Stroh's. It also owns a few regional stalwarts (Lone Star, Rainier, Old Style) and malt liquors (Colt 45, St. Ides). Its top seller, with about 1 percent of the U.S. beer market, is Old Milwaukee.

Along the way, Pabst shuttered its Milwaukee brewery, eliminating nearly 250 jobs and touching off a legal battle over pension obligations to former workers. This might explain another quirk of the Pabst resurgence – that it has radiated out from a part of the country that had no particular historic tie to the brand. "They really alienated people in Milwaukee," Dennis E. Garrett, a marketing professor at Marquette University in that city, told me. In 2001, Pabst finalized an outsourcing deal with Miller, becoming a "virtual brewer," as one executive put it at the time. Having virtually wiped out its blue-collar workforce, Pabst employed just 166 people, about half of them selling beer in the field and the rest in the home office. This, in other words, is exactly the kind of scenario that people like Lasn and books like *No Logo* were complaining about.

That is to say, PBR's blue-collar, honest-workingman, vaguely anticapitalist image – the image attached to it by consumers – is a sham. You really couldn't do much worse in picking a symbol of resistance to phony branding.

Does it matter? I actually doubt that a single PBR drinker who hears the history of Pabst Brewing will give up the beer as a result. PBR may be a political, "social protest" brand, as Alex Wipperfürth suggested, but not in a 1960s sense of political, which assumes a kind of zero-sum ideological game. In this new politics, symbolic solidarity with the blue-collar heartland trumps the real thing. (Actually, even as the brand made its comeback, that was thanks to growth in urban centers; it was still losing share in the rural Midwest.)

You could argue that no-benefits line cooks, bike messengers, and temps add up to new blue-collar equivalents, but perhaps the way to think of it is that the PBR base is less concerned with protesting boorish and heartless corporate behavior than with protesting boorish and invasive corporate sales tactics. It's very much a politics of individual freedom, of rejecting overt pitches and elite tastes. Pabst did not set out to fill that niche, but it was well positioned to do so. It turned out that PBR actually did have an image, but it was an image that its anti-image consumers can hardly complain about. After all, they're the ones who created it.

chapter seven

click

IN EVERY LIVING ROOM . . . THINGS THAT CAN'T BE TIVOED OUT . . . NEW PUBLICS . . . IN EVERY POCKET . . . DEODORANT AS CULTURE

in every living room

Late teens and twenty-somethings, *The Economist* argued in late 2000, "are the first young who are both in a position to change the world, and are actually doing so." The magazine's case was that this was largely because of the Internet and other new technologies – the click that's breaking up the passive media audience of the past.

What we think of as a media audience seems like something eternal, but it's really not that much older than youth culture. The media audience as we know it first came about in the 1930s or so, by way of radio. Before radio, a group of people experiencing something in real time (like a play, a concert, or a sporting event) were also experiencing it in real space. They were, in short, a crowd. The readership of a widely published newspaper or magazine or book might all consume a secondhand account of an event, but they were not actually *experiencing* it together. Radio listeners were. Listeners were a new kind of crowd – a disembodied one – and radio connected people to an experience or a message in a new way. That connection could center on a musical performance or on someone telling you that Pillsbury makes the best flour.

By 1933, more than 62 percent of U.S. households had radios, up from about 10 percent in 1925. "The simple fact is that never before in the history of the world have five or ten or fifty million people listened to the same sound at the same time," a vice president of the advertising firm BBDO declared in 1935. (He went on to explain the popularity of radio by noting that it "provides a vast source of delight and entertainment for the barren lives of millions," which is not the sort of thing you'd catch an ad executive saying today.) A radio host named Ida Bailey Allen, who was popular in the 1930s, spoke explicitly of radio forming a community. "There is Magic today," she wrote. "The Magic of great manufacturers who have taken drudgery away – the Magic of gas and electricity – the Magic of books and libraries – and we have Radio – that makes the Whole World Kin." Her "National Radio Home-Maker's Club," she claimed, had "a membership in the thousands" and more to come. "Rich or poor – sick or well – through your Radio, you can belong to this club." Her show had a variety of sponsors, and the positive effect of their association with her was also noted.

Naturally, the companies that made flour and any number of other products were keen to know who, exactly, was out there listening and what, specifically, they were listening to and how many of them, precisely, there were. These were "not only metaphysical questions but also economic ones," writes scholar Susan J. Douglas in her book *Listening In: Radio and the American Imagination*. She recounts how in the late 1920s and 1930s, a handful of people invented what we now call market research, to study the listeners as empirically as they could. "The object of this scrutiny – the audience – was itself an invention, a construction that corralled a nation of individual listeners into a sometimes monolithic group that somehow knew what 'it' wanted from broadcasting," she writes. Taken for granted today, the study of "how the audience spent its leisure time" was new then. Scholar Sharon Zukin takes this a step further: "Because they were studied – and appealed to – as reasoning subjects, consumers formed a new, modern *public*."

This "new, modern public" became, in effect, the dominant public for the next sixty years or so: the mass audience. Radio begat television and the Big Three networks, all built on the premise of massness – the maximum number of people looking in the same direction at the same time. Even before television sets were available to the general public, Gilbert Seldes, writing in *The Atlantic* in 1937, acknowledged that radio had proved an "incomparable engine of social influence," but argued that "the audience which television will create will be more attentive and, if properly handled, more suggestible even than the audience of radio." He had in mind extending radio's positive effects, such as (he asserted) the improved "oratory" of political campaigns. But all this is also what made the television set, as it was once described in the early days of TV power, "a selling machine in every living room."

The glue holding this mass together was, of course, advertising. Producers of consumer goods are often described as "buying advertising time" on networks, but that's not really what they're buying at all. What they are buying, and the networks are selling, is access to you. You are a commodity; you are part of an audience. Companies that sell products need to buy audiences. In essence, those companies say, "Here's $1 million, we want this kind of audience." The network says, "Okay, I'll get you that kind of audience," and designs its shows to draw the sorts of crowds that the companies want to reach. That's the transaction Jamie Kellner was pilloried for talking about. Technology makes it possible. Money makes it practical. Everybody gets something.

It's worth pointing out that cynicism about this transaction, criticism of the advertising model, and weariness with the pervasiveness of commercial persuasion predate the click.

Magazines like *MAD* in the 1960s and *Ballyhoo* in the 1920s mocked the hollow and ham-handed sales pitches of their eras. The advent of radio advertising was "hotly debated" in the 1920s, Susan J. Douglas observed in her book about the form, partly because for a brief time radio had seemed to offer some relief from the "visual onslaught" of billboards and magazines. One of the more amusing mainstream responses to commercial creep on the dial was a piece in the *New York Sun* in 1926, a fanciful account of a football broadcast in which sponsorship cluttered every sentence. ("It is a forward pass . . . a long forward pass under the direction of the Great Western Soap Powder Company, makers of the world's finest soap and cleaning fluids. The pass was caught by Schnapps, the Harvard back, who slipped on the wet ground under the auspices of the Hector M. Milligatawney Chocolate works, the world's leading manufacturer of bon-bons and almonds," and so forth.)

Popular novels, movies, and even *I Love Lucy* made fun of advertising. In one classic 1952 episode of the sitcom that commanded something like 68 percent of the television-viewing audience of its time, Lucy wheedled her way into a gig as the spokesperson for Vitameatavegamin, one of Ricky's sponsors. "It's so tasty," she says brightly, then takes a spoonful and makes an acrobatic series of miserable faces before choking out, "It's just like candy." Her director points out that "you're supposed to *like* the stuff," and she does her best, even though it turns out to be spiked with alcohol. The audience howls with laughter as she completely misrepresents an awful, addictive product that instead of pepping her up, as promised, makes her need to lie down. Evidently, even a 1952 audience could "see through" advertising hucksterism.

Still, the selling-machine-in-every-living-room model that made Lucy a megastar (and presumably did all right by her real-life sponsors) is the thing that's lately being clicked to pieces – hundreds of millions of pieces. TiVo, really, is the least of it.

Wireless devices, for instance, create a wholly new kind of public. If you were sitting in an auditorium, and I was standing at the front of the room lecturing you about all of this, then you and everyone else sitting there would be an audience, a public, in the sense that you were all listening to me. But at the same time, you could also be text messaging one another with a real-time critique of everything I said. Or about something totally different – a party tonight, or a movie you saw last week, or what time the bike polo starts this Saturday. You could also be texting people in other buildings. Or other cities. You could create your own public, and it would not have to be limited to people you know: If you had the right kind of phone, you could take my picture, write a rebuttal to my ideas, post it on your blog, and text message all your friends about it. All before I could even shut up.

Apply this scenario on a larger scale and you can see what the problem is for the top-down messages of traditional advertising: They have no authority – no control – over the new forms of public in the postclick world. No wonder Faith Popcorn, the famous futurist, is among the gurus who have declared that the advertising business is "on its way to extinction."

things that can't be tivoed out

I met Faith Popcorn late one windy morning at the offices of BrainReserve, her trend-spotting and consulting company, which had recently moved from its old home base in her town house on the Upper East Side of Manhattan to an imposing office building near the United Nations. The BrainReserve office was a bunch of cubicles, occupied by fifty or so employees who all wore black, with no visible logos.

Popcorn founded her business in 1974. Previously, she had studied acting at NYU and worked for an advertising agency before deciding to launch a venture built around the spotting of trends and the selling of insights related to those trends. She used to tell a colorful story about her memorable surname deriving from an Italian grandfather named Corne telling officials at Ellis Island that he was "a-Papa Corne." Eventually, *Newsweek* reported that she had simply made this up; her surname at birth was Plotkin.

In any event, by the mid-1980s she had dozens of employees and annual revenues estimated at $20 million. At least since 1996, she has been arguing that "people don't have faith in big companies anymore" and that this was bad news for major brands and their marketing efforts. Midway through the first decade of the twenty-first century, as many large companies seemed to be drawing the same conclusion, BrainReserve's business doubled.

I was ushered into a crisp conference room. There were pads and pens; the seating arrangement had been worked out in advance, so I sat where I was told. Popcorn, with a dyed purple streak in her hair, sat to my left. Three young BrainReservists, all women, took their seats. They all wore black. Salads were served, and there was a PowerPoint presentation. First I was debriefed about the structure of BrainReserve (the trend department, for example, is charged with "brailing the culture") as well as its 9,500-person "talent bank." This is not merely a Rolodex, I was informed, but a web of contacts. A slide listed some of the names from the talent bank, such as designer Karim Rashid and personal finance writer Jean Chatzky. I was told that one of the questions often asked of BrainReserve is: "How come we're always right?" The answer involved a thirty-eight-step process. My hosts clicked through more slides.

What interested me about BrainReserve was not the general contention that the new generation is too smart to be persuaded by traditional advertising methods – which I'd obviously heard before – or even that this idea guided their thinking. What interested me was that they were applying this point of view to the selling of Tylenol. Do these cultural shifts matter to something so mundane and workaday? Surely this is a product that consumers buy for purely practical reasons, not for public status, trendiness, or identity formation. Well, the BrainReserve crew told me, Tylenol was a widely known name at the top of its category – but it had a problem. Most of its sales volume was coming from consumers age fifty and up. And among those Tylenol users who were switching to other brands, the majority were in the eighteen-to-twenty-eight-year-old age group. According to one published report, Tylenol sales had fallen 10.5 percent between 2002 and 2003. So its corporate owners, McNeil Consumer & Specialty Pharmaceuticals, of Fort Washington, Pennsylvania, had decided that, yes, the seismic changes that people like Faith Popcorn are talking about applied to their product. The owners of the brand had to change the way it communicated with this new, postclick generation.

BrainReserve conducted (they say) six thousand interviews. They looked at "styles" of pain. And eventually they hatched a multiphase plan. The first phase targeted the world of extreme sports, skateboarding, and the like. In a more lavishly funded version of the outside-of-traditional-media strategy PBR had employed, they signed up "pain partners," such as underground filmmakers and artists; underwrote the building of a skateboard park; created zines that were distributed in youth-oriented magazines. Toward the end of the PowerPoint summation of all of this, they showed me a parody commercial from *Saturday Night Live* for a nonexistent product called "Tylenol Extreme." Here, they said proudly, was proof of the way their ideas had infiltrated the mainstream. Apparently, they showed the same presentation to *Fortune,* which ran a glowing article about BrainReserve's early Tylenol efforts that ended: "That kind of exposure is priceless: It can't be TiVoed out."

new publics

Wherever a new kind of audience or public forms, a new ad venue is created. The clicky world of video games, for example, is hardly a refuge from the messages of commercial persuasion. The music business figured out that getting a song into the sound track of a popular video game meant millions of "spins"; angst-pop band Good Charlotte, to take an early example, boosted its sales from 300,000 records to 3.5 million after getting into the wildly popular Madden football video game.

Consumer brands followed, working with new specialty agencies that brokered deals to get logos onto in-game billboards, posters, soda cans, and so on; in some cases, the same game-world surface could be tweaked to show different ad images at specific times. Activision's games had paid product placements from Puma, Nokia, and McDonald's. Electronic Arts made deals with 7UP, Honda, and even Old Spice. In the more highbrow game the Sims, you could set up (again) a McDonald's, thanks to a paid placement deal. Starting in 2003, the most popular NBA video game offered gamers the freedom to choose from forty Nike shoes in 130 color variations to put onto the virtual feet of athletes in the game – or at least those who had real-life endorsement contracts with the shoe giant; you couldn't put Nikes on a player who had made the mistake of endorsing Reebok.

In late 2005, Pepsi launched a version of Mountain Dew called MDX – an eight-ounce Red Bull – style product with a high dose of caffeine – aimed specifically at gamers. It launched at the E3 Electronic Entertainment Expo, where gaming fans were invited to participate in a "beta test," giving their input on package design and the like. E3 was an "amazing targeting" opportunity, one of the marketers explained.

Plenty of other brands found ways to have a presence at E3, too. Including Tylenol.

Video game players turned out to be the target for the second phase of BrainReserve's Tylenol work. Again they were studied exhaustively, and here the research resulted in the discovery of what Popcorn called "a new indication." This was jargon she had picked up from the McNeil people, and what it meant was that they had found a previously unknown constituency for pain relief – a new public for Tylenol. Gamers, it turned out, were hurting. Hands, neck, and eyes. Headaches, soreness, blisters, cramps. Not to mention "gamer's butt." They talked of video game characters invading their dreams and of seeing the characters in their peripheral vision as they went through life. It impaired their driving; they got the shakes. There were, my hosts told me, "a lot of pain occasions" in gamer life. For these people, pain was not so much a badge as something to be tolerated silently, stoically: They deny their pain, I was told, because the *real* pain was the pain of not playing.

Having discovered all of this, the BrainReserve team set about figuring out how to sell Tylenol to the new public it had identified. A few months after my meeting at BrainReserve, I got an update from some of Faith Popcorn's people. (Curiously, they said that any quotes I wanted to use from this follow-up discussion should be attributed to Popcorn herself and not to them. So I'll simply paraphrase what they had to say.) In essence, BrainReserve decided to build its own team of gamers and insert them into the game community. They wanted leaders of the community, people who believe in gaming as a lifestyle. Heroes. Influencers.

Some weeks later, the USA Championship round of the 2005 World Cyber Games was held at the Hammerstein Ballroom, more often a venue for midsize rock shows, on 34th Street in Manhattan. Billed as "the world's largest e-Sports festival," the World Cyber Games is a global tournament for the best players of several computer and video games. Although organized game competitions remain outside the mainstream consciousness in the United States, they are a major pastime in South Korea and some other countries, and at least some people see the U.S. audience as one that has grown quickly and will not stop anytime soon.

There were a few hundred young fans and game players milling around when I arrived, which wasn't a bad turnout considering that it was the middle of the day on a Friday, and it was only the first round of the competition. People settled into chairs to look up at two giant monitors above the stage, where we would watch someone else's battles in the virtual world of a computer game called Counter-Strike. This basically consists of two teams of five individuals each, shooting and throwing bombs at each other in various computer landscapes. All the teams were located off to the side in a few rows of computer terminals. I stood near this area, talking with Craig Levine, a clean-cut recent New York University graduate, who served as the "managing director" of Team 3D – winner of the world championship in Counter-Strike for two years straight.

Levine was exactly the kind of young guy that Jeri Yoshizu (the Toyota marketer I mentioned earlier) was talking about: He wasn't worried about selling out. In fact, he proudly explained to me that his was the first Counter-Strike team to wangle corporate sponsorships, getting deals with Samsung, Intel, and NVIDIA (a maker of graphic- and digital-media processors), which meant its players got paid around $30,000 a year. "You're going to see more of these the next three to five years," he said matter-of-factly. And not just from technology companies, which have done most of the sponsoring so far – all kinds of companies. In fact, he was starting another business, which he hoped would serve as a kind of agency to broker relationships between gamer stars and Fortune 500 companies. He was betting that those companies were figuring out that they need to get involved with games. He gestured around the room. "These kids aren't watching TV," he informed me sagely. "They're not reading magazines."

It was right about this moment that I was shoved out of the way by a cameraman, walking backward, recording the arrival of a Counter-Strike team called Ouch! Five young guys wearing matching jerseys strutted past like celebrities. On the back of their jerseys: each player's last name. On the sleeve: the word *Tylenol*. This was the team that Faith Popcorn and her

BrainReserve experts had conjured up – with a little help, it turned out, from Craig Levine. He was actually the guy who got the call from someone at BrainReserve who was looking for help in building a team to represent Tylenol. They didn't want simply to sponsor an existing team; they wanted a group of players with a certain profile, a certain fame and respect in the gamer community. They wanted a team that could instantly compete at the highest level. And they wanted the team to be called Ouch! The captain of the Ouch! team, Levine explained cheerfully, had actually been poached from Team 3D.

Team Ouch!'s opening-round match was coming up, and I wandered over to the area where the five players had lined up before their screens, wearing headsets. The contest began, and along with it the jacked-up play-by-play of two "shoutcast" announcers on a stage nearby, describing how each battle was going, how many "frags" this or that player had racked up. Whatever the reaction was to the incongruous presence of Tylenol in this world, it certainly wasn't resistance. To the contrary, in the slower moments, the play-by-play guys talked about how exciting it was that a big sponsor like Tylenol had gotten involved in their sport. "Absolutely huge," one said.

in every pocket

Not long after Zenith first tried to sell the freeing click of technology to the masses, there were public debates about, of all things, billboards. In the 1960s, an advertising man named Howard Gossage wrote an essay for *Harper's* magazine, making the case against them. "An advertising medium," he wrote, ought to be something "that incidentally carries advertising but whose primary function is to provide something else: entertainment, news, matches, telephone listings, anything. I'm afraid the poor old billboard doesn't qualify as a medium at all; its medium, if any, is the scenery around it, and that is not its to give away.

Nor is a walk down the street brought to you through the courtesy of outdoor advertising."

Gossage obviously lost his argument (outdoor advertising is a multibillion-dollar business today and actually growing), but his line of thinking is worth considering again. Because he is saying something that is quite similar to what Turner executive Kellner was trying to say, albeit from a very different angle. That is, a broadcast media audience has the freedom to choose to watch or not watch a given program; a person walking down the street, or stuck in traffic, doesn't have that same freedom. There ought to be some line, in other words, between what can be converted into a marketing medium and what cannot.

It's worth recalling Gossage's critique today, because whatever effect TiVo and other enablers of click culture end up having on the transaction model of the commercial persuasion industry, they are also helping a new murketing culture that obliterates all such lines. Advertising, after all, is so far showing no signs of extinction, and anything the click makes popular soon becomes popular with advertisers – Facebook and YouTube included. Big companies like Proctor & Gamble and GM have cut their TV budgets, but they are shifting money to "new-media experiments and branded entertainment," not rolling over and giving up. The creation of advertising that can't be TiVoed out has moved at a much more explosive rate than TiVo itself spread through the consumer marketplace. (According to Nielsen Media Research, about 18 percent of American households had digital video recorders by 2007. That put the DVR well ahead of outhouses, but well behind, for example, the huge flat-screen TVs that had already found a place in 34 percent of homes.)

Within a year or two of the first declaration that the clicks would tear down the old culture of control and replace it with a nirvana of consumer freedom, it became clear to anyone who was paying attention to what was actually happening in the media and advertising marketplace (or who had spent more than five minutes surfing the Internet) that, even if the most doomsaying of these experts are correct, and the thirty-second commercial dies out completely, or that "mass-media marketing is going the way of the horse and buggy," as one advertising trade journal report asserted, it won't actually matter to most of us: Our clicky new world will be defined by more commercial messages, not fewer.

Consider again that symbol of tech-enabled freedom, the cell phone. The abstract audiences that cluster around wireless devices – or the "third screen" (after the television and computer), as marketers say – are becoming, like video gamers, another target platform for commercial persuasion. The earliest commercial persuasion experiments with the new medium played to its "interactive" properties. Text message voting – on whether, for instance, you thought a woman in a Dove soap ad was "wrinkled" or "wonderful" – was one popular tactic. (Ironically, network television shows were among the most enthusiastic proponents of text voting, as a new way to keep a live audience stuck in front of the ads and paid product placements of various competition shows decided by viewer votes.) Bud Light launched a contest involving consumer-submitted cell phone photos. As the technology improved, so did the ad strategies: If you could use your phone to surf Web sports headlines, you might encounter the question "Hungry? Click to find a Burger King." By 2007, the number of cell phone owners in the United States was two hundred million, and the factors that have kept the development of third-screen marketing relatively slow (notably certain technical issues with older phones and cautious attitudes on the part of cell service providers) were fading: Verizon, AT&T, and Sprint Nextel all allow banner ads to appear on the home screens of Web-enabled phones that use their services. Other companies explored using a model quite similar to the one that network television was based on, giving users free content or services in exchange for accepting more ad messages.

To young people, "cell phones symbolize freedom," *American Demographics* explained, and consumer companies seem to agree. "We're seeing text messaging as an important enabler for communicating with teens and young adults," an associate brand manager for the Coca-Cola Company observes, not sounding particularly threatened by this freedom-granting device.

Japanese and European consumers can already use mobile devices to buy from vending machines or at store cash registers, linked directly to debit or credit accounts. Or, in Japan, consumers can (and do) opt to get messages from, for example, the makers of a Lipton drink. Such tactics are making their way to the American market. Coke, Pepsi, McDonald's, Timex, Claritin, and Heineken are a few of the many companies and brands already experimenting with wireless advertising, and at least half a dozen new marketing firms have been formed, devising sweepstakes and discounts and whatnot to get you to "opt in." Often this is achieved by some kind of giveaway. For instance, a convenience store chain called Sheetz gave away things like Xboxes and iPod nanos: All you had to do was send in a special text code, which about thirteen thousand people did, and around three-quarters of these were responsive to subsequent text messages and coupons from the chain, according to *Brandweek*. The creation of minishows for these miniscreens has also attracted miniads from not-so-mini marketers. For 2007, Procter & Gamble planned no fewer than thirty-five marketing programs built around reaching consumers via mobile devices.

"This is the one medium you carry with you," one marketer says. Another says that, yes, television spots just don't have the reach they used to, but: "The mobile phone is very personal, and it's always with you." A third agrees: "By communicating with consumers through the mobile phone, you can deliver your message right to their hip pocket."

Thus a symbol of freedom becomes a selling machine in every pocket.

deodorant as culture

The strongest case for the power of the click is in the realm of television. In 2007, the media-buying firm Mindshare reported that the average amount of TV time taken up by either ads or network promotions had leveled off – at about fifteen minutes of every hour. This figure had, of course, been rising steadily for years; advertisers refer to it as "clutter." Clutter annoys viewers, but advertisers see it as a problem, too, since the more of it there is, the harder it is for any single commercial to stand out. (The advertising trade has been complaining about and coping with this issue in one form or another since at least the 1890s – though they were referring to print media and outdoor advertising at the time. By the early 1960s, celebrated ad man David Ogilvy blamed clutter for consumers having "acquired a talent for skipping advertisements in newspapers and magazines and going to the bathroom during television commercials.")

A clutter slowdown sounds like great news for everybody. But looking at the amount of the television hour devoted to clearly labeled commercial time doesn't quite give us the whole picture. The findings of another firm, TNS Media Intelligence, suggested that branding is increasingly escaping from the thirty-second confines of actual commercials and cluttering its way into shows themselves, in the form of paid product placements. In 2006, six minutes and twenty-two seconds of a typical prime-time hour were devoted to paid product placements – a leap of 89 percent over the prior year. On newly popular unscripted "reality" shows, the figure was close to eleven minutes. In the third quarter of 2006, episodes of one CBS show, *Rock Star: Supernova,* included an astonishing 1,609 product or brand image shots.

Meanwhile, Nike, Procter & Gamble, and Toyota are among the multinational brand owners that have taken to bankrolling entire documentaries that happen to tell stories related to products made by Nike, Procter & Gamble, and Toyota. And while the

Web has emerged as an alternative venue for some television-style storytelling and entertainment, it has not been immune to its own clutter problems. Even the makers of *Lonelygirl15*, the fake video diary that was lauded as a grassroots media hit, cut deals with consumer companies, resulting in things like paid-for close-ups of Ice Breakers gum and a character who, by sponsored arrangement, was identified as a Neutrogena staffer. (Neutrogena liked that "the show specifically attracts teen and twentysomething consumers – the demo that the company is trying to target with its products," *Variety* explained.)

Clearly, then, brand owners are learning to cope with the click both in new media forms and in the old-fashioned realm of television. But to truly comprehend the click, you can't look just at the way marketers use one specific communication realm or another. Transcending any single medium, and making the line between commercial expression and cultural expression as murky as possible, certainly helped one brand that established itself in the U.S. market at the precise moment when consumer control supposedly had commercial persuaders on the ropes. That brand was Axe, a line of body sprays and deodorants that arrived in the U.S. market in 2002.

Certainly the owner of Axe, multinational consumer products conglomerate Unilever, faced a media landscape that was cluttered and clamorous and fractioned. Its target was that fickle and media-smart creature, the young American male in his teens and early twenties. Yet Axe has been a runaway hit. In fact, it quickly became the best seller of all Unilever's deodorant brands (which also include Degree and Dove), and within two years it was reportedly outselling all rivals, from Right Guard to Old Spice. In 2007, annual U.S. sales of Axe products were estimated at $500 million, and it had inspired a range of knockoffs from other companies.

Probably the last time there had been a truly significant shift in how deodorants are sold was in the 1920s. In the urbanizing America of the early twentieth century, perspiration had been recognized as a problem (possibly an unhealthy one) worth solving, but print ads for products like Mum and Odorono tended to be small and discreet, and placed in the back pages of magazines. The tone changed right around the time Listerine was introducing consumers to the concept of halitosis, and increasingly bold ads did so in a similar way. For example, Lever Brothers – a predecessor company to Unilever – blared warnings about "B.O. (Body Odor)."

The advertising agency that devised Axe's click-era marketing campaign is Bartle Bogle Hegarty, and a BBH executive in New York, Kevin Roddy, later explained to me the brand's twenty-first-century approach. Deodorants and antiperspirants had long remained "a pretty rationally marketed category," he pointed out. "Usually, about things like 'This lasts twenty-four hours or thirty-six hours,' or, 'It smells good.'" True enough. But really, how else *could* this particular product be sold? Much like dish soap, deodorant seems a pretty poor candidate for a "badge."

To find an answer to that question, Unilever had commissioned a massive study of the consumers of all the deodorant brands in its portfolio, overseen by Barbara Perry, one of the best-known corporate anthropologists working today. The "Axe man" study involved videotaping extensive ethnographic-style interviews with twenty-eight male consumers, aged eighteen to twenty-two, and their friends, in Pittsburgh and Los Angeles. This material was in turn presented to Axe's marketing and PR teams at a special off-site event exploring the sex lives and mental outlooks of Axe target males, who were divided into categories such as "pimp daddy," "player," and "sweetheart." An *Advertising Age* columnist called it "the deepest and most awkwardly personal dive into the young-male sexual psyche I've ever seen." He seemed to mean this as a compliment.

At first glance, the tone of the campaign that Unilever and BBH came up with seems drastically out of step with the times. That is to say, the tone was totally ridiculous – Axe was portrayed as an all-powerful, surefire babe magnet, the kind of thing that will not only attract pretty girls to the young male consumer, but attract them in groups, and right to the shower. The website included phony home videos of women being converted into instant sex maniacs upon exposure to Axe-wearing men, some ripping off their clothing. "The Axe effect feels so good," a related website winked, "and there are so many ways to do it." There were those who questioned whether the risqué tone of Axe's marketing wasn't a bit much, but a Unilever executive explained: "Everything that we do, we test with both moms and young women. We want to make sure that people know it's an over-the-top, tongue-in-cheek take on the mating game."

Operating in the click era, BBH took what is sometimes called a "media neutral" or "media agnostic" approach. What this means, as a practical matter, is that *all* media were used: television, radio, print, the Web, and real-world events, including "sampling" events featuring scantily clad "Axe Angels" as well as "Axe After Dark" nightclub parties. For radio ads, the company threw in a toll-free number that led to a voice-mail box for an obviously fake ad firm; guys called and left amusing or ribald stories about their Axe adventures. An online game called Is Your Shower Hottie Ready? brought in two million visitors in three months, about half of them drawn in by someone who had forwarded it to them. People not only forwarded the online videos, they also actually bought a "limited edition" publication called *How to Cope with All the Ladies,* which was basically an entertaining piece of Axe marketing. Later, the brand invented a kind of girl group called the Bom Chicka Wah Wah Girls, who dressed as strippers and sang vapid, processed music in ersatz videos (basically long-form Axe ads) that were uploaded to YouTube – and promptly viewed hundreds of thousands of times. One estimate has it that Unilever spent more than $100 million advertising, marketing, and promoting Axe in the first couple of years it was on the market.

Roddy offered me one particularly compelling example of

how Axe had circumvented the click. In musing on ways to be relevant to the life of the Axe Man, BBH pondered what it called "game killer" men whose sole mission in life is to undercut other guys, especially around girls. Maybe this means the game killer one-ups everything you say (you ran a marathon? He just did the Ironman Triathlon), until you lose your cool – and the girl. "We created a television show revolving around the idea of all these game-killing characters," Roddy continued. "It's a quasi sort of reality show." They pitched the show, called *Game Killers*, to MTV, where it was picked up and debuted in early 2006.

This certainly trumps product placement or "branded content," in which a brand tries to soak up the reflected meaning of some established cultural property. "We've actually created the content from scratch, using the same brief that we use to create advertising," Roddy concluded.

The click world, then, is not a place where marketers have lost control. It's a world where they have gained new freedom – to be practically everywhere. Similarly, thinking of a product in terms of meaning first and Pretty Good functionality a taken-for-granted second removes all sorts of limits. "We don't really think of it necessarily in competition with other deodorant brands," another BBH executive, William Gelner, explained to me. "To be successful as a youth brand is to realize that's not what you're competing against."

Well, I asked, if a deodorant isn't competing against deodorants, what *is* it competing against? "Pop culture," Gelner replied. "You're competing against things like movies, television shows, sporting events, other advertisers, the Internet." So to sell something like Axe, he concluded, "you have to become part of pop culture."

chapter eight
very real

WHAT SCION UNDERSTANDS . . . THE BIG IDEA . . . "KEEPING
EVERYTHING VERY REAL" . . . RICKETY BRIDGES

what scion understands

It doesn't particularly matter what a Scion is. Never mind who made it, or how much it cost, or whether it is any good. All you need to know is that a few years ago, it was a brand-new brand. The people who created this brand set out to get members of Generation Y to buy the thing – whatever it was – and if they knew anything about the new consumer in the TiVo-Internet-wireless-video-game era, they knew that their target audience would not stand for the clumsy, crass marketing style that worked on its parents. They knew that these potential customers, in other words, hated to be *pitched*. Just know that Scion got this; Scion understood.

So Scion showed up at graffiti block parties on the Lower East Side of Manhattan and outsider art events in San Francisco and Los Angeles. Instead of running ads during prime time, its marketers distributed custom magazines at an alt-film festival called RESfest. Instead of buying splashy spreads in *Time* and *Vanity Fair,* Scion loaned its product to an editor of *Art Prostitute,* a magazine based in Denton, Texas, with a print run of 2,500.

This process had started before the product was even available. Later, Scion – with a reported $50 million budget to fuel these "underground" efforts – inched toward the spotlight, but carefully, like an underground rapper trying to move from mix tapes to MTV without losing street cred. Scion's brand czars said they didn't want their customers seeing the marketing in the wrong place – a TV spot might be okay if it appeared during *Aqua Teen Hunger Force* (but certainly not *The O.C.*) and included no voice-overs, no sales pitch, hardly a mention of the brand. It was as if they were trying to keep it all under the radar, as if the Scion were a secret they didn't want the vast majority of the consuming public to find out about.

Perhaps none of this would be terribly remarkable if Scion really *were* a rap artist, or even if its makers were trying to compete with PBR or Converse. But Scion was a brand of car. A car is a major durable good – for most of us, the second largest purchase we will make, after housing – not an impulse buy or a fad. Cars are not supposed to be sold with winks and whispers and secret handshakes.

Scion is made by Toyota, and unlike the Pabst Brewing Company or the makers of Tylenol, Toyota is not ailing or losing market share. Its production innovations, copied around the globe, helped bring the Pretty Good Problem to the auto industry. Thanks in large part to the Japanese auto giant, *The Economist* has argued, "the quality, content, and economy of today's cars is incomparable with what was on offer 30 years ago." The auto business remains "the epitome of mass production, mass marketing, and mass consumption," the magazine argued, but to match sales levels for prior hits like the Ford Cortina in Europe or the F-150 truck in the United States, companies now had to offer "a plethora of niche models designed to attract particular groups," and ultimately production runs would have to get smaller to accommodate this dynamic (which the automakers themselves had helped create). Toyota offered many niche models – sixty in the Japanese market (although the company was particularly adept at making models that *seem* different, with lots of standardized components hidden out of view).

Nobody wants to drive their parents' car of choice, and that's a particularly thorny issue for Toyota, whose U.S. success was definitely a Boomer phenomenon: Around the time of Scion's launch, the average age of Toyota buyers was nearing fifty (Buick's was sixty-three), and Toyota's first attempt at bringing in Generation Y drivers, a compact called the Echo, had fizzled. For its second attempt at decoding the new young consumer, the company would travel a very different road.

Interestingly, the car that had been the biggest hit with under twenty-fives when the Scion was being positioned for the U.S. market was the Honda Civic, a model that was never marketed to that demographic. The car-customizing crowd – "tuners," as they're called – adopted (or hijacked, if you like) the Civic, apparently, because it was reliable, inexpensive, and a good blank slate for individualization. In another example of consumer-driven meaning, the Civic became an icon of tuner culture, which went mainstream through the 2001 movie *The Fast and the Furious;* the Civic was the top-selling car among young people in 2002.

Which brings us into Sixes and Eights, the lower Manhattan club filled with hip youths waiting to hear Qool DJ Marv and DJ Jazzy Jeff. They drank $4 cans of PBR, and smoked openly, which in Michael Bloomberg's New York was what passed for being off the grid. But we weren't *that* far off the grid, seeing as how the whole thing was actually a marketing event and the evening's organizer was one of the largest corporations in the world. And in fact, a few of the hipsters were dutifully paging through the latest issue of a Scion magazine or tucking away free copies of *Scion CD Sampler Volume 8* (featuring tracks from Madvillain and Pete Rock). A guy with a digital camera darted around documenting the clutches of cool people with their Scion paraphernalia.

Obviously nobody was fooling these kids. There's no way they couldn't "see through" the event; they had to know that it was murketing. But unlike a Converse or a PBR, Scion wasn't a brand whose meaning originated with consumers and was subsequently amped or nurtured by a company. This time, the "collaboration" was built into the brand right from the beginning. And it seemed to be going exactly according to Toyota's plans.

the big idea

Randall Rothenberg's 1994 definitive study of auto marketing, *Where the Suckers Moon*, focused on the efforts of ad agency Wieden+Kennedy on behalf of Subaru of America, in the early 1990s. The agency was, and remains, best known for its work with Nike (including coining the famous "Just Do It" slogan). In the late 1980s and early 1990s, its successes in both business and creative terms had built it a maverick image and a reputation for an almost postmodern approach to advertising. When he described the way people at Wieden thought of themselves, Rothenberg referenced "image scavengers" like Cindy Sherman and Roy Lichtenstein, "roaming the cultural landscape and mining from it bits and pieces of the mass-cult past to use in their pastiches." Wieden creatives built a Honda scooter ad around Lou Reed and his song "Walk on the Wild Side." They used a Beatles song ("Revolution") in one Nike ad and hired Spike Lee to direct many others. Often those ads built in a critique of advertising – as with Lee's Mars Blackmon character patiently explaining that you can buy a pair of Nikes, but you still won't be able to dunk like Jordan. Of course, as Rothenberg pointed out, Wieden employees were not *really* artists, whatever they thought; they were marketers. However postmodern their sensibility, the end result was still commercial persuasion.

The target market for the Subaru was Baby Boomers (who were seen, you will recall, as a uniquely marketing-resistant generation). On a purely functional and rational basis, one adman quoted by Rothenberg summarized, "the consumers' perception is that it *doesn't matter* which car to buy, because they're all reliable, they're all well-engineered." Wieden was concerned not so much with mere fashion or styling as with a kind of ideology: The agency believed it should stress the idea of Subaru as an "alternative to the mainstream" – just the thing for Boomer individualists who didn't want to get caught driving the gray flannel suit of automobiles.

Car advertising was ultimately about the Big Idea, as Rothenberg put it, "a new American myth, an Idea so Big that it would immediately integrate [a brand] into the collective national consciousness." Practical selling points like price, performance, fuel efficiency, and style, bound together by a larger-than-life image: That's how cars have always been sold, from the early Ford promise "Worth more when you buy it. Worth more when you sell it," to Mercedes-Benz's "Engineered like no other car in the world," to "Baseball, hot dogs, apple pie, and Chevrolet." Loud. Conspicuous. Big. The spine of *Where the Suckers Moon* deals with the creation of television commercials (and the astonishing difficulties of putting the aforementioned theories into practice) that would communicate that idea in a big way, to as many people as possible – very much in line with the way Big Ideas had long been sold.

By the time Scion came along, the whole auto industry had begun shifting its focus from Baby Boomers to their children – for the fairly obvious reason that most of this enormous generation would be old enough to drive by 2010 – but despite aggressive attempts, no one had created a car that truly rhymed with Generation Y.

Maybe the Big Idea was finally over, or maybe no one had found the right one yet. Or maybe the Big Idea had to be delivered through whispers and secret handshakes now. Maybe it had to be murketed.

"keeping everything very real"

Scion launched in California in early 2003. "Authenticity" was the core of the brand, one of Scion's marketing executives later told *The New York Times Magazine*. "Just keeping everything very real," one of them explained, as if that were some kind of breakthrough idea.

When I first encountered the brand, it barely existed but had popped up in an unusual Los Angeles art exhibition called "Sponsorship." There was no actual art in the show, at the BLK/MRKT Gallery – just corporate logos, each displayed at a size that depended on how much the company had paid to be included. While there was clearly a critique of the relationship between corporations and the art world at work here, several big brands had decided to play along and buy their way in, including Levi's, Red Bull, and Scion. This was the occasion for my first conversation with Jeri Yoshizu, the Toyota marketer I mentioned earlier. "Scion is branding by as many noncorporate methods as possible," she explained to me at the time. She was mildly annoyed that the company's logo in the show identified the car as the "Toyota Scion" rather than simply Scion. "Other than that," she said, "I thought it was supercool." Then she added: "I did feel that we were being mocked, but what the hell."

I didn't know if that was an authentic answer, but it sure was interesting, and I kept an eye on Scion. Its advertising agency of record was an obscure San Francisco shop called Attik, which did things like parking Scions outside of raves and spreading around posters with (kind of hokey-sounding) slogans like "No Clone Zone."

Attik claimed credit for hatching the strategy that the best way to approach young people was by selling them tuner-style customization and personalization. The brand offered dozens of custom options from the dealer itself, from special lights to alloy wheels to turbochargers and clutch-pedal covers. Its slogans included "Personalization begins here" and "What moves you." One not particularly subtle print ad simply announced, "Self-expression is what it's all about. . . . You are unique. Your car should be too." All of this sounded a lot like an echo of Wieden+Kennedy's Boomer individualistic "alternative to the mainstream" positioning. And in any case, those expressive Scion options – blue or red covers for the pedals cost $79 – all carried excellent profit margins for Toyota.

Yoshizu's job involved keeping up with youth culture, networking with underground artists, knowing the relative standing of LRG or A Bathing Ape clothes, and deciding whether or not Sonotheque was still a good club for Chicago Scion events. But she had help: To keep things very real, Scion had hired plenty of experts on that subject.

Any big automaker introducing a new line or model generally gives members of the automotive trade press a look at it well before the official launch. The opinions of these expert gatekeepers are important: Their test drives and evaluations set a tone for the way a car or truck or sport utility vehicle might be received. For the Scion, Toyota also took another, far more unusual step. In addition to *Car & Driver* and *MotorTrend* and similar publications, Toyota (working with a marketing agency called Inform Ventures) previewed the Scion for editors of magazines like *While You Were Sleeping, Frank,* and *Yellow Rat Bastard,* among others.

No one associated with any of these publications had any particular car expertise; at least one of the editors didn't even have a driver's license. Nor did these shoestring-budget magazines command huge circulations or even mainstream name recognition. They were closer to the homespun zines of the "Beautiful Losers" generation than to the distribution power and glossy impact of a *GQ* or an *InStyle*. For lack of a better word, they were underground magazines, heirs to a long tradition of alternative publishing. But Toyota did not see them as threatening or representative of a counterculture that would cause problems. It saw them as a window on the new youth market. So Toyota invited the editors of these edgy little magazines to San Francisco. The editors of the edgy little magazines accepted.

Toyota put them up at the W Hotel. The weekend was described to me as a bit debauched by people who were there – why not get drunk and enjoy a lavish sushi dinner on Toyota's dime? – but by and large, everyone seems to have gotten along swimmingly. Before long, the underground magazines included both editorial coverage of Scion – and Scion ads. One of the twenty-something editors who was there later told me he was excited that a big company might be interested in, and actually listen to, his and his peers' opinions and ideas about marketing. Giving out marketing advice didn't sound to me like a very alternative or underground thing to do, but one of his colleagues had taken that very notion a step further. The founder of a pocket-size alternative-culture journal called *Frank* ended up landing the Scion as a client. *Frank* – like several other such publications – was in the process of building a marketing arm: Malbon Brothers Farms is based in New York, and as it happens, the party at Sixes and Eights was one of its events for Scion. Which turned out to be a good place to learn how murketing might pull the triggers of the Desire Code more effectively than any traditional commercial could – precisely by "keeping it very real."

rickety bridges

In what has since become a widely cited social psychology experiment conducted in Canada, researchers had a good-looking young woman approach various men and ask them to fill out a questionnaire. In each case, she would tell the man that she was working on a study having to do with creativity and that if he had any questions to ask later on, well, here was her phone number – she would write it on a torn-off corner of the question sheet.

The study was not really about creativity, of course; what the researchers actually wanted to know was how many men would call this woman back and ask her out. All the men were approached in the same park, in one of two scenarios: either while sitting on a bench or while crossing a footbridge over a gorge. This particular bridge swayed in the wind and did not seem to be very well made; it was a bit of a nerve-racking thing to be on. So at the moment this attractive woman was handing over her phone number on the bridge, she was handing it to men whose hearts were pounding, who were breathing quickly, maybe even sweating. Physiologically speaking, they were aroused.

It's not that these guys somehow didn't know or forgot that they were on a rickety bridge and that this was what was making their hearts pound. Naturally, they knew that. But the researchers wanted to know, basically, how the men's interpreters would handle the situation – if the men might, without really knowing they were doing so, associate their arousal not just with the situation, but with the woman. Of the men who were approached while sitting on a bench, 30 percent called her. Of those approached on the rickety bridge, 65 percent called.

Surely none of these men would have drawn a conscious link between their apparent attraction and a rickety bridge – any more than a young consumer would draw a conscious link between having a great time at a party and liking a particular brand.

But the rickety bridge is a good way of understanding one of the most widely used tactics of murketing. Chris Nagy, one of the Malbon Brothers partners, explained to me the way his firm thought about events. Part of the point, he said, was to keep them small, maybe two hundred or three hundred attendees, tops. He used a different client as an example: Molson, whose corporate owner (the Coors Brewing Company) wanted to throw a huge bash for the brand, on Miami Beach. Malbon Brothers suggested that this would be a waste of money; instead of a memorable rickety bridge, it would be a big, crowded, totally forgettable overpass. So the agency organized a series of smaller events in markets like Syracuse, Pittsburgh, and Columbus, targeting "average guys, the ex-frat guys, the guys in white shirts and ties who work in buildings downtown" and treating them like VIPs. They brought in New York–style DJs as well as "eye candy," he explains, "like girls that – you didn't know were working – but they were flirting with all the guys." The idea was that the guys who went to those parties would never forget it – or Molson. They'd tell all their friends.

They had been on a rickety bridge.

Waiting around for Sixes and Eights to fill up, I chatted with Jim DiCarlo, a mellow young guy in a baseball cap, a year or so out of college. He also worked for *Frank* and for Malbon Brothers Farms. I asked him his title, and he said they really don't do titles at Malbon Brothers, then he settled on "account executive."

How, I asked him, does an event like this help sell cars? "You might not see a spike in sales for the quarter," DiCarlo said. "But I really believe in the long run that these types of things are beneficial to the brand. Because ultimately it's your consumer's perception, the way they feel about the brand, that really affects how the brand does."

Perhaps he was right. Not long after we spoke, J. D. Power and Associates reported that the Scion was already the top-selling car brand among buyers age twenty-five and under, with 19 percent of that market. Toyota was reported to have a target goal of selling 125,000 Scions in 2005 and sold more than 150,000. Sales kept rising, and by early 2007, Toyota had sold more than 400,000 Scion vehicles; one auto industry researcher told *The Wall Street Journal* he believed Toyota could sell 250,000 a year if it removed certain limits placed on production. The brand gradually moved toward more mainstream marketing efforts but continued to rejuvenate its murkier strategies. Aside from the events, it launched a line of clothes, commissioned original films (one of which I caught at the TriBeCa Film Festival), and started a small record label called Scion Release. Jim Farley, who oversaw the brand for Toyota, was promoted in April 2005 to the VP marketing title for the company and was soon pressuring its main advertising agency (which had not been involved in the Scion launch) to move away from television advertising; he also added a variety of smaller, nontraditional agencies to Toyota's roster, basically applying the Scion way to the entire company; *Advertising Age* named the carmaker its "Marketer of the Year" for 2006, and *Brandweek* picked Farley as that year's "Grand Marketer."

The Big Idea still seemed like a sales pitch from a huge corporation to me, just one that had been packaged in a novel way that, as it happens, gave complete priority to image. But midnight passed, and Sixes and Eights was packed. There still wasn't much dancing, but people had put away their two-ways and were paying attention to the DJ set or to a couple of girls-gone-wild types who kept charging back and forth to the bar. Apart from a logo projected on one wall, all the marketing material had been shoved aside. It was all feeling very rickety, and very real.

the murkiest common denominator

the unknown publicity stunt

The day was so perfect, it looked just like a commercial. The sky was blue, the sand was white, and although it was December, the temperature was in the low seventies. Among a handful of people milling around on a broad stretch of Miami Beach shorefront, three guys were fussing with kiteboards – contraptions that consist of large, crescent-shaped parachutes rigged atop miniature surfboards. Two more people wielded videocameras, and several others clutched little silver cans of the peppy refreshment that was paying for all this activity: Red Bull, the "energy drink" that was already on its way to becoming a global phenomenon.

Created by a privately held Austrian company, Red Bull was introduced to the United States in 1997. At the time, there were no "energy drinks" in the American beverage market, but within a few years of its arrival, it had attracted a swarm of shameless knockoff competitors and spawned an entirely new answer to the question of what you might drink if you happen to be thirsty. Anheuser-Busch put out a drink called 180. Coca-Cola tried one called KMX, then another called Full Throttle, and one called Tab Energy. Pepsi introduced SoBe's Adrenaline Rush, a Mountain Dew spin-off called Amp, and another Mountain Dew spin-off called MDX (the gamer-targeted drink hyped at E3 the same year that Tylenol was being promoted at the trade show). There were also plenty of smaller start-up rivals, like Crunk Juice. Despite heavyweight competition, Red Bull has remained dominant, with annual global sales reported at more than $1.5 billion.

Red Bull comes in small cans (8.3 ounces), usually costing $2 or more and featuring a silver-and-blue pattern and two red bulls about to head-butt each other. "Improves performance, especially during times of increased stress or strain," it says on the can. It also says, in bold red letters: "With Taurine."

As it made its way into the American market, the company did not do anything so banal as sponsor an established skateboarding star. Instead, it devised and underwrote its own stunts and competitions in obscure disciplines. Red Bull ran an event for "competitive freeskiers," for instance. It created a "street luge" contest that involved shooting down San Francisco hills strapped to a wheeled board. It sponsored a guy who set a world record by kayaking over a ninety-eight-foot waterfall.

And on Miami Beach that December day back in 2001, the Red Bull forces were preparing something particularly audacious: A small flotilla would ride wind-powered kiteboards eighty-eight miles from Key West to Varadero, Cuba, a distance that would set a new world record for the emerging sport. Kiteboarding involves standing on a four-to-six-foot board, secured by foot straps or boots, and being propelled by a billowing kite that is controlled by manipulating a hand bar that guides one-hundred-foot-long tethers. When the wind is right, those who know what they're doing can pull off astonishing forty-foot-high jumps. Not surprisingly, the number of people who can do this is pretty small.

As I joined the beach crew, Kent Marinkovic, one of the kite-boarders, was talking to the cameras. Marinkovic, thirty-three, was national sales manager for a Miami extreme-sports equipment retailer. He was preppy-looking, very tanned, and very, very motivated. "I'm *super*motivated," he said. "I don't get nervous." He held a can of Red Bull. Nearby was another kiteboarder, Neil Hutchinson, who co-owned a Fort Lauderdale – based water sports company, scorned vegetables of any kind, and smoked Marlboro Reds. He was British, thirty-one, and with a tan deeper still than Marinkovic's, he looked like a leather-hided Peter O'Toole. When he took his turn explaining his equipment and tactics to the lens, he was immediately heckled by Oliver "Mowgli" Butsch, the third kiteboarder. "Neil has *tactics!*" Butsch bellowed in mock disgust. "Buddy, I'm going *over*. I'm *arriving*. Fuck tactics!" Butsch was Austrian, so it was hard not to think of Arnold Schwarzenegger when he spoke, which was often. A thirty-eight-year-old model with long hair, he wore shades and had the most stupendous tan of all.

I took a seat under a beach umbrella and opened a can of Red Bull. You drink this stuff not for the flavor – it's been described, accurately, as tasting like liquid SweeTarts – but for the effect. It's supposed to give you a boost. As the can puts it, Red Bull "Vitalizes body and mind." Marinkovic joined me, and I asked about Red Bull's appeal. He stared at the can in his hand. But he didn't say anything about the various promises printed on the back ("Increases endurance," "Stimulates the metabolism," and so on). He said: "It makes a good mixer with vodka. And it's kind of a hangover cure."

The beach scene struck me as odd. It wasn't the fact that the puny cans cost three or four times more than a twelve-ounce Mountain Dew, or the curious rumors about "taurine," or even the bizarre particulars of this particular promotional stunt. The weird thing about this promotional stunt was that *no one knew about it*. There was no advance press release. There were no carefully recruited coolhunters to tell their influential friends. There was no Red Bull tent set up to attract local news crews or hand out free samples to curious onlookers. For that matter, there were no curious onlookers. (One white guy with dreadlocks wandered up to ask if we were giving lessons; that was it.) This was one of the most outrageous marketing events I'd ever heard of – kiteboarding to a nation that's under a strict U.S. trade embargo! – and it seemed to be happening in a vacuum.

How could this possibly work? I've followed Red Bull ever since that curious day on Miami Beach, and although I didn't know it back then, what I was watching was the beginning of the modern era of murketing. Red Bull was not a brand with a history, like PBR, or a reputation for functional quality like Timberland or Apple. Unlike the Scion, it was not seen by its owners as a product for a rarefied consumer niche. Unlike Tylenol, its brand name was not established in the traditional mass-media era. Yet Red Bull became perhaps the quintessential example of how brands become established in the early twenty-first century. Its story is a direct rebuke to the supposed impossibility of going mass in the postclick era, to the insistence on authenticity, and to the idea that the end of top-down marketing and the supposed capitulation of commercial persuaders to consumer "collaboration" adds up to a triumph of rationality. It's the brand whose story makes you wonder: If consumers are in control, is this really the best we can do?

explaining red bull

Red Bull is headquartered in Fuschl, Austria, a lakeside village outside Salzburg. The official corporate creation saga says it was invented by a Fuschl resident and entrepreneur named Dietrich Mateschitz. Traveling in Asia in the 1980s, he supposedly came across a syrupy tonic favored by rickshaw drivers in Thailand, called Krating Daeng. The key ingredient (the story goes) was an amino acid called taurine, which occurs naturally in human and animal bile. He adapted it to something more palatable and launched Red Bull in his home country in 1987.

Red Bull grew into a widely known brand in Europe, but when it came to the United States, it did not roll out a big, flashy ad campaign or orchestrate massive, coast-to-coast distribution. There was no announcement or even explanation as to what this new stuff was and who was supposed to drink it and why; there was no big bang. Mateschitz, meanwhile, remained a largely unknown figure. "He doesn't like the media," offered Emmy Cortes, Red Bull's spokeswoman, who was assigned to answer my questions at the time. She said he was "a very charismatic gentleman," age sixty or so, single, and "kind of a playboy." This coyness, she explained, was of a piece with "the mystique of the brand."

As Red Bull gained momentum, marketing experts jumped on the bandwagon and tried to explain its strategy with a shower of adulatory slogans. "We live in an emotional society," purred Marc Gobé, president and CEO of the New York–based branding firm Desgrippes Gobé Group and author of a book called *Emotional Branding*. He identified a key to Red Bull's success in its association with exotic and risky physical feats. "Extreme sports deliver on that need to, to ... *vibrate*, in a way. Red Bull is one of the first products I've seen that delivers on that energy." According to Nancy Koehn, a Harvard Business School professor, the key was that "cosmopolitan" young people view Red Bull as a product of the "global village."

Later, gurus Al and Laura Ries argued that the key was positioning Red Bull as not simply a drink, but a whole new category with a clever name. "*Energy drink* works as a category name even though there is little relationship between the ingredients in a can of Red Bull and the ingredients in energy bars like PowerBar" and others. "Red Bull became a powerful brand because it is perceived as a drink that improves performance especially during times of increased stress or strain, which some people take to mean sexual performance. (*Energy* is just a way of expressing that idea in a socially respectable way.)" Others held up Red Bull as an example of a brilliant "stealth" brand, built by "brand evangelists" who stoked a "grassroots" marketing wave – "building an image for next to nothing," enthused the business magazine *Fast Company*. The experts all agreed: A didactic, top-down, fuddy-duddy, *traditional* mass-market product like Coke could learn a few things from Red Bull.

It was certainly true that Red Bull was not following what had been the dominant strategy of the dot-com era that was still in full flower when the drink made its U.S. debut: a big explosion onto the scene, epitomized by something like a Super Bowl ad. But really, all those marketing experts were not describing the mystique of the brand, they were helping create it. Because Red Bull's street vibe didn't just happen, and it certainly wasn't created on the cheap. Bankrolling those extreme sports is a pricey proposition. The Cuba crossing, after all, involved a crew of at least twenty people, including a meteorologist, several boats, a lot of equipment, and a video team.

Red Bull also invested in an array of other projects that had nothing to do with extreme sports. For a while, it ran Red Bull Lords of the Floor break-dancing competitions. Remember that computer game tournament I attended in Manhattan? Red Bull was distributed freely to the top gaming teams. Another interesting example: Red Bull Music Labs. The company picks a dozen or so cool young people in several cities and enrolls them in a free multiday workshop where they learn how to create original music using the latest electronic technology. I once visited a Music Labs session in New York; it took place in an expansive downtown loft rented for the occasion, with sleek and elaborate computer terminals for everyone and recording studios at the ready. The main instructor was a famous San Francisco DJ and producer called Bassnectar. At the end of a three-day binge of learning and music making (punctuated by visits to the refrigerator full of Red Bull), everybody attended a party at a fashionable nightclub, where the participants' tracks were played before Pete Rock did a set. In addition to a CD of their new creation, all the Music Labs attendees got to keep a copy of Reason, a $600 piece of software.

Meanwhile, as Red Bull spread from city to city, it deployed "mobile energy teams" that traveled about in supermodified Suzuki Vitaras, all done up with the company logo and a big silver can mounted on the back. Cortes told me these teams show up at any place where people might "need a boost," like gyms, office buildings, and construction sites.

And as I've mentioned, the first time I came across Red Bull, it was in a bar in the French Quarter of New Orleans, where I lived at the time. Red Bull turned out to be fairly easy to find in the Quarter, in the company of such good-time classics as the Hurricane and the Hand Grenade, which didn't seem to make much sense for a drink that postures as an aid to sporting achievement, given that the Quarter is arguably the most unathletic neighborhood in the world. Those "mobile energy teams" Cortes was talking about would also show up at, say, certain bars and hand out samples. If all went well, the bar owner would notice that the kids loved this stuff and start to sell it. From there, it moved to convenience stores and other retail venues. I was told that bar visits happened only occasionally – at the time, the drink was getting bad publicity because there had been deaths allegedly associated with its use as an alcohol mixer at raves and other party settings – but Red Bull also spent money installing displays in nightclubs. And in New Orleans, at least, the first place to sell Red Bull was in fact a bar on Bourbon Street.

In other words, Super Bowl ads or no, Red Bull was spending real money. Within a few years of its first appearance in the United States – and right around the time Red Bull was first coming to the attention of marketing watchers who would praise its supposedly low-cost image-building strategy – *Brandweek* reported that the company was spending $100 million a year for its American "stealth" efforts. Company spokeswoman Cortes disputed the figure but admitted that "the perception that these events don't cost much to produce is good for us." She explained, "We don't want to be seen as having lots of money to spend."

The key thing in the creation of the so-called mystique of Red Bull wasn't so much about what the company did – it was about what it *didn't* do. There was something oddly unfocused and inconsistent about the Red Bull message. Most notably, nobody ever really explained what the Big Idea was. Red Bull's various sales strategies never involved clearing up the rumors about the drink or defining taurine once and for all. The company really never offered any rational explanation of what the stuff was all about and who was supposed to drink it. It never sent a clear message to the masses.

When I spoke to college-age people about Red Bull, they did not associate the stuff with extreme sports at all. They thought of it as a bar drink. One typical Red Bull drinker was Kaytie Pickett, a Tulane dormitory resident assistant who heard about Red Bull from sorority girls. She didn't say anything to me about cosmopolitan youth or Red Bull's global origins. "It's really a kind of fashionable drink," she said. "You see the fashionable sorority girls buying their can of Red Bull with their Marlboro Lights. It's like 'Look, I can afford to pay three dollars for this ridiculous drink.'" This from a person who bought Red Bull on a regular basis.

And like many others, she'd heard a few of the rumors. These tend to focus on the drink's ingredients, especially taurine – it's bull testosterone, it's bull semen, it's bull urine, it's an aphrodisiac, and so on. The company simply laughs off the more outlandish of these.

Pickett had also heard the less amusing rumors. Pretty much from the beginning, health officials in other countries have had questions about Red Bull; in some European countries, its sale was limited to pharmacies. The controversy stemmed from a handful of deaths in which an overload of Red Bull (sometimes in concert with alcohol) allegedly played a role. Some pointed to the drink's caffeine content, and one theory was that Red Bull with liquor acts like a poor man's speedball. The company didn't laugh these off but did assure the press that the reported problems had more to do with using the product unwisely than with Red Bull itself. As for the caffeine, Cortes said it is about 80 milligrams per can, equal to that in a cup of coffee. (It's also about twice what's in a twelve-ounce Coke, along with roughly two teaspoons of sugar per can.)

Kaytie Pickett was no fool. Her rationale for drinking the stuff was a Zen statement on young adult ambivalence. "Maybe I think it works just because they say it works," she said. "I'm a slave to peer pressure." Then she laughed, just a little.

the murkiest common denominator

The easiest way to think about popular culture, or fashion, is to think in sweeping strokes: Everybody wakes up one morning, throws away their Ecko hoodies, and starts buying Lacoste again, revising their vision American style, and their very aspirations, in lockstep.

The real world is nothing like that. An "urban" brand might lose strength in the inner cities but explode in the suburbs. Meanwhile, "street" vernacular reaches for establishment symbols, while the children of the established middle class aspire to connect with authentic street, which in turn aspires to upper-crust validation. You can buy baggy jeans at Abercrombie & Fitch and an argyle sweater from Phat Farm. Somewhere in this Möbius strip of branding metaphors is the consumer.

Indeed, hardly anyone seems to believe – in our click-fragmented age – in the idea of a single America. Political pundits suggest there must be at least two Americas (red and blue, as they say). In the 1970s, sociologist Herbert J. Gans argued that there are five Americas, or at least five American "taste cultures," defined partly in terms of class and income. At around that same time, researchers at a firm called SRI International created the Values and Lifestyles Program, which suggested there are nine Americas. Paul Fussell's 1983 book, *Class: A Guide Through the American Status System*, finding the usual lower-middle-upper-class distinctions inadequate, also settled on nine Americas, defined in no small part by their consumption habits. And of course there are those who think that in a post-mass-market, one-to-one marketing world, there are three hundred million Americas.

In a mass-market culture, it's important for anyone trying to send a message – whether it's a politician or a brand creator – to be consistent about it. One way that such message senders have dealt with this problem is a phrase you've heard before: the lowest common denominator. That is, what is the most basic thing that can be said or offered that everyone will agree on? In the new, niche-y, post-mass marketplace, that's less important. In fact, some suspect that it may even be counterproductive. Once a brand is established as being *for* a certain slice of the population (hip-hop fans, for example), this could be taken by others (NASCAR enthusiasts, let's say) to mean that it is *not for* them.

Perhaps that's the kind of thing Timberland, for instance, was worried about back in the 1990s. In 1999 – when Timberland racked up its fourth straight year of record revenue – the company launched a new subbrand called Timberland Pro, for "the professional trades-person." This was created, as the company's chief operating officer, Ken Pucker, explained to me, to serve a consumer Timberland had lost touch with: the blue-collar worker.

Joe Butler – the crusty factory foreman who inspired the original Timberland work boot – remained at the center of the company's official self-identity, but the reality was, the Joe Butlers of the 1990s didn't buy Timberland anymore. Pucker had a hypothesis that although the company could make products that blue-collar workers would buy, it was probably best to do it under a new brand name, since Timberland was "no longer as relevant to them, because of how the brand had expanded in terms of products and distribution."

The company conducted three hundred one-on-one interviews with "blue-collar guys" in about half a dozen markets. These confirmed part of Pucker's hypothesis. The latter-day Joe Butlers didn't buy Timberland because it was not sold at the places where they bought boots and because they needed steel toes, nonmarking soles, or boots approved by the American National Standards Institute for electrical hazard protection. "Those are all things we didn't do anymore," Pucker observed. "Our boots hadn't evolved that way."

But what's interesting is the part of Pucker's hypothesis that proved wrong: The interviewees had no problem with the Timberland brand. "They actually loved the brand," he said, and would be more than willing to buy it if the functional attributes were there. So Timberland Pro became a distinct line, with a slightly different logo that incorporated the famous Timberland tree but had an orange-and-black color scheme. New boots that resembled Timberland classics but were functionally loaded were placed in a distinct distribution pattern – not so much Nordstrom as Sears. Timberland Pro worked out sponsorships and partnerships with the Future Farmers of America and NASCAR. It has enjoyed double-digit growth in each year of its existence. More to the point, it created no particular confusion in the marketplace. The Timberland name and iconic logo can be on a NASCAR racer and an OutKast album cover, and neither has any particular effect on the other.

In a way, Timberland inadvertently found something more powerful than unified, top-down, centrally defined meaning. Just as the key to the success of the LiveStrong bracelet or the iPod was not *one thing* about those objects, Timberland discovered success in the diverse, even contradictory, ways that consumers found personal narrative relevance.

And this is essentially what Red Bull figured out, too: Murky, it turns out, is not only okay, it's the whole point. Murky is why rumors are not a corporate headache – they help. Murky is why being embraced by extreme athletes and clubgoers and gym rats and middle-class office workers and computer gamers and break-dance fans is just fine – at worst, each group simply thinks Red Bull is something for them, partly because they have never been told otherwise. That silver can is able to stand for whatever you want it to stand for. If meaning can flow from consumer to product, not the other way around – then let it. Let the same "projectability" that allows Hello Kitty's fans to read a mood into her expressionless image take over. Let the rationale thinkers spot the pattern that works for them and fill in all the blanks.

roots of murketing: the 1890s

Much like Red Bull founder Dietrich Mateschitz, Angelo Mariani invented a drink with a mysterious foreign ingredient. Famous actors and singers in Paris soon took it up, feeling that it enhanced their performances. Soon Mariani, a Corsican with a family background in pharmaceuticals and medicine, was selling his Vin Mariani all over Europe and in the United States and Canada and even as far away as Egypt and Vietnam. He, too, attracted a swarm of imitators and was called a promotional "genius" more than once. He made the most of celebrity endorsements, not just from entertainers, but from politicians, royalty, and even religious leaders; some of these notables were introduced to the stuff (or as they say today, "seeded") with a free case. He published books filled with tales of Vin Mariani heroics and commissioned scores of leading artists to produce original posters and postcards. He was, in short, a brilliant user of murketing tactics, from the debut of Vin Mariani in 1871 until his death in 1914.

Vin Mariani consisted of Bordeaux wine mixed with coca leaves; so in this case, the mysterious foreign ingredient was cocaine. Eventually this, along with Prohibition, would cause serious problems for the once global brand, which withered away after it was reformulated. But among its imitators, there was one man worthy of some notice: John Pemberton of Atlanta, Georgia. Pemberton borrowed not just the key ingredient of the coca leaf for his French Wine Coca, but also the notion of targeting the educated, the upper class, the "intellectual," as the primary consumers (and brand evangelists) for "this great invigorator of the brain." His innovation was two more exotic ingredients: something called damiania, and the kola nut, from Africa. Both were touted as having energy-enhancing effects, and the drink was, according to an 1885 advertisement, the perfect thing for "all who are afflicted with any nerve trouble, dyspepsia, mental and physical exhaustion," among other things. It was hinted that the drink might be an aphrodisiac as well.

Pemberton later changed the name of his murkily powerful tonic and adjusted his formula to remove the traces of cocaine in 1903. Of course, his invention, now known as Coca-Cola, is no longer marketed using hokey means like playing up the "invigorant" powers of some mysteriously potent ingredient discovered in a faraway land. But it remains famous for its "secret formula" a century later and has surpassed the worldwide success of Vin Mariani many times over.

Today, the phrase "snake oil peddler" means anyone selling something useless, probably to a bunch of gullible rubes. But what the snake oil salesman actually sold was snake oil, and that was exactly what he wanted his potential customers to know: Snake oil was considered a virtuous ingredient; it was used in remedies to treat joint pain in China and, later, the United States, particularly in the frontier West. Increasingly spectacular "medicine shows" were a fixture of American life by the end of the nineteenth century. These were extravaganzas and in some cases promoted brands that were thoroughly national. Hamlin's Wizard Oil sent its rigidly controlled "concert troupes" to perform "open-air advertising" concerts, using horse-drawn mobile stages with a built-in organ, all over the country. The Kickapoo Indian Medicine Company, seller of salves, oils, cough cures, and "Sagwa," was perhaps the biggest of the medicine show companies, with one hundred units or more, typically consisting of half a dozen tepees, a twenty-foot-wide stage, and ten or more performers, traveling as far as the West Indies.

The patent medicine companies also advertised heavily. Their often outlandish claims appeared not just in newspapers – many of which basically depended on the business – but in all manner of outdoor advertising, from billboards and posters to the sides of trolley cars.

Charitably, one can imagine a physically ailing consumer, in a time when a visit to a reputable doctor was not necessarily a routine event, becoming diverted by an entertaining extravaganza long enough to let down his or her guard and – in a rickety bridge moment – decide that it was worth trying a bottle of Wizard Oil. Less charitably, one can simply think about how easily people used to be suckered, hoodwinked, and fooled. When an exhibition of "quack" advertising from the nineteenth century appeared at the Philadelphia Museum of Art in 2005, wall tags explained that the wild claims for the benefits of these dubious products and treatments were "widely believed in an era when double-blind studies for effectiveness were nonexistent."

But as that same "quack" art exhibit made clear, vociferous public criticism of patent medicines and other fishy-sounding products of medicine show culture were a constant presence. The critiques climaxed with the rise of muckraking journalism near the turn of the century, which eventually inspired government regulations like the Pure Food and Drug Act of 1906, cracking down on the fantastic – and, crucially, *specific* – claims of the patent medicines. (The medicine show was bound to die out anyway, with or without government rules: "The end came, in large part, because of competition from other forms of free entertainment," Brooks McNamara wrote in his study of the form, *Step Right Up*. "The premise of the medicine show was that a free performance would sell a product. The premise was a sound one and radio and television merely borrowed it and developed it on a scale far beyond anything dreamed of by the traveling medicine showman." And kept on developing it – right up through today.)

The vast majority of patent medicines were not so much dangerous as useless, and in many cases the pitchman simply responded to regulation by being a little murkier – "cough cure" became "cough syrup"; instead of patent medicine offering "cures," tonics offered "pep." They let the consumer fill in the blanks. This was what Vin Mariani did. And Coca-Cola did, too, with its "secret formula." At the very least, some of these consumers were tricking themselves. They were, you might say, collaborating with the pitchman in the creation of a product's meaning.

Jackson Lears, in his books *Fables of Abundance* and *Something for Nothing*, has explored a history of America that is not simply a triumphant march of progress, but an ongoing competition between two visions of life: one guided by doctrines of science and technology and rationality, the other by beliefs that transcend the measurable and controllable and tilt over into the realms of fate, providence, and even magic. "The recurring motif in the cultural history of American advertising," he has written, "could be characterized as the attempt to conjure up the magic of self-transformation through purchase while at the same time containing the subversive implications of a successful trick."

Sometimes this could be pulled off simply through lying. But sometimes, perhaps, some of those buyers were engaging in "magical thinking," an element of what Lears terms the Other Protestant Ethic: not the plodding approach of the Puritans, but rather the "fascination with the ecstatic experience of conversion, the moment when the soul transcended its human limits." This tendency plays well into the "carnivalesque" tradition that has waxed and waned throughout the history of commercial persuasion.

Still, most of us surely assume that to the extent that this tradition exists, it has little effect on us.

After all, we live in the age of the double-blind study.

the interesting effects of energy drinks

This brings us to an interesting question: What, exactly, is "taurine"? Taurine is important, a Red Bull spokesperson told me, because "in times of stress and strain, your taurine levels are depleted, and Red Bull replaces them." The key to the "kick," I was informed, comes from the combination of caffeine, taurine, and glucuronolactone, a "carbohydrate that rids your body of toxic substances." When I ran this by Gregory Stewart, co–medical director of the Institute of Sports Medicine at Tulane, he dismissed the idea that boosting taurine level has a meaningful impact on physical or mental performance – just like most medical professionals who have been asked. A study in the journal *Nutritional Neuroscience* reported that the only ingredient in energy drinks found to have a measurable impact on mood and performance was caffeine (energy drinks generally have extremely high caffeine content). As for taurine, another nutrition expert, at Rutgers, has summarized: "We haven't got a clue to what it does." A Canadian study examining the effect of taurine on cycling performance found that it had "no effect . . . on anything," one of the researchers involved told me.

A Coca-Cola executive explained to *The New York Times* that the beverage giant's entry into the lucrative energy drink category included taurine and various other exotic-sounding ingredients because, basically, the consumer is boss, and that's what the consumer wants – whether it has any real effects or not. "We make no claims about any of them," she continued. "We believe in marketing our brand by focusing on the brand's personality rather than the ingredients."

Here, perhaps, is the true lesson of the energy drink boom: The real secret of Red Bull is there is no secret.

But there's another study to consider. It was organized by Dan Ariely, a management science professor at MIT, along with collaborators Baba Shiv and Ziv Carmon. They were interested in how the effectiveness of something like an energy drink might be affected by its price and by third-party claims. Rationally, of course, such things can have no direct effect on whether or not Red Bull or any other energy drink "gives you a boost." Just because a Vin Mariani poster promised that the tonic "fortifies and refreshes body & brain," just because a satisfied consumer of Kickapoo Indian Oil claims that the stuff cured his "nervous headache" – none of it has any *real* meaning. Everyone knows that.

The 204 participants in Ariely's experiment were split into four groups. In each group, everyone drank a can of SoBe Adrenaline Rush, waited ten minutes, and then were asked to solve a series of puzzles; a set of written instructions explained that the subject had thirty minutes to solve 15 puzzles. An earlier pilot study – that is, one not involving energy drinks – had established that the average number of puzzles solved was 9.1.

For half the subjects, the written instructions also included this statement: "The website of SoBe includes references to over 50 scientific studies suggesting that consuming drinks like SoBe can significantly improve mental functioning." The other half got the same note, except that in their version the claim was downgraded: Energy drinks were said to "slightly" improve mental function. There was a second variable. Each of the two groups were divided again: Half were told the drink cost $1.89, the normal retail price, and the rest that it would cost half the regular price, thanks to an institutional discount (that is, nothing to do with the quality of the drink).

Members of the group that drank full-price SoBe and had been told the drink "can significantly improve mental functioning" were by far the puzzle-solving stars of the experiment; they completed an average of 10.1 each – better than the energy drink–free norm of 9.1.

The other groups, curiously, all performed well *below* normal. The worst was the group told that SoBe might "slightly" boost mental functioning and that they were drinking 89-cent cans; those subjects managed only 4.2 puzzles on average.

This seems bizarre. It's one thing for the power of suggestion to lead a person to believe that a certain beverage tastes better than another – or even that it is better than the same thing in a different package. But here the change occurred not in the subjective realm of taste, but in the measurable realm of a kind of mental performance. The experiments, the researchers argued, suggested that "marketing actions" and price changes can affect "not only *perceived* quality, but also *actual* quality" of a product.

Perhaps what Lears calls "magical thinking" – that belief in the transformative power of certain, right stuff – is not just an artifact of a vanished, prerational age. Perhaps it is, instead, one of the most powerful forces of the world of marketing. Perhaps it is powerful because it comes from us. And because we believe it's real. Maybe if we believe that it's real, then somehow it is.

all about marketing

Since that day I first encountered Red Bull's murketing efforts, its profile has continued to rise – as has its spending on its oddly flexible image. At this point, practically everybody knows what Red Bull is; it's in every supermarket and is the stuff of late-night talk-show punch lines. There's even a diet version now. Red Bull, in other words, is totally mass. Somewhere along the line, Dietrich Mateschitz even started to give interviews and was quoted saying things like "Everything we do is about marketing."

Much of the brand's approach has continued to be, while not cheap, decidedly unconventional. Rather than simply sponsor sports teams, Red Bull preferred to buy them: It owns two Formula One racing teams and one soccer club in Europe, and in the United States, it announced plans to start a NASCAR team, bought the New York MetroStars, a major league soccer team, and promptly renamed them the New York Red Bulls. The company also carried on with its more obscure sports endeavors – involving some eight hundred official Red Bull athletes – such as the Red Bull Air Race (small planes slaloming through air-filled pylons over the river Thames) or a Red Bull-created sport called "Crashed Ice" (a cross between hockey and snowboarding). It continued the club-culture-focused projects, like Red Bull Music Labs, and began dabbling in video games through a partnership with a game developer. In 2006, it cut a deal with the Independent Film Channel to produce five-minute alt-sports documentaries about its various stunts and extreme-sports activities, never shilling directly for the drink but not exactly turning the camera away if it happened to come to rest on a Red Bull logo worn by a participant. (This fit into IFC's efforts to create "TiVoproof" revenue sources, *Brandweek* noted.)

In time Red Bull did run television commercials, as it gradually increased its distribution to truly mass scale. And as it happens, they demonstrated that murkiness is not just about the medium, it is also about the message: Its TV spots were vague and pointless things featuring a bull animated in a sort of *Schoolhouse Rock* style. The slogan "Red Bull gives you wings" could mean anything and almost sounded like a kind of secret code. The ads did nothing to specify the Red Bull claim or clarify the Red Bull idea. It was still up to the consumer to decide what this stuff was for and what it supposedly did, how it was relevant to him or her.

And in this way, at least, not much had really changed since my initial encounter with the brand back in 2001. The morning after my rendezvous with Red Bull on Miami Beach back then, I sat in the little breakfast room of the Key West Comfort Inn. It had been made over into Command Central, with a laminated map taped to the wall. The organizer of the "Cuba Crossing," Gilles d'Andrieux, a dashing thirty-two-year-old Frenchman, arrived and led everyone through the basics. The eighty-eight-mile trip was expected to last eight hours, touching down on the coast one hundred miles east of Havana. Winds on launch morning would likely gust to twenty knots or better. Everyone going on the trip got forms to sign that said things like "I agree that upon my transport to any medical facility or hospital, Red Bull shall not have any further responsibility for me."

A few days later, d'Andrieux debriefed me on how it turned out. Neil, Kent, and another rider made it all the way to Cuba. Oliver, the model, got his kite tangled and barely got off the starting line. A fifth rider, Paul Menta, who insisted on going even though he was battling the flu, passed out about halfway through the trip, falling off his board facedown in the water, arms akimbo. D'Andrieux fished him out, apparently saving his life. (I spoke to Menta later, and he said he flew back to Florida the next morning because he had blood in his urine.) All in all it was a rough ride, d'Andrieux concluded, but a clear triumph: The party arrived at 6:38 p.m., after eight hours and thirty-eight minutes on the water. The sun had set by then, and it was too dicey to kiteboard all the way to shore, so they stopped five hundred feet short of Cuban sands and took the boats the rest of the way. All five kiteboarders told me the same story.

So I was surprised when I later got a press release from Red

Bull, which presented a somewhat different version of events. It had the three kiteboarders "arriving in Cuba at 5:55 p.m., one minute before sunset." A tape of the "video news release" put together by the company responsible for documenting the event included a few minutes of highlights and some comments from a couple of the kiteboarders. This footage was what went out over the wires and was picked up for use by more than forty local news broadcasts around the country. In the video, oddly, the three kiteboarders surf all the way onto the shore and celebrate with high fives in light that is obviously presunset. The release didn't say so, but the scenes of the boarders' "arrival" – unbeknownst to the folks who used the footage in their evening news broadcasts – had been shot the following day.

Questioned about this, my Red Bull contact called the video release "a huge mistake not in line with our brand values." But it doesn't really matter. This is the final lesson of modern murketing theory, one that would be familiar to those who have built businesses off quenching our various thirsts for more than a century: When the truth doesn't quite work, substitute something better.

And whatever the facts may be, the *truth* is that any Red Bull drinkers, or potential drinkers, who might be impressed by the Cuba crossing are going to get exactly the message Red Bull wants them to get. People who are receptive to the idea that Red Bull's involvement makes the drink cool will decide that without additional prompting. Other Red Bull fans will never hear about it or just shrug when they do and dream up some other, murky reason to buy the next can.

They won't even need to see a commercial.

chapter ten

the commercialization of chitchat

unhidden persuaders

Many of the guests arriving at cookouts on a particular July 4 weekend not so long ago – at a family gathering in Kingsley, Michigan, at a small barbecue in Sag Harbor, New York, at a sixty-guest picnic in Philadelphia – had something in common: They brought, for the grill, packages of Al Fresco brand chicken sausage. We can know that this happened, and even how various party guests reacted to their first exposure to Al Fresco, because the Great Sausage Fanout did not occur by chance. The sausage bearers were not official representatives of Al Fresco sausage, showing up in uniforms to hand out samples. They were invited guests, friends or relatives of whoever organized the get-togethers, but they were also – unknown to almost all the other attendees – "agents," and they filed reports. "People could not believe they weren't pork!" one agent related. "I told everyone that they were low in fat and so much better than pork sausages." Another wrote, "I handed out discount coupons to several people and made sure they knew which grocery stores carried them." A third observed that "my dad will most likely buy the garlic" flavor, before closing, "I'll keep you posted."

These reports went back to the company that Al Fresco's owner, Kayem Foods, had hired to execute a "word of mouth" marketing campaign. And while the Fourth of July weekend was busy, it was only a couple of days in an effort that went on for three months and involved not just a handful of agents, but two thousand of them. The agents were sent coupons for free sausage and a set of instructions for the best ways to talk the stuff up, but they did not confine themselves to those ideas or to obvious events like barbecues. Consider a few scenes from the life of just one agent, named Gabriella.

At one grocery store, Gabriella asked a manager why there was no Al Fresco sausage available. At a second store, she dropped a card touting the product into the suggestion box. At a third, she talked a stranger into buying a package. She suggested that the organizers of a neighborhood picnic serve Al Fresco. She took some to a friend's house for dinner and (she reported back) "explained to her how the sausage comes in six delicious flavors." Talking to another friend whom she had already converted into an Al Fresco customer, she noted that the product is "not just for barbecues" and would be good at breakfast, too. She even wrote to a local priest known for his interest in Italian food, suggesting a recipe for Tuscan white bean soup that included Al Fresco sausage. The priest wrote back to say he'd give it a try. Gabriella asked me not to use her last name. The Al Fresco campaign is over – having notably boosted sales, by 100 percent in some stores – but she was still spreading word of mouth about a variety of other products, and revealing her identity, she said, would undermine her effectiveness as an agent.

The sausage campaign was organized by a small company in Boston called BzzAgent, part of a wave of firms that have sprung up in recent years to serve the growing number of companies that concluded they needed to find new, postclick forums for consumer seduction. The forum they had in mind was not TV ads or billboards or even video games, but rather the conversations we have in our everyday lives. Word-of-mouth marketing agencies joined the various other persuasion professionals who had been organizing veritable armies of hired "trendsetters" or "influencers" or "street teams" to execute "seeding programs," "viral marketing," and "guerrilla marketing." What were once fringe tactics were becoming, despite some controversy, increasingly mainstream. By 2006, JWT Worldwide estimated that of the top one thousand marketing firms in the United States, about 85 percent used one word-of-mouth strategy or another. There is even a Word of Mouth Marketing Association.

Marketers bicker among themselves about distinctions among the various word-of-mouth tactics and strategies, but to those of us on the receiving end, this debate is largely academic. They are all attempts, in one way or another, to break the fourth wall that used to separate the theater of commerce, persuasion, and salesmanship from quotidian life. To take what may be the most infamous example, an agency working on behalf of Sony Ericsson once hired sixty actors in ten cities to accost strangers and ask them: Would you mind taking my picture? Those who obliged were handed, of course, a Sony Ericsson camera-phone to take the shot, at which point the actor would remark on what a cool gadget it was. And thus an act of civility was converted into a branding event.

This fresh frontier of murketing – the commercialization of chitchat – resembles a scenario from some paranoid thriller about a world in which corporations have become so powerful that they can bribe whole armies of flunkies to infiltrate the family barbecue. That level of corporate influence sounds sure to spark outrage – another episode in the long history of mainstream distrust of commercial coercion and marketing trickery. Fear of unchecked corporate reach is what made people believe in things like the popcorn hoax and turn Vance Packard's book *The Hidden Persuaders* into a best seller in the 1950s; it is what gave birth to consumer rights movements from the Progressive era through the 1970s; and it is what alarms people about neuroscientists supposedly locating the "buy button" in our brains today. Quite naturally, many of us are wary of being manipulated by a big, scary, Orwellian *them*.

But as it turns out, it is not just them. Gabriella and the rest of the sausage agents are not paid flunkies trying to manipulate Main Street Americans; they *are* Main Street Americans. Unlike the Sony Ericsson shills, Gabriella was not an actress. She was an accountant, with full-time work and a twelve-year-old daughter, living in Bayonne, New Jersey. Aside from free samples, she got no remuneration. She and her many fellow agents had essentially volunteered to create "buzz" about Al Fresco sausage and dozens of other products, from books to shoes to beer to perfume. By 2006, BzzAgent claimed to have more than 125,000 volunteer agents in its network.

And it has rivals. Tremor, a word-of-mouth operation that is a division of Procter & Gamble (maker of Crest, Tide, and Pampers), said it had an astonishing 240,000 volunteer teenagers spreading the word about everything from toothbrushes to TV shows to motor oil. A spin-off, originally called simply Tremor Moms and later renamed Vocalpoint, is now even bigger: By early 2006, the company claimed to have 500,000 carefully screened "influencers" in this network of moms, spreading word of mouth about P&G products like Crest Whitestrips as well as for outside clients, like the makers of the WD-40 No-Mess Pen and a nature show on the Discovery Channel.

A company called BoldMouth reportedly recruits twelve-year-olds on behalf of certain films. Girls Intelligence Agency targets girls age eight and up for Mattel, Hasbro, Disney, and Fox. Various youth-oriented firms have put up websites recruiting teenagers to serve as "secret agents." One example: Alloy.com, a teen chat site, searched through its data to find seven thousand teenagers who had, in their discussions on the site, said something that suggested interest in the UPN show *America's Next Top Model* and culled a battalion of five hundred to help UPN, its client. (The girls got "party kits" with the idea that they'd have their friends over to watch the show.) A Massachusetts company called Communispace, meanwhile, claimed to have set up more than two hundred invite-only brand-oriented social networks, with memberships ranging from four hundred to one thousand, for clients like Kraft, Hewlett-Packard, Reebok, and Starwood Hotels. "The communities have had tangible effects," *Advertising Age* reported. "Community members assured Unilever's Axe that its Tsunami body spray wasn't insensitive following the 2004 disaster, and they helped Kraft decide which Asian foods it should include in a line of diet products."

Given that we are a nation of busy, overworked people who in poll after poll claim to be sick of advertisers jumping out at us from all directions, the number of individuals willing to help market products they had previously never heard of, frequently for no money at all, is puzzling to say the least. BzzAgent, with its particularly intense relationship with a growing legion of volunteers, offered a rare and revealing case study of what happens when word-of-mouth theory meets Desire Code consumer psychology in the real world. In finding thousands of takers, perfectly happy to use their own creativity and contacts to spread the good news about, for instance, Al Fresco sausage, it has turned commercial influence into an open-source project. It could be thought of as not just a marketing experiment, but also a social experiment. The existence of tens of thousands of volunteer marketing "agents" raises a surprising possibility – that we have already met the new hidden persuaders, and they are us.

what motivates the agents?

Dave Balter, who founded BzzAgent in 2001, when he was thirty, is a smart guy, but he would be poorly cast as a slick Madison Avenue mastermind. Fresh-faced, good-humored, almost goofy, he cheerfully told me that he had no definitive explanation for why it was that tens of thousands of average citizens want to be, in company parlance, BzzAgents. In the beginning, he had a theory about what would motivate regular people to generate word of mouth for his clients – but that theory was full of holes.

For example, it assumed, reasonably, that agents would require some kind of quasi-financial motivation to do legwork for consumer companies. Balter's background was in loyalty marketing – those frequent flier-style programs that give rewards to dedicated users of a particular product, service, or credit card. He read up on word-of-mouth marketing theory, raised some money, hired a right-hand man, and put the word out among family and friends that he was looking for "agents." The idea was to build a network of people who would get points for spreading "honest word of mouth" and could cash in the points for cool products. "The whole concept," he said, "was rewards, rewards, rewards."

The first full-fledged Bzz campaign was for a book called *The Frog King*. It lasted one month and focused on New York City. Balter persuaded Penguin Publishing to let him do it by charging the publisher nothing. *The Frog King* was a quirky, comic first novel by a young writer named Adam Davies. Davies wasn't exactly going to get a giant publicity blitz. "We didn't expect much" from the campaign, recalled Rick Pascocello, a Penguin vice president.

The guide for the agents, a no-frills seven-page document in those early days, welcomed them as members of "an elite group" of word-of-mouth spreaders and listed the contact information for "your BzzLeader," BzzAgent JonO. (That was Jon O'Toole,

Balter's right-hand man.) It summarized some of the novel's highlights, noting a few passages in particular that might be useful "conversation points," and suggested tactics like reading the book on mass transit with the cover clearly visible, posting a review on Amazon.com, and calling up bookstores and chatting with the clerk about this great new book about New York publishing with lots of sex and drinking whose title you can't quite recall. JonO signed the cover letter assuring agents that the folks back at the hive found the book laugh-out-loud funny.

Local events for *The Frog King* drew larger than expected crowds of 100 or 150 people, according to Pascocello, who said that, thanks to the word-of-mouth campaign, the book sold in three months what he had hoped it would sell in a year. Soon there were more than fifty thousand copies of *The Frog King* in print, and BzzAgent has had a steady flow of paying clients ever since (including Penguin, which has used BzzAgent to promote other books, like the novel *The Quality of Life Report*). The fee it charges varies according to the size and nature of the campaign, but in 2005 a twelve-week campaign involving one thousand agents cost $95,000.

Before long, BzzAgent had about seventy-five paid employees. Many were young, without backgrounds in traditional marketing. When the company took on a new client, a group huddled to figure out whatever is most buzzable about the product at hand. One summer day, for instance, I sat in as they handed around and discussed a new line of Johnston & Murphy dress shoes, which featured a fiberglass shank rather than a traditional metal one so they wouldn't set off metal detectors at airports. A whiteboard was filled with suggested conversation starters and likely sites for word-of-mouth opportunities. This was later refined and transferred to a slick Bzz guide for the agents.

As the number of agents grew, the company was able to meet increasingly specific requests for, say, agents of a certain age or income level or who live in certain parts of the country. It has done campaigns for a wide array of goods and for major companies and brands like Anheuser-Busch, Lee jeans, Ralph Lauren, even Du Pont. The company has also worked with clients to convert existing loyal customers into private, well-organized, word-of-mouth forces.

Although Balter told me he was pleased with his agents' efforts from the start, he did worry early on that the system could not be sustained. The problem was that while agents were spreading buzz and thus earning and piling up points, most were not cashing them in. That is, they weren't bothering to collect their rewards. "We've built a broken model," Balter thought. He asked his colleagues from his loyalty marketing days: Is it that the rewards aren't good enough? Are they too hard to get? After many hours of listening to the conflicting analyses of experts, he and O'Toole decided to ask the agents themselves about the points. "We didn't realize the agents would want to talk to us," Balter said. This was another miscalculation; many of the agents very much did want to talk. In essence, they told Balter that there was nothing wrong with the rewards; it was just that the rewards weren't really the point. Even now, only about a quarter of the agents collect rewards, and hardly any take all they have earned.

Ginger Powell, a woman in her early thirties living in a working-class section of an outer borough of New York, was among the firm's earliest agents and became one of its most effective. (I have changed her name here.) When she signed up for her first BzzAgent campaign – *The Frog King* effort, in fact – she was working with a pharmaceutical researcher, mostly doing paperwork, and thinking about finding a more fulfilling way to spend her days. An enthusiastic reader, she heard about BzzAgent through a website called Bookcrossing.com, an online community where someone had posted about the firm. Like everyone who signs up at the BzzAgent site, she was accepted.

During active stretches, Powell told me, she put in between

five and ten hours a week talking up products and writing reports about her activities. (She signed up for many campaigns, including a perfume called Ralph Lauren Blue, a line of jeans for Lee, and something called No Puffery, a gel to soothe skin below the eyes.) What, I asked her, if not the potential to get some free prizes for her effort, made her bother to volunteer with BzzAgent? First, she told me, she gets the chance to sample new products shortly before they hit the stores, so she gets to feel a bit like an insider. Second, she has always liked to give people her opinion about what she's reading or what products she's using, and BzzAgent gives her more to talk about. Third, if she *does* like something, then telling other people is helpful to them. In other words, participating is both a chance to weigh in and be heard and something close to an act of altruism.

What Balter said he learned from his agents is that *lots* of people like to tell others what they are reading and what restaurant they've discovered and what gizmo they just bought. In his view, BzzAgent is simply harnessing, channeling, and organizing that consumer enthusiasm. This is presumably why it's so easy, so natural, for someone like Ginger Powell to work word-of-mouth efforts into daily life. When, for example, a friend mentioned to Powell that she would have to get up early after a late night out on the town, she brought up No Puffery. When a pharmaceutical representative visiting her office worried about looking lousy at a meeting she had to fly to, Powell mentioned No Puffery. At her grandfather's wake, "a relative told me how well I was looking," she wrote in one report back to the BzzAgent hive, "and I mentioned that No Puffery helped to keep me looking calm instead of puffy-eyed and as horrible as I felt."

magic people

The endless chatter of American consumer life that BzzAgent has infiltrated is not simply a formless cacophony; it has its structures and hierarchies, which have been studied exhaustively for decades. Tremor, the Procter & Gamble word-of-mouth unit, was founded in 2000 with those structures in mind. A key Tremor premise is that the most effective way for a message to travel is through networks of real people communicating directly with one another. "We set out to see if we could do that in some systematic way," Steve Knox, Tremor's CEO, told me. He added a second, closely related premise: "There is a group of people who are responsible for all word of mouth in the marketplace." The idea is that some friends are more influential than others, and those are the ones who are chosen to join Tremor.

Who are they? The answer seems to be found in the word-of-mouth industry's favorite graph. This graph is meant to show the pattern by which ideas or products or behaviors are adopted, and it looks like a hill: On the left are the early adopters; then come the trend spreaders; the mainstream population is the big bulge in the middle; then come the laggards, represented by the right-hand slope. This is not new stuff – Knox himself cites research from the 1930s, as well as the 1962 academic book *Diffusion of Innovation,* by Everett Rogers – but it has become extremely popular in the twenty-first century. Seth Godin (whose ideas partly inspired BzzAgent) uses it, as do dozens of other marketing experts. Malcolm Gladwell's *The Tipping Point* made an argument about these ideas that was simultaneously more textured and easier to digest than most of what had come before (or since) and put them firmly in the mainstream.

But whatever the intentions and caveats of the various approaches to the subject, the most typical response to the graph is to zero in on the segment that forms the bridge over which certain ideas or products travel into the mainstream – influentials, trend translators, connectors, alphas, hubs, sneezers, bees, and so on. Let's just call them Magic People.

Knox told me that (teen-focused) Tremor's approach to finding the Magic People was intensively researched. The company tried to isolate the psychological characteristics of the subset of influential teenagers and developed a screening process to identify them. The details of this were a secret, but as an example, Knox noted that most teenagers have 25 or 30 names on their instant-messaging "buddy list," whereas a Tremor member might have 150. Tremor recruited volunteers mostly through online advertisements and accepted only 10 or 15 percent of those who applied, he said. The important thing, he added, was that they were the right kinds of kids – the connected, influential, trend-spreading kind. Knox mentioned a focus group of Tremor kids in Los Angeles, where several teenagers showed up with business cards. Magic.

Tremor was certainly not the first outfit to be entranced by the idea of Magic People. In the mid-1990s, firms like Sputnik, the Zandl Group, Teenage Research Unlimited, and Lambesis were getting hired by companies such as Reebok, Burlington, and PepsiCo to enlist and study allegedly trendsetting teens. "We did no research," Irma Zandl, who has been in the trend business since 1986, once told *Time* magazine of her early days as a professional Magic Person. "I just had a golden gut." By the early 2000s, her company claimed a network of three thousand carefully selected young people whose take on the zeitgeist was funneled into a newsletter sold to the likes of GM, Coke, and Disney, for $15,000 a year. Some key people from Lambesis formed Look-Look, which claimed a network of twenty thousand. The results of these businesses have been mixed. Aprons for men was one legendary trend-spotting gaffe that emerged from the mining of Magic People thoughts. In the mid-1990s, Sputnik predicted such trends as "guys in vinyl skirts," "see-through track shoes," and "suspenders with African-print shirts."

Around the same time that these trend companies were attracting attention, Steven Rifkind, a hip-hop fan from Long Island and the son of a longtime music industry executive, was being given credit for inventing the "street team," a term that he apparently coined. Rifkind wasn't studying or polling the young Magic People – he was simply hiring them. He founded his company in 1987, formalizing what he had seen on the hip-hop circuit – the way DJs and store clerks and fans traded information. The idea was for a small pack of hired cool kids to go to cool places and, for example, hand out mix-tape samplers to guys wearing a Walkman or to pretty girls. The strategy was credited with launching Wu-Tang Clan: The group's second record, released in 1997, debuted at number one, and *Spin* reported at the time that its success was "all built strictly on word of mouth, without the benefit of radio or MTV airplay." In 1992, Rifkind landed his first nonmusic client: Nike. (Phil Knight, after all, had used former University of Oregon track and field athletes to build a grass-roots network when he launched his company.) By the late 1990s, Rifkind's firm was working for Miramax and Tommy Hilfiger.

By the time Tremor and BzzAgent and others came along, this was an established tactic for companies targeting the urban market. Cornerstone, which *Brandweek* called "the king of mixtapes," distributes to ten thousand (according to Cornerstone) "influencers" promoting not just music and movies, but brands like Sprite, Hennessy, and Converse. The way that P&G tweaked the combined formula of rounding up and enlisting armies of young Magic People was simply to bring the idea out of the urban market and add massive scale.

Janet Onyenucheya was chosen by Tremor, and she is pretty much what you picture when you picture a trend influencer. When I met her she was an intern at an independent music publishing company in Manhattan: eighteen, African American, beautiful, smart, and wearing a really cool pair of (Converse) sneakers. She was preparing to enter the Berklee College of Music in Boston in the spring. She'd gotten involved with Tremor a couple of years earlier, while attending LaGuardia High School.

Onyenucheya got free stuff from Tremor and sometimes even

a small check for taking surveys and participating in focus groups. She got to vote on the design for a T-shirt for the tenth anniversary of the Vans Warped Tour and of a Crest toothbrush. She was once invited to an advance viewing of two soon-to-debut television shows at a screening room in downtown Manhattan. There were about seventy teenagers there and pizza and sodas for everybody. Onyenucheya particularly loved one of the shows, *Lost*. "When I came home," she said, "I immediately told my five closest friends, like 'Oh, my God, you just missed the greatest show. I got to go down to the Millennium and saw a show called *Lost* and it was so good, and we have to watch it when it comes out.' And I felt like I had the upper hand. Like 'You don't know what I know.'"

non-magic people

By and large, the word-of-mouth literature tends to describe our influence and degree of connectedness as something hardwired. Magic People like Onyenucheya are born, not made, is the idea, which is why companies spend so much effort developing psychological profiles to find them.

But one of the fascinating things about the BzzAgent experiment was that it largely discarded this premise. Its agents were not screened. They were not chosen. They simply signed up. They were all kinds of people, all over the country: a fifty-something bookstore owner in suburban Chicago, a young housewife near Mobile, Alabama, a college student in Kansas. Many were teenagers or even younger. At least one was eighty-six years old. Yet it seems they were ready, willing, and able to persuade.

Jason Desjardins was a regular guy, a good guy, accommodating and polite. At twenty-eight, slim, clean-shaven, with close-cropped hair, he was the dairy manager at a supermarket in rural New Hampshire, part of the same supermarket chain he had worked for since high school. Although he was wearing a Brooklyn T-shirt when we met, the truth is he bought it at the Old Navy in the Concord mall and had never been on an airplane or even traveled outside of New England. Jason Desjardins was sweet and guileless, but he was not, by any expert definition, a Magic Person.

Desjardins stumbled across a reference to BzzAgent online, and he was interested. How could this thing work? He signed up, and soon after, they sent him *Purple Cow* – Seth Godin's most recent book at the time – and his life changed. It's hard to overstate how enthusiastic Desjardins was about BzzAgent. He joined campaigns for several other books, as well as for a beer called Bare Knuckle Stout, a spam-blocking service called Mail-Block, and, yes, Al Fresco sausage. He figured he spent about ten hours a week either buzzing or writing reports about buzzing. I visited him at his apartment in Bradford, New Hampshire. We were joined by his wife, Melissa, a pretty woman with a stylish haircut and a big smile, and their two-year-old daughter. I wondered how Melissa felt about her husband spending so much time on a no-money hobby. In fact, she was thrilled. She said she thought it had made him more open to other people. He used to be the kind of guy who just hated to call a mechanic about a noise the car was making; he would wait until the car actually broke down and he had no choice but to bother someone about it. He was in a shell. But that has changed – partly because of Melissa, Jason wisely interjected – but also partly because of his involvement in BzzAgent.

For starters, Desjardins said, BzzAgent "turned me on to reading." And having enjoyed *Purple Cow*, he wanted to do his best to spread the word. The Bzz guide suggested he call a bookstore. For a while, he put it off. He would look at the phone and tell himself, "I can do this," and he would try to rehearse what he would say, and this would go on for fifteen or twenty minutes. "I thought: 'What have I got to lose?'" he said. "'I'm never going to see this person.'" Finally he called and pretended he did not know the name of Seth Godin's new book. "He'll call anybody now," Melissa said, smiling.

He printed slogans from *Purple Cow* ("Be Remarkable or Be Invisible") onto card stock and hung them where his fellow employees could see them. He posted reviews on Amazon. He started conversations with co-workers, customers, strangers. He submitted a rave review for a fantasy novel he was buzzing called *Across the Nightingale Floor* to the *Concord Monitor,* and it was published; there's a laminated copy of the review on the fridge. He wrote to the governor touting Mail-Block. At the grocery store, when a co-worker moaned about not liking her job, Desjardins practically turned into a motivational speaker, waving his hands and quoting from another book called *The 5 Patterns of Extraordinary Careers,* telling her that if she wasn't happy, she needed to take control of the situation. "She did end up finding another job after that," he observed. By then Desjardins was ranked the forty-fifth most effective BzzAgent, out of sixty thousand nationwide, and proud of it. He had learned to influence.

Now, this was all good for Desjardins, but it doesn't really square with what the experts say about word-of-mouth influence. The whole premise of the Magic People is that the rest of us take our cues from them because they have some special credibility, in the form of reputation or expertise or connections. In April 2003, that premise was put to the test when BzzAgent began a thirteen-week campaign for a restaurant chain called Rock Bottom Restaurant and Brewery, which had about thirty locations around the country. This particular campaign was studied by two academics: David Godes, an assistant professor at Harvard Business School, and Dina Mayzlin, an assistant professor at Yale School of Management. The experiment involved more than one thousand subjects; some were devoted Rock Bottom customers, and the rest were BzzAgents – none of them Rock Bottom loyalists; only a few had even heard of the chain.

Rock Bottom wasn't running any other significant marketing program at the time.

Sales increased markedly. Godes and Mayzlin found that, consistent with past research, word of mouth traveled more effectively when it was spread not through close friends, but through acquaintances (meaning that networkers – the people with the big buddy lists – are more valuable). But curiously, it turned out that the agents – the "nonloyals" – were more effective spreaders of word of mouth than the chain's own fans. Godes and Mayzlin hypothesized that the Rock Bottom's most devoted customers had probably already talked up the restaurant to all the friends and acquaintances they were likely to tell.

The researchers also looked at the tendency of marketing efforts to focus on "opinion leaders," who often gain that social status by way of expertise. The results here were somewhat mixed, in an interesting way. A loyal opinion leader – someone who was seen by her social network as an expert on restaurants and who was also a Rock Bottom fan – was pretty effective; if that restaurant expert was ambivalent about Rock Bottom, she was of little use. In contrast, it didn't really matter if the nonloyal agents knew much about restaurants. What mattered was that they told a lot of people (and presumably that they were enthusiastic). The implication is that it doesn't matter if you know what you're talking about, as long as you are willing to talk a lot.

When I spoke to Godes, he offered some caveats to that particular conclusion. He pointed out that expertise may be much more important to real-world word of mouth – the kind that occurs absent an orchestrated effort to create buzz from scratch. He also emphasized that willingness to talk doesn't mean much if you have no one to talk to.

Maybe so. But when Dave Balter saw the results, it provided strong evidence for a position he had been coming to for a while: He didn't quite believe in Magic People anymore. BzzAgent's system did, of course, try to identify who has a large network of friends, who is an expert, and who is outspoken, just as Tremor does in its screening. (Actually, a number of BzzAgents are Tremor members as well.) "But we also know that sometimes those people aren't the best at spreading word of mouth," Balter said. "We all get information from people around us who don't fit any type of profile that would make them more intelligent or more focused on products than someone else." And the information we share changes, too. "We might go from influential to noninfluential, from trendsetter to nontrendsetter all year long," he suggested, "because we have continued interactions that change our opinions."

On some level, then, participating in a voluntary marketing army serves as a kind of consumer-status enabler that is tailor-made for the interpreter. Maybe you weren't the first on your block with a LiveStrong bracelet; at least you can be the one to tell your friends about Al Fresco sausage. And the more people you can persuade that Al Fresco sausage is good, the better you'll feel about your discovery. BzzAgent, in turn, will help you be a better persuader. Pretty much everyone likes the feeling of having "the upper hand," as Janet Onyenucheya put it. Even in the small orbit of your own social circle, knowing about something first – telling a friend about a new CD or discovering a restaurant before anyone else in the office – is satisfying. Maybe it's altruism, maybe it's a power trip, but influencing other people feels good.

As an example of how powerful the desire to have the upper hand can be, consider that some participants in a campaign for a new scent called Ralph Cool simply could not wait for their free sample to arrive and rushed out to buy the $40 product so they could start buzzing. Word-of-mouth marketing leverages not simply the power of the trendsetter, but also, as Balter puts it, "the power of *wanting* to be a trendsetter."

the "mere ownership" effect

BzzAgents are under no obligation to push a product they don't like. In fact, if they think it's awful, they're encouraged to say so. Yet of all the agents I spoke to, and the hundreds of reports I read, there were hardly any examples of outright dissatisfaction with a product. Most of the agents seemed genuinely excited about most of what they were buzzing.

Part of the reason is that most people tend to join campaigns for things that interest them. Perhaps just as important was that the volunteers, hearing that BzzAgent turns down 80 percent of potential clients, seemed to believe that the folks at BzzAgent spend their days sorting through the morass of consumer culture, choosing only the best of the best. BzzAgent does want to keep lousy products out of the system, of course, but it also wants to make money. It's a business. And its ability to keep the system relatively free of flat-out awful products probably has much less to do with acting as a consumer-culture curator than with the Pretty Good Problem: The same embarrassment of choices that makes consumer decisions complicated was good for BzzAgent's prospects. There was no shortage of stuff out there it could flow into its system without much worry.

Still, people's tastes differ, and it seemed remarkable that agents are so rarely disappointed. What explains this? One oddity the behavioral economists Daniel Kahneman and Amos Tversky discovered in their research was "the endowment effect." They found that when two items of equal value are handed out randomly to a group of people and given the opportunity to trade, hardly anyone does. It's very unlikely that all the participants were randomly handed the objects they would have preferred had they been asked in advance, so the economists concluded that once something has been given to us, we value it more.

In another experiment, conducted in the early 1990s by a

psychology professor at the University of Louisville, two groups of subjects were given nine similarly valued objects and asked to rate the desirability of each. One group was informed in advance it would get to keep one of the items – one of those insulating tubes that keeps canned drinks cold. The other group, which didn't get to keep anything, rated the desirability of all the objects roughly equal. The first group's ratings, however, pointed to a clear favorite: the drink-insulating tube. That is, they concluded that the thing they'd been told they would get to keep was better than all the others. A follow-up experiment found that this "mere ownership" effect was essentially instantaneous.

This research on how we value – or irrationally overvalue – things that are given to us might help explain why BzzAgents and other word-of-mouth volunteers get excited about whatever they are asked to push. And not only does the process make the product inescapably salient to the agent, it encourages him or her to ruminate on all the ways it might be relevant. Perhaps such rumination even explains why, during the course of that Johnston & Murphy meeting, I gradually went from being indifferent to the shoes to wishing I could have a pair. (And if you're curious why, in light of this, you're not crazy about every product you've ever bought, the answer may be "adaptation" – our tendency to get used to our possessions and, in effect, fall out of love with them. For the word-of-mouth volunteer this hardly matters, since by the time it happens the campaign is over. I'll have more to say about adaptation in this book's final chapters.) But it doesn't address another mystery: Why would the volunteers work so hard to get other people excited about these products?

Another line of research suggests a possible answer. This school of thought would characterize word-of-mouth volunteers as operating not in a traditional money-in-exchange-for-effort "monetary market," but rather in a "social market." A social market is what we engage in when we ask our friends to help us load up the moving van in exchange for pizza. The research suggests that we are likely to get a better effort out of our friends under the social market scenario than by offering the cash equivalent of the pizza. (An article in the journal *Psychological Science* found that "monetizing" a gift, like the pizza, by announcing how much it is worth effectively shifts the whole situation from social market to monetary market.) Under some circumstances, we will expend more effort for social rewards than we will for monetary rewards. This suggests that the agents may do more to spread word of mouth precisely because they are not being paid.

Add to all of this the idea that they have been granted status as "agents" in an "elite group" that most of the world doesn't even know about and have received a free sample of a brand-new product from a source that they trust, and unless the thing is definitively flawed, they are almost certain to expend some kind of effort.

honest opinions

There was another advantage to the social market. Since the agents were not being paid, and had the option to ignore any Bzz object they didn't like, they tended to see themselves as not being involved in marketing at all. Almost all of the BzzAgents I interviewed made this point. "In marketing, obviously, those people are paid to pump a product, whereas I'm not really getting paid to do this," explained Powell, the agent from outer-borough New York. "I don't talk about a product if I don't feel strongly about it. I'll give my honest opinion."

The notion of the "honest opinion" came up again and again in conversations with the agents and with Balter. Can any conversation be honest if one participant has a hidden agenda? I asked several agents and Balter himself several times. Of course the agents believed in their own integrity, but that was the easy part. Do we really want a world where every conversation about a product might be secretly tied to a word-of-mouth "campaign"? Doesn't that kind of undermine, you know, the fabric of social discourse?

"The key is," Balter replied, "people already talk about this stuff. They already talk about things they love." Manufactured word of mouth is indeed a bad and scary thing, he maintained, but that's not what his company is doing. "For whatever reason, we have this natural instinct to tell a friend about a product – and to get them to believe what you believe. We're not trying to change that. All we're trying to do is put some form around it, so it can be measured and understood. That's not changing the social fabric."

It is certainly easier to defend the voluntary buzz spreaders as less devious than the paid model pretending to like a product in public – but the honesty and openness came with an asterisk or two. Those suggestions in the Bzz guides to call bookstores and pretend you didn't know the exact title or author you were looking for were pretty hard to define as "honest." Similarly, it's most unlikely that Amazon.com (let alone the *Concord Monitor*) would consider the reviews of a BzzAgent quite as unbiased and helpful to readers as a review from someone who hadn't consulted talking points compiled with input from the publisher. The whole tone of the Bzz guides – which read like a cross between a brochure and a training manual – was a bit difficult to square with the idea of genuineness.

As BzzAgent's profile rose, it attracted some controversy – at least some of which, I should disclose, was partly the result of an article I wrote about word-of-mouth marketing in *The New York Times Magazine* – and some of its practices have changed. (Also, for the record, the *Concord Monitor* stopped using Desjardins as a reviewer.) A debate about ethical standards took shape within the word-of-mouth community, in light of the actions by various consumer groups to get these new murketers regulated.

In late 2005, Commercial Alert, a consumer advocacy group, asked the Federal Trade Commission to investigate the tactics of various word-of-mouth marketers, particularly those focused on teenagers. "There is evidence," executive director Gary Ruskin wrote in a letter to the agency, "that some of these companies are perpetrating large-scale deception upon consumers by deploying buzz marketers who fail to disclose that they have been enlisted to promote products." About fourteen months later, the FTC replied that, while it had chosen not to "issue guidelines" on the matter, it did suggest that if a company is "paying" a person – a "sponsored consumer," as the FTC put it – to spread word of mouth, then he or she must disclose as much to his or her targets. This still left a good deal of uncertainty over what constitutes "payment," but the FTC said it would evaluate specific future complaints on a "case-by-case basis."

In any event, BzzAgent had already changed its code of conduct by then. Previously, while the company had told its volunteers that they were under no *obligation* to hide their association with the company and its campaigns, it seemed to me that most of them hid it most of the time. And so a new policy theoretically *required* its agents to identify themselves. (Other members of the Word of Mouth Marketing Association agreed to similar policies.) This seemed to address the FTC's main concern preemptively.

Sometime after this new rule went into effect, a research project conducted by Walter J. Carl, an assistant professor of communication studies at Northeastern University, tried to gauge its effects. His study found that 37 percent of buzz targets reported afterward that they did not know they were talking to an "agent." That finding suggests – new policy or no – that a pretty significant amount of undisclosed buzzing continued. (Curiously, the vast majority of the targets claimed that the revelation had no effect on their reaction to whatever the agent had said to them.)

And in the real world, it's hard to imagine how any word-of-mouth agency can police its disclosure policies. After all, the reasons that agents had given me for not mentioning their affiliation in casual conversations seemed to have less to do with consciously nefarious motives than simply avoiding awkwardness. "It just seems more natural, when I talk about something, if people don't think I'm trying to push a product," Ginger Powell had explained to me. Other agents had said the same. Jason Desjardins had told a few people about his efforts for BzzAgent, with mixed results. Some people thought it sounded exciting. Others, however, said they felt "used." One friend he had tried to recruit later responded with suspicion when Desjardins talked up something he has done: "Are you buzzing me?" the friend would ask. Telling me about this, Desjardins shrugged. "I've been honest about everything." Similarly, Gabriella insisted to me that she really did think Al Fresco made the best sausage around. Basically, they all trusted BzzAgent, and they all trust themselves, so they didn't see a problem.

One reward Powell did collect from BzzAgent was, of all things, the William Gibson novel *Pattern Recognition* – paranoid thriller about a world in which corporations have become so powerful, they can bribe flunkies to infiltrate your life and talk up products. "It made me think, when somebody says something about a product – I wonder. That gave me a little pause," she said. Earlier in our conversation, I had touted my iPod. Wouldn't she feel differently about my comments, I asked, if it turned out that I'd gotten it from Apple or a BzzAgent equivalent? "That's true," she said. "But you know what? If you start questioning everyone's motives, then you'll be in a home with tinfoil on your head."

Moreover, the motives of chattering consumers can be biased in all kinds of ways, whether they are "agents" or not. If your friend is bragging about his great new cell phone, he may not be doing so on behalf of the company that made it – but he may not be the purely rational information source you assume. He says it's the best phone around, and maybe he even believes it – but the truth may be that he bought it because it looks cool and he read that Vince Vaughan has one just like it. Your friend may simply be in effect telling a story about himself – that he's a well-informed, clever guy who of course was smart enough to buy the best phone around. It may be true that we trust our friends more than TV ads, but that doesn't actually mean they've become more reliable.

stronger than persuasion

The most interesting thing about the BzzAgent system was the small team of young people in Boston who read and answered every single Bzz report. They offered encouragement, tips on how to improve word-of-mouth strategies. Every report was rated and every agent ranked according to a complicated formula, one that is constantly being tweaked, taking into account everything from how often the agent reports to how many people they tend to buzz to the quality of their summaries – plus intangibles like originality. (This system was part of BzzAgent's defense against people signing up for free stuff and simply making up fake reports about their buzz activities; the home office was said to be trained to spot such things.) Along with the feedback, they almost always threw in a joke or a comment so it was clear that they had actually read the report.

No doubt because of this, many agent reports were full of personality. Some were almost confessional; others were revealing perhaps without intending to be. Casual mentions of boyfriend or girlfriend problems came up, as did complaints about bosses, friends, strangers. One of the most memorable was from a young BzzAgent who reported that a man she met in a bar complimented her on her Ralph Cool perfume, one thing led to another, and they spent the night together. The next morning, he asked about the perfume again and said he liked it so much, he might have to buy some for his wife. (These reports are ultimately handed over to the client; entertainment value aside, they are a trove of anecdotal research from the front lines of consumption.)

Along the way, Agent JonO became a kind of celebrity, or at least a figure of mystery. There are more calls and e-mail messages and instant messages to "JonO" than Jon O'Toole himself can possibly deal with, so eventually JonO became more of a construct than a person. Jason Desjardins sounded honored to have had a chance to meet the real JonO: O'Toole lined up a dinner in Cambridge with several BzzAgent volunteers, to meet them and hear their thoughts and ideas. Desjardins was so excited about this that at first he overlooked the fact that it was on the same night as his wedding anniversary. (Melissa encouraged him to go anyway. "But we'll see if JonO is still there for you ten years from now," she joked.)

Balter did not count on the agents taking BzzAgent so seriously. He still doesn't seem to know quite what to make of it. When he met agents, they often seemed almost apologetic about not doing more – about not buzzing enough on this or that campaign. One agent resigned because he said he was unsure whether he could live up to BzzAgent's ethical standards. The biggest complaints came from people who said they had not been invited to join enough campaigns.

This might be the most peculiar thing about BzzAgent: Not only are its volunteer agents willing to become shock troops in the murketing revolution, but many of them are flat-out excited about it. At his apartment, Desjardins told me about another book he had read because of BzzAgent. Called *Join Me*, it's about a guy who decides he wants to start some sort of voluntary group – a commune, a cult, whatever you want to call it. He puts an ad in the paper that just says, "Join me," and to his surprise, people are interested. They didn't know what they were joining or why, but they joined anyway. The guy, whose name is Danny

Wallace, decided to turn his followers into a good-deeds army, basically on the "pay it forward" method. The book is nonfiction.

Why, I asked Desjardins, did people join a group without even knowing what it was? Well, he explained, Wallace's theory was that they just wanted to be part of something. That made sense to me. Some people are lucky enough to find meaning and fulfillment through their work, civic engagement, or spirituality. But many don't. Many people have boring jobs and indifferent bosses. They feel ignored by politicians. They send e-mail to customer service and no one responds. They get no feedback. It's easy to feel helpless, uncounted, disconnected. Do you think, I asked Desjardins, that there's some element of that going on with BzzAgent?

"I think for some people it probably is," he answered. "For me, it's being part of something big. I think it's such a big thing that's going to shape marketing. To actually be one of the people involved in shaping, that is, to me, big." That made sense to me, too. After all, being part of something bigger than oneself is half the fundamental tension of modern life. That's why there's one thing that is even more powerful than the upper hand and more seductive than persuading: believing.

chapter eleven

the brand underground

a new form of cultural expression

I'd been hearing about Aaron Bondaroff for a while before I
finally met him, in 2006. He was twenty-nine, part Puerto Rican,
part Jewish, Brooklyn born, and a high school dropout; his life
weaved through the most elusive subcultures of lower Manhattan.
A-Ron, as he was also known, was one of those people who
embodies a scene. "I'm so downtown," Bondaroff was fond of
saying, "I don't go above Delancey."

Even so, he longed for something bigger, like the cultural
noise made by the Beats in the 1950s or Andy Warhol's Factory
in the 1960s or the bands and fans who clustered around CBGB
in the 1970s. He wanted to "make history" and join "the timeline"
of New York. He was not an artist, an author, a designer, musician,
filmmaker, or even a famous skateboarder or graffiti writer. In
another era, Bondaroff might have had to settle for his cameos
in some of the acclaimed images of youthful outsider debauchery
captured by his photographer friend Ryan McGinley. He could

be, in other words, a counterculture muse, like Neal Cassady or Edie Sedgwick.

In the murketing era, however, he may not have to settle. There's an alternative, one that's summed up neatly in a question that A-Ron had been asking himself around the time that I first met him: "How do I turn my lifestyle into a business?"

The answer he came up with is worth paying attention to because it captures the relationship between youth culture and branding in the time of murketing – and thus hints at the direction of American consumer culture. Young people have always found fresh ways to rebel, express individuality, or form subculture communities through cultural expression that often subsequently becomes part of the mainstream: new art, new music, new literature, new films, new forms of leisure, or even whole new media forms. A-Ron's preferred form of expression, however, was none of those things. When he talked about his chosen medium, which he called aNYthing, it sounded as if he were talking about an artists' collective, an indie film production company, a zine, or a punk band. But in fact, aNYthing was a brand. A-Ron put his brand on T-shirts and hats and other items, which he sold in his own store, among other places. He saw it as fundamentally of a piece with the projects and creations of his antimainstream heroes.

We have already seen plenty of examples of how corporations labor to associate their brands with bigger ideas – individuality, community, and the like – but of course, traditional companies don't go into business to express a particular worldview and then gin up a product to make their point. Corporate branding remains a function of the profit motive: Companies have stuff to sell and hire experts to create the most compelling set of meanings to achieve that goal. A keen awareness of and cynicism toward this core fact of commercial persuasion – and the absurd lengths that corporations will go to in the effort to infuse their goods with, say, rebelliousness or youthful cool – is precisely the thing that is supposed to define the modern consumer. And if we can all see that corporate branding is fundamentally a hustle, then guys like A-Ron are supposed to see it better than anybody.

Which is why the suggestion that his brand possesses counterculture attributes sounds a little suspicious at first. Manufactured commodities as artistic media? Branding as a form of personal expression? Indie business as a means of dropping out? Turning your lifestyle into a business as rebellion?

Yet this is one aspect of what lies beyond murketing's final front lines: not simply infusing some company's material objects with fresh meaning, but creating meaning by creating objects – branded objects. And the reality is that thousands and thousands of young people who are turned off by the world of shopping malls and Wal-Marts and who can't bear the thought of a nine-to-five job are already doing precisely this, pursuing a path similar to A-Ron's. Some design furniture and housewares. Many leverage do-it-yourself craft skills into businesses – as we'll see in a later chapter. Still others make toys, paint sneakers, or open gallery-like boutiques that specialize in the offerings of product artists. And some convert their consumer taste into blog-enabled trend-spotting careers. Many of these people clearly see what they are doing as not only noncorporate, but also somehow *anti*corporate: making statements against the materialistic mainstream – but doing it with different forms of materialism. In other words, they see products and brands as legitimate forms of creative expression.

It is easy enough to see one big attraction for the new upstart branders who seem to jump into this realm every day. They don't have to worry about the credentialing procedures that now define the traditional high arts, like getting a master's degree from a well-connected art school or hobnobbing on the writer-retreat circuit. They don't even need to study marketing. For most founders of underground brands, their apprenticeship was the act of growing up in a thoroughly commercialized world.

Certainly A-Ron didn't need training or credentials. Through aNYthing, he saw himself as part of a "movement," a brand underground. And maybe there was something going on here that could not simply be dismissed just because of the apparent disconnect between the idea of a "brand" and the idea of an "underground." Maybe what matters isn't what outsiders think about a subculture, but what the participants think.

cool guys

Bondaroff dropped out of high school at age fifteen to spend more time partying, getting into trouble, and hanging out with the people who were worth hanging out with. He ended up getting a job in lower Manhattan at the Supreme store. Theoretically a skateboard brand, Supreme was really an attitude brand, and the store had a reputation as a place where clerks would insult you to your face if you weren't cool enough. A-Ron was not only cool enough, he was photographed for Supreme ads and became its "unofficial face." He offered his opinions about what would make the photo shoot work better or which underground artists the brand should work with. Supreme caught on in Japan, and by the time Bondaroff was twenty-one, he was visiting Tokyo and getting asked for autographs by kids who had seen his picture in magazines. "I was always bugged out by that – people are like 'Oh, you're that guy,'" he told me. "You get famous for nothing."

While still basically working a retail job, he was also becoming the cool guy who is flown to Australia to sit on a trendsetter panel or whose elaborate birthday party is underwritten by Nike. He was a full-on Magic Person, and he was figuring out that because of this he had the option of becoming, in effect, a corporate muse. But he concluded that there was no reason to rent his coolness and knowing-ness to other companies. The point of aNYthing was to turn his lifestyle into *his own* business.

He devised his brand not long after September 11, 2001, and it was deeply tied to his love for New York City and his own status on the downtown scene. The "NY" in the logo resembled that of the New York Giants football team, and aNYthing designs often blended familiar New York iconography (from the *New York Post* nameplate to Lotto signs) with the brand's name. He opened a boutique in 2005 on Hester Street on the *lower* Lower East Side.

One reason an underground brand sounds nonsensical is that countercultures are supposed to oppose the mainstream, and nothing is more mainstream than consumerism. But we know the postclick world cannot be divided into the Mainstream and the Counterculture. It's a world of multiple mainstreams and countless counter-, sub-, and countersubcultures. Bondaroff's brand was built both on the sort of microfame that such a finely cut cultural landscape enables and on his absolutely exquisite ability to analyze that landscape. He knew that he was seen by the various trendhunters or Japanese magazine editors or marketing types who hit him up for the latest news as a professional Cool Guy. He recognized that taste was his skill.

He and his friends even turned downtown demographics into a kind of parlor game: There are Cool Guys and the Art-Damaged crowd, the Parent Haters, the Dropouts, and so on. "I like to label all the different scenes," he explained to me. "I coin the phrase, and people use it, and it goes back to me." In fact, he made a related set of T-shirts. He called up his friend Futura, the veteran graffiti artist, and asked him to write "Kool Guys"; that was one of the shirts. "I'm exposing everybody," Bondaroff said, and included himself in the critique. ("I'm definitely a Cool Guy – the top Cool Guy on the scene," he said. "I'll say it loud and proud.") This was the quintessence of the postmodern brand rebel, hopscotching the minefield of creativity and commerce, recognizing the categorization, satirizing it, embracing it, and commoditizing it all at once.

If A-Ron and his crew were the ideological descendants of the scenesters who clustered around Warhol in the Factory period or hung out at CB's in its heyday, then perhaps they were trying a new tactic in the eternal war against the corporate suits who co-opt the rebellion, style, and taste of every youth culture and sell it right back to the generation that created it. Perhaps the threat that brand-smart young people really pose to commercial persuaders is not that they have stopped buying symbols of rebellion. It is that they have figured out that they can sell those symbols, too – and the next big thing will be a million small things.

what i (finally) learned about nike

Many of the success stories that the brand underground upstarts aspired to replicate – like A Bathing Ape, Supreme, and Stussy – have been around since the early 1990s or longer and began as adjuncts to the spectacular subcultures associated with hip-hop or the DIY "Beautiful Losers" generation. Countless others have come and gone. Among the survivors are Lenny McGurr and Josh Franklin, better known as the graffiti writers Futura and Stash.

McGurr, who had recently turned fifty when I met him, has seen many iterations of the dance between subculture and mainstream. He made the transition from painting on subway cars to selling paintings in East Village galleries back in the 1980s. The Futura-Stash creative partnership began around 1990. Separately and together, they made T-shirts, and they struggled to get by. But by 2006, the brands and products they created or oversaw – from clothes to vinyl toys to rugs and pillows – were sold in boutiques around the world. Franklin had his own stores, Recon and Nort, in New York, San Francisco, Tokyo, and Berlin; Futura had stores in Fukuoka, Japan, and Bangkok. Futura and Stash's Williamsburg headquarters was a rambling series of rooms filled with boxes of merchandise, ten or so employees, and a skate ramp.

One thing that had changed since the days when they scrambled to make a living was that Japanese consumers embraced certain small New York brands as something culturally significant and worth a price premium. Nigo, a Japanese designer, built a fanatical following for his A Bathing Ape brand partly because he collaborated with so many graffiti writers and others who had an aura of street cred that impressed young, hip Japanese consumers. "The legacy of our history from New York gave us a lot more credibility over there than it did here," McGurr told me. He compared it with the black jazz musicians who had to go to Paris to be appreciated.

The second change was the click. Technology allowed production to become more accessible – it is easier than you think for a two-person brand to work with factories overseas, using computer files and the occasional package – and the Internet in particular has acted as an amplifier of salience and relevance. Ten years ago, a new T-shirt design could not be flashed around the planet minutes after completion. Nor could it be championed in blogs like Hypebeast and Slam X Hype, dedicated to this practice, reporting dozens of new products or design collaborations from the brand underground every day.

And there was a third factor: Manufactured commodities have in fact become accepted as quasi–art objects. As it happens, there is no more stark example than the sneaker. I began my education on sneaker meaning not long after having my personal epiphany about Converse – realizing, that is, that I cared about brands more than I thought I did. This was when I met Yu-Ming Wu. He was twenty-three and the cofounder and "sneaker editor" of a website called Freshnessmag.com. Part of what had made Converse my sneaker of choice, and the reason I'd ended up having a consumer dilemma, was my resistance to wearing what I considered a particularly annoying mainstream brand: Nike.

Like Apple users disdainful of Microsoft or PBR drinkers turned off by obnoxious big-beer-brand marketing, I had found an antidote to one brand in the form of another, and that's largely why I was bothered by the news that Chuck Taylor was becoming a Nike product. I had assumed, given all I'd heard about the new generation of young consumers shunning mainstream brands, that I'd find plenty of skepticism about a megabrand like Nike in the brand underground.

Meeting Wu and his Freshnessmag cofounder, Danny Hwang, was a big clue that I had no clue. Hwang was wearing a pair of Nike Shima Shima 2 Air Max 1's ("a U.K. exclusive," he explained). Wu wore Air Max 90 Pythons and noted that he owns twenty identical pairs. In their world, Nike, with its ubiquitous swoosh, was somehow not a staid mainstream brand to be avoided. It was the undisputed king.

Hunting for unusual sneakers and modifying them with markers or different laces had been cool for decades, a phenomenon defined in Harlem and the Bronx that developed right alongside the brand remixing of Dapper Dan and the Shirt Kings. "We were the first generation, and only one, to enjoy sneaker consumption on our own terms," Bobbito Garcia asserted in his book about sneaker hunting in the 1970s and 1980s, *Where'd You Get Those?* – a blend of memoir, sociology, and the cataloglike history of urban sneaker collecting that made the case for sneakers as nothing less than symbols of personal identity.

If there was a consumer base willing to think of athletic shoes made by multinational corporations that way, then a new breed of boutique stores, which started to appear in the early 2000s, would serve them. Eventually the sneaker companies got wise and began to cater to this market, manufacturing rarity through "limited editions," commissioning small runs of sneakers made for specific stores or designed with the help of people like Mister Cartoon or Neckface. (If you don't know who they are, these shoes aren't for you.) Instead of stealing ideas from the underground, the big sneaker makers positioned themselves as supporting it. The strategy seemed to work. Both Stash and Futura have designed co-branded products with Nike.

Hwang, who grew up in Queens, and Wu, who is from the Bensonhurst section of Brooklyn, met at the Parsons School of Design in Manhattan but really bonded while exploring the nearby Lower East Side. A lot of what they did there was shop – or, as Wu puts it, "collect." Talking to them made it clear that Nike was hardly seen in the marketplace as a stodgy and vulnerable brand. Time and again, Wu told me, Nike has innovated in the quality of its actual sneakers (appealing to athletes), in the way those sneakers look (appealing to the "lifestyle" wearer), and in edgy ways to promote them – limited editions, collaborations with underground artists, and so on. "Everybody tries to copy Nike," Wu summarized.

Neither seemed to take seriously the politically grounded exploitation-of-Asian-labor critique that dogged Nike in the 1990s as it moved its manufacturing overseas – the issue that Naomi Klein had theorized in *No Logo* would be Nike's undoing. And that's worth noting, given that Wu and Hwang are not just members of the most educated, plugged-in, and coveted consumer demographic, but also both of Chinese descent. They told me that low wages in Asian factories are better than no wages. "The worst joke I tell is, 'They're employing my people,'" Wu said with a deadpan shrug.

Wu was a kind of superconsumer; he called himself "a hunter" and loved seeking out limited-edition Nikes, gathering information on new offerings and where and when they'd "drop." I went with him one day when a rare Nike Laser Cortez – part of a series of shoes decorated with a new laser-etching technique – was set to be released. There was never a formal announcement for these events, let alone an advertisement; word just got around. We met on the Lower East Side, outside one of the first rarefied sneaker boutiques, the Alife Rivington Club, which had no sign and required the customer to press a button and get buzzed in.

It turned out that the Alife Rivington Club wasn't getting any sneakers for that Cortez release – even store owners don't seem to know for sure until the day of the drop – but Wu had a list of other places we might hit. As we dashed from one shop to another, Wu kept bumping into fellow travelers through the world of exclusive sneakers, trading information here and there.

This information hunt was what his site, Freshnessmag.com, was largely about. Subcultures are often built, in one way or another, around exclusivity, sharing information, being in the know. Freshnessmag.com collected what Wu and Hwang gathered about their obsessions – from art openings around the world to exclusive photographs of prerelease sneakers – and built an audience. The site helped Hwang and Wu pick up invaluable contacts, from Vancouver to San Francisco to Hong Kong, who help them get ever better information. (Over time, they also heard from pretty much every major sneaker maker.) Meanwhile, sites like theirs made sneaker hunting more accessible – and more visible. With the Web, a relative handful of fanatics scattered around the world can look like a scene, and if enough people buy into that idea, then eventually it *becomes* a scene.

This created a new layer of people – half consumer, half entrepreneur – who snapped up hot commodities with the sole intention of reselling at a profit. A T-shirt that Futura or Stash designed ten years ago, and made in small numbers because that was all the market would support, might now trade hands on eBay for $100; today, some of the most successful minibrands keep production runs well below demand in order to maintain an image of specialness and rarity (just as the sneaker giants do). You can say the Internet made the market or that it simply made the market visible, but these are the same thing. Nothing draws people like a crowd, virtual or otherwise.

Soon there were sneaker and streetwear boutiques all over the country; people slept on sidewalks outside some of them because they had heard about some new limited-run product and wanted to be first in line for it. Occasionally, things got out of hand and the police were called. There were magazines about sneakers, a sneaker show on ESPN, a sneaker podcast called *Weekly Drop,* and a sneaker documentary, *Just for Kicks.* NikeTalk, a community and gossip web-site created by and for sneakerheads, claimed to have more than fifty thousand registered users.

Several years ago, some sneaker fans in Australia decided to mount a show of their collections, and this became Sneaker Pimps, which has been on a permanent world tour ever since. When it hit New York in 2005, the line outside the club Avalon, where the sneakers were on display, stretched well down the block. Inside was a cross between a trade show, a museum exhibition, and a nightclub. Walls were lined with notable sneakers, famous customizers were on hand, and an artist named Dave White, who paints impressionistic portraits of sneakers on canvas, was on a platform, working under a spotlight, while DJs spun. Later, Public Enemy performed. If Warhol's Factory laid the foundation for giving consumer objects fine-art scrutiny, and Keith Haring's Pop Shop built on that foundation, it is still hard to imagine that either artist could have predicted such a thorough product-as-medium spectacle. Later, Sneaker Pimps even launched a clothing line.

Freshnessmag.com, meanwhile, became a popular destination for sneakerheads – as well as a way for Hwang and Wu to convert their passions into revenue streams. They collaborated with a Singapore-based artist and "sneaker customizer" called SBTG, who made a set of eighteen custom Nike sneakers that went on sale exclusively through their website at $350 each. These sold out in ten minutes. And perhaps inevitably, they started designing and selling sets of limited-edition T-shirts of their own. When Nike and Apple released a collaborative product called Nike+ that linked sneakers to an iPod, the companies invited about twenty-five "global influencers" to a private party at the Gansevoort Hotel in New York to hobnob with Steve Jobs, Nike CEO Mark

Parker, and Lance Armstrong; the list included Futura, Stash, various other brand underground designers – and Yu-Ming Wu.

All of that came to pass long after my morning spent with Wu on one of his sneaker runs, but even back then it was clear that something remarkable was going on. We ended up at an obscurely marked basement shop called Nom de Guerre. A clutch of other young Nike superconsumers were on line – white, black, and Asian. After a bit of a wait, a store employee announced that there were exactly ten pairs available; following the custom in these situations, each shopper would be limited to one pair (price: $140), though by enlisting me, Wu scored two. The moment the transaction ended, he headed back upstairs to try one more shop, even though he knew that since it was by then a bit after noon, he had little chance of finding anything more than, perhaps, some new rumors about what might be next. He didn't even bother to open the boxes to look at his new sneakers.

the hundreds revisited

Scores and scores of tiny streetwear brands were working this newly discovered territory by the middle of the first decade of the 2000s, with names like Crooks & Castles or Married to the Mob . . . or the Hundreds. That, you will recall, is the T-shirt brand we encountered at Magic in the first chapter of this book. It was cofounded by Bobby Kim (one of three children of Korean parents who came to America and made good; his father is a physician) and Ben Shenassafar (another child of successful immigrants, his father is an accountant from Iran), who met in law school, came up with their underground brand idea, and became Ben and Bobby Hundreds in 2003.

I'd kept in touch with the Hundreds since that meeting at Magic, as both their brand and the brand underground in general gathered strength. Their site, TheHundreds.com, had become quite popular, featuring Bobby's essays and interviews with people he admired: "The culture's finest brands, artists, designers, photographers, retailers and media," the site said. It wasn't fancy, but it made clever use of technology and was updated regularly with gossip from the scene and pictures of the Hundreds' friends (and of parties and girls). There might be a clip from YouTube of an evening news report on the crowd lining up to get the latest Stash-Nike collaboration from a boutique in San Francisco. Or maybe a clip of Los Angeles teenage skaters showing off in free Hundreds Ts. These kids were just doing what kids do, goofing around and trying to look cool; but they were also, technically speaking, Hundreds "team riders," happy to find themselves with an impressive sponsor while still in high school.

The Hundreds kept adding new stores to their distribution list, from New York to Paris to Tokyo – the right kinds of stores, of course, stocked with other independent, properly underground brands. Ben and Bobby remained focused on "the Hundreds lifestyle" – Los Angeles, skateboarding, music, art – that they'd first peddled to the buyer at Fred Segal. You can get some sense of what this is supposed to mean through a specific Hundreds T-shirt graphic, like the one on a shirt they titled "Jerky Boy." The design took the logo of Tommy Boy, the pioneering hip-hop label, and reimagined its three silhouette figures in the style of the moshing cartoon teenager used as an emblem of the legendary Southern California punk band the Circle Jerks. Looming over the Circle Jerks mascot, who is repeated in three Tommy Boy poses with props including skateboards and handguns, is "the Hundreds" and the phrase *California Culture*.

Streetwear designers often refer to graphics that riff off some other logo or icon or brand name as "parodies." Kind of like the Ramones' logo, which took the presidential seal but substituted a baseball bat for the arrows the eagle clutches in its talons. But the word *parody* can be misleading: Often the visual references are more like a sampled bass line – recognizable to some but not to others – that makes a remix add up to more than the sum of its parts. A descendant of what Dapper Dan and the Shirt Kings were up to back in the 1980s, these graphics can be tribute or mockery or something in between, but the new cultural (and monetary) value that results accrues to the minibrand that did the remixing.

It's these symbols and references and logos that the minibrands create that are usually said to "represent" a culture or lifestyle. But I found myself asking, What, exactly, did that culture or lifestyle actually *consist of* – aside from buying products that represent it? Bobby did his best to clue me in. "It's just the idea of trying to be rebellious," he said. "Or trying to be a little bit anti, questioning government or your parents. Trying to do something different."

Those are familiar answers, and the brand underground hardly counts as the first time that vague rebelliousness has been translated into an aesthetic: Spectacular subcultures from skateboarding to hip-hop (to the Red Hat Society) do it routinely. And the style and iconography of, say, punk arguably did more than music – let alone ideas – to fulfill the crucial subcultural function of group identity. It just happens that in this instance the symbols, products, and brands aren't an adjunct to the subculture – they *are* the subculture.

In 2006, the Hundreds had a breakthrough. Their spring line, still dominated by T-shirts, included a hoodie with an all-over paisley print. The day these arrived, a number of their cool-guy friends dropped by the new office space they had rented in West Hollywood; Bobby took pictures and posted them on TheHundreds.com. One of these images ended up on the front page of Hypebeast, a popular streetwear blog. Bobby put the whole line up for sale on the website at 1:30 in the morning; then he turned off his cell phone and went to bed. A few hours later, his girlfriend was pounding on the door of his apartment. Ben, unable to reach Bobby, had called her with the news: The entire line had sold out. Bobby posted a new entry on the site: "Which one of you sickos is up at 4 a.m. buying T-shirts?"

Soon the paisley hoodies were going for $250 or more on eBay, two or three times the retail price. Of course, Ben and Bobby had made only about five hundred of them and under the orthodoxy of the scene would look greedy if they manufactured more. (Ben's accountant father has softened on the Hundreds as a potential business but couldn't understand why they refused to make more of those "stupid paisley hoodies," Ben told me.) A few weeks later, the retail consulting firm Doneger, whose clients include major department store chains, sent out a bulletin called "Streetwear – The Next Generation," naming brands that trendsetting kids in New York City were wearing. The list included Nike and Stussy but also upstarts like Artful Dodger, Triko . . . and the Hundreds. Their T-shirt orders were climbing every season.

Not surprisingly, the Hundreds were optimistic – for themselves, but also for their fellow travelers in the brand underground. On the site, Bobby posted pictures of the latest line outside the Supreme store in Los Angeles. "It's a great sign for our industry/culture/scene/whatever-it-is. It shows how fast we're all growing," he wrote. "Another notch for the independents."

the dog whistle narrative

Maybe you buy the idea that brands can be a legitimate form of subcultural expression, and maybe you don't. But there is a reason the commercial persuasion industry pays a lot of attention to what cutting-edge young people are up to: They represent, perhaps, a proxy for the future. I spent a good deal of time with these young minibrand entrepreneurs, and what I concluded was that what they were up to had very little to do with the rejection of brands as a source of meaning. To the contrary, it had everything to do with *accepting* that brand meaning is a given and using this notion to their own ends. This, I think, does tell us something about where the market, the culture – the dialogue between what we buy and who we are – may be headed.

For a clearer sense of where that might be, consider one last example – not through the prism of what the brand underground suggests about the nature of subcultures, but through the prism of how commercial persuasion is changing.

Daniel Casarella was a young man who had something to say. At twenty-eight, he was fascinated with the gritty, turn-of-the-century New York underworld described in Luc Sante's book *Low Life*. His brother, Michael, twenty-three, was writing his college thesis about nineteenth-century New York literature, and the Casarella brothers came to believe that the depths of the forgotten past offered an intellectual antidote to the superficial, surface-driven present. The first time we met, Casarella told me the story of the Collect Pond in lower Manhattan: drained because of pollution in the early 1800s, it was filled in and became the brutal Five Points slum. "My brother and I have this theory of the Collect being the original sin of Manhattan," he said, launching into a riff on man's betrayal of nature and its consequences.

He wanted to get these ideas across to others, but instead of writing a novel or making a series of paintings, he started making T-shirts. He learned screen printing at the Fashion Institute of Technology but never considered actually joining the industry to work long hours for somebody else. Instead, in 2003 he founded Barking Irons – the name is nineteenth-century slang for pistols – a line of T-shirts with stark but intricate graphics that look like old woodcuts, paired with mysterious phrases that refer back to the secret history of New York. One was inspired by the Collect Pond and another by a Washington Irving story. After he had printed some of his first designs, Casarella dropped off samples at Barneys, the high-end Manhattan department store, in a paper bag.

A pricey department store doesn't seem a likely place for expressing ideas, but the store's buyer called him the next day.

It turned out "new ideas" were exactly what the company was hungry for, according to Wanda Colon, a Barneys vice president. Its "young-minded" Co-op spin-off stores cater to consumers who seek self-expression specifically through nonmainstream brands, like Gilded Age or Imitation of Christ, she told me. Barking Irons got attention in the fashion trade press and on blogs such as Coolhunting.com – and from an apparel distributor called Triluxe. The brand's T-shirts popped up in *GQ, Elle Girl, Maxim,* and elsewhere. The main character on the HBO show *Entourage* wore a Barking Irons shirt, and this fact was reported in *People* magazine.

A Triluxe executive told me that what the Barking Irons brand had going for it was "point of view." Adam Beltzman, the owner of a Chicago store called Haberdash – one of many boutiques serving the same shoppers Colon describes – agreed. He liked the Barking Irons aesthetic, but what sold him on the brand were the background narratives. "There's something meaningful behind it," he told me. "There's something to talk about."

Beltzman is on to something: Whether brand underground consumers *literally* talk about their T-shirts or whatever other products of the scene they might buy is not the point. The reason these material objects find an audience is that they fit into those stories of the self that Gerald Zaltman, the Harvard psychologist, described. They are part of the consumer's personal narrative.

Back in this book's first section, I made the point that the real audience for this personal narrative is not the Joneses or strangers on the promenade – it's the individual consumer. As I argued then, this is why I believe it is time to set aside the old conspicuous consumption argument that consumer behavior is all about status – all about badges. I want to underscore that point here, because the broadcasting status theory of consumption is particularly inadequate in explaining what brand undergrounders are up to.

Casarella had declared to me that his project is part of a

"revolution against branding." That sounded like a call for the snuffing out of commercial expression. It was not. In fact, it was a call for the elevation of commercial expression. What had really bothered Casarella about mainstream branding were big, blatant logos that turn the wearer into a walking advertisement. What had bothered him, in other words, were simplistic – *conspicuous* – badges. That approach, he suggested, was what makes big brands as shallow as most top 40 music or Hollywood movies. It is not that these forms (music, movies, or brands) are inherently bad; it is that they always seem built for the lowest common denominator. The contemporary consumer, he argued, demands more – more originality, more sincerity, more not-in-the-mainstreamness, a greater goal than just making money. That was what he saw Barking Irons as doing in the realm of the brand. Barking Irons does have a logo, but it appears *inside* his T-shirts, where only the consumer sees it. And the point is: Only the consumer needs to.

If it seems a little incongruous to combat superficiality by way of T-shirts that retail for $60 in exclusive boutiques, well, in Casarella's view, that's the best place to find an audience that "gets it." I'd already learned through the stories of PBR and other brands that understanding or recognizing or "seeing through" marketing culture and logos was not the same thing as being immune to or even rejecting those things. But here was something new. It made me realize that it wasn't just commercial culture that the brand underground was co-opting – it was the most exclusive and elevated form of it.

In his book about luxury, *Living It Up*, scholar James Twitchell compared the effect of certain rarefied, high-end brands with a dog whistle. As an example, he pointed to the various sorts of logo treatments on a Prada bag. A bag with a small logo would likely be more expensive than one with a big logo – and one with no logoing whatsoever would be the most expensive of all: Only true cognoscenti would "hear" it. "This was connoisseurship applied to consumption," he wrote.

A brand like Barking Irons – or the Hundreds, or aNYthing – may communicate participation in a subculture, but it does so in a way that has a lot more in common with Twitchell's dog whistle than with the aggressively flamboyant regalia of the punk or other spectacular subcultures. As in the luxury arena, you had to have the proper background to understand what you were seeing. To everyone else – underground arrivistes, Twitchell might say – the brand symbols meant nothing and probably don't even register. They were, in effect, invisible. And this was not a failure; it was the goal. It suggested a tighter relationship between the brand producer and the brand consumer but also spoke more directly to that most crucial relationship: the relationship between the consumer and consumed. If the underground logo is a badge, it's one that is most noteworthy for how few people can see it.

the grammar of branding

When I last checked in with the Casarella brothers, in mid-2007, they had begun to produce "better garments," like polo shirts, thermals, hoodies, and belts. (Printed inside these items was a Walt Whitman quote: "Whatever satisfies the soul is truth.") They were feeling pressure to expand quickly to fend off imitators but struggling with their factory suppliers, retail accounts, cash flow, and other headaches. A-Ron, meanwhile, was said to have fallen out with the financial backer of aNYthing, and had started a different brand, called Off Bowery, that he hoped would help him turn his lifestyle into a business. The Hundreds, however, seemed to be thriving, having opened their own store in Los Angeles, moved into new products like jeans and button-down shirts, begun a spin-off brand for women (called Tens), and hired nearly a dozen employees.

I had no idea – and still don't – if any of these particular mini-brands would survive. The more important fact, though, was that whatever the fate of any single upstart brand, more were popping up all the time. The brand underground had become an established part of this generation of youth culture. Its lasting significance was not in any single brand, but in what the "movement" said about changes in the secret dialogue between what we buy and who we are.

Back in the mid-1990s, when James Twitchell began writing a series of books about consumption, he passed along to his readers an anecdote about quizzing his students over their familiarity with some of the historical figures and concepts that E. D. Hirsch had named as the things that every "culturally literate" person in the United States ought to know about. "Federalism" and "Herman Melville" and so on drew mixed responses at best. Then Twitchell offered his own list, all drawn from mass marketing. And of course, everybody knew "Just Do It" and "Colonel Sanders." And they were thrilled at this evidence that they had a "common culture" after all.

As more media fragmentation and clicks continue to separate us into discrete demographics, it seems possible that this mutual recognition of old mass-culture slogans and mascots will fade. But the culture of murketing turns on something quite a bit more deeply ingrained than that. In our present era, branding and marketing are more pervasive, and more influential, and more meaningful, not less so. Regular citizens will carry out this process in collaboration with corporate brands. And at the bleeding edge of youth culture, smart and creative young people are not just aligning with brands, but creating brands of their own. The murketing era isn't about memorizing slogans. It's about having mastered the grammar and syntax of commercial persuasion. That language is the one that everyone has, for better or worse, learned to speak.

part three
invisible badges

Imagine that you are not particularly thirsty.

Imagine that you are not naked, that you're well fed, have adequate shelter and pretty much everything else you really need. Today, this would seem to describe most consumers in most of the developed world, most of the time. "Really," asked Peter Franchese, the founder of *American Demographics* magazine and now an analyst for the advertising agency Ogilvy & Mather, "how many households need two homes, three vehicles, and four TVs? It's clear that a great deal of, if not most, consumer spending is driven by desire, not need."

This is a familiar scenario – not just for the commercial persuasion professionals that Franchese was addressing, but for our society and for us as individuals. Cultural observers have been declaring that developed world economies deliver all we "need" for the better part of a century now. The good news for Franchese, the agency that employs him, and the rest of the commercial persuasion industry is that of course the line between what we feel we *need* and what we *desire* is not so easily drawn, and it shifts constantly. In 2006, the Pew Research Center polled U.S. consumers about "things they say they can't live without" and found that we needed more than ever. In 1996, 32 percent had named the microwave oven as a necessity; in 2006, it was 68 percent. Almost half named the cell phone, which wasn't on the list in 1996. (Nor was the flat-screen TV or the iPod, which were granted necessity status by 5 percent and 3 percent of respondents.) The higher the income level of the respondent, the more items he or she was likely to need.

Clearly, consumer culture – American culture – has changed since that day back in 2001 when I pondered the mysteries of Red Bull in Miami Beach. But the change is not that there are suddenly great masses of people whose most pressing thirsts are not physiological but psychological. That's been true for a long time. In the murketing era, what seems new is rather the degree to which they – we – have embraced branded material culture as an acceptable way to quench those thirsts. Thus commercial persuasion is more thoroughly integrated into our lives than ever. Thus consumers have not resisted branding and marketing, they've shown a willingness to participate in the process: Rather than reject the idea that a manufactured symbol can have meaning, many have even manufactured symbols of their own. And thus there is every indication that we'll keep moving in this direction – contrary to what so many observers of commercial culture suggest.

But I have not spent so much time in the past several years exploring what I think is really happening in consumer culture in order to merely debunk expert commentary. I have done it because I believe that understanding the real nature of the secret dialogue between what we buy and who we are is something that actually matters, especially in our specific age of abundance. The "consumer is in control" theorizing seems so counterproductive to me because it merely panders to rationale thinking, offering new reasons to behave just as we have for decades, only more so. It offers nothing useful – to business, to society, to individuals – about how to deal with the world we actually live in.

I'm sure, for example, that many of us are quite sincere when we tell pollsters that we are sick of the world being drenched in marketing. Or that we are concerned about the downsides of materialism. (According to a survey by an organization called

New American Dream, 93 percent of Americans agree that "we are too focused as a society on working and spending and not enough on family and community.") In fact, I suspect that plenty of people in the commercial persuasion industry share some of these same feelings. And if that is so, then there is nothing to be gained by simply believing we are immune to branding and the trappings of material culture. But maybe something can be gained from our understanding that we are not immune at all.

Back in the first chapter of this book, I listed what I called the four and a half rational factors in any given consumer decision: price, quality, convenience, pleasure – and the half factor, ethics. I certainly don't mean to minimize the idea of consumption ethics. In fact, I want to underscore it. I think it's a quite rational thing to consider, and I am convinced that many of us want to consider it. I gave ethics less weight than the other factors, however, because I am not convinced that we do consider it as often as we wish we did. This is why I have saved the subject for this final section of the book.

The broad subject of ethics comes up all the time in "Consumed," my *New York Times Magazine* column, usually in some more narrowly defined context: "fair trade" products for which developing-world farmers are paid prices more generous than what the open market might give them; organic products; "sweatshop-free" products; eco-friendly products; products that give a portion of proceeds to a particular cause; and so on. Eventually, I began to think of the myriad issues addressed by these items and brands under the general heading "consumer ethics." It seems to me more useful to think in this broader way, because what each of these issues gets at is the connection between our consumer behavior and its real-world consequences. Yes, symbolic meaning is real meaning, brands can play a role in the stories we tell about ourselves and help us resolve the tension between individuality and belonging. But none of us wants some bit of rationale thinking on our part to have measurably negative consequences. Everyone wants to consume ethically.

Here, then, is a different way to think about what the consumer "in control" can mean. The relationship between consumers and brand owners and product makers can be about something more tangible than assigning value to symbols. The ethics of consumption serves as a framework for understanding how the dialogue between what we buy and who we are might be changed, by business and by society – but most of all by each of us as consumers. After all, if there is one thing we really ought to be "in control" of, it's our own behavior.

chapter twelve

murketing ethics

consumer ethics

Of the things that make us uneasy about material culture, one of the most compelling is the broad question of whether consumers in the developed world consume too much, too recklessly, and are thus in the process of depleting natural resources, unleashing vast environmental damage, and destroying the Earth.

In 2005, Yale's *Journal of Industrial Ecology* published a special issue on consumption and left little doubt about its point of view on these matters. "The resource use and pollution of the global consumer class is already too much for the planet to bear," Edgar G. Hertwich announced in the journal's opening editorial. "Because the consumer class is growing both in extent and in affluence, its environmental impact keeps rising." We live in a "world in danger," argued another article in the journal. "Oceans, forests, and rivers are being degraded. More fresh water simply does not exist." A third article insisted: "We must dramatically reduce consumption of certain renewable and nonrenewable resources to avoid further harm."

The good news, we are often told, is that ethical consumption is on the rise. Various forms of "green" – or eco-conscious, or sustainable – consumption have become trendy in recent years, and consumers consistently describe themselves as quite concerned with the ethical dimensions of what they buy. A consultancy called Wirthlin reported that 40 percent of consumers say "corporate citizenship" has "a lot of influence" on their purchase decisions, and another 42 percent say it has "some influence." One estimate has it that thirty-five million U.S. adults are "LOHAS" consumers – this stands for "lifestyles of health and sustainability" and refers to "goods and services focused on health, the environment, social justice, personal development, and sustainable living." The trade publication *Brandweek* has even argued that this consumer demand is creating a "fifth column in the business world," including big companies like Ford and Estée Lauder. Trend watcher and consultant Piers Fawkes, when asked what fashion and lifestyle trend would "have resonance in the consumer goods market" in the coming years, replied:

> Eco-consciousness . . . I have a feeling that mass-adoption to eco-consciousness will be led by fashion, not by carmakers. Fashion talks to the right people who stimulate conversation in the greater public domain. Once people start wearing their eco-clothing, I hope they'll take a look at all the other products around them – the plastic products, the products with high waste packaging – and reconsider those choices, too.

An article in that same special issue of the *Journal of Industrial Ecology* passed along a wide variety of consumer responses to various surveys that offer similarly reassuring views. About 70 percent of U.S. consumers consider themselves environmentalists. Around 70 percent say they would choose a "greener" product if it were offered; 65 percent say they would do so even if it meant paying more; 30 percent report that they have avoided ungreen products; 75 percent insist that they won't buy something if they know it was made under bad working conditions; 86 percent maintain that they would pay an extra $1 for a $20 apparel item from a guaranteed "sweat-free" factory, and 76 percent say that they would pay $4 extra for such a garment.

The only problem with this happy thesis is that what many of us tell pollsters has very little to do with our actual behavior. Appeals to the ethical concerns of consumers – not just on issues related to the environment, but on labor conditions, global trade practices, and so on – have yet to transcend niche success in the actual marketplace. Perhaps, in time, that will change, and the broader market will fall in line behind the taste-making influencers, as some contend. But the click-fragmented world that gave rise to the culture of murketing makes that kind of near universal consensus harder to attain, not easier. Perhaps there's a different way for brand owners and businesses to think about how they communicate their ethical practices in the dialogue between what we buy and who we are – or even how they *don't* communicate those practices.

"it fucking failed"

Dov Charney was naked from the waist down. He was in his office with three of his employees – a man and two women – and me. The door was closed.

By the time I found myself in the scenario, I'd known Charney long enough to be unsurprised. I had first met with him in 2004, at an apartment he kept in New York. Back then, his company, American Apparel, had only a handful of stores. By the end of 2005, it had opened its 101st, with locations all around the United States and in Paris, Berlin, Zurich, Tokyo, Mexico

City, Tel Aviv, and Seoul. By 2006, American Apparel's revenues were in the $250 million range, and it had more than 3,500 employees at its Los Angeles headquarters, the largest garment-manufacturing operation in the United States. Once obscure, the brand had become famous.

Or maybe infamous, since much of the attention Charney and his company got along the way tilted toward the sensational. His idiosyncratic lifestyle received much scrutiny following a curious article in *Jane* magazine in which the writer vividly mulled Charney's sex life, right down to descriptions of his masturbation habits. And let's face it, when a successful entrepreneur stands with no pants on in front of a journalist, the journalist is likely to mention it.

I wanted to see Charney again, a year and a half after our first meeting, to talk not about his lifestyle, but about his business. Several times on this journey through consumer behavior, I have examined the ways in which adding symbolic brand meaning to a simple item, the T-shirt, transformed it from a commodity to a thing of meaning and value. Charney's business was also built on the selling of T-shirts, but the ones he sold carried no logos or symbols at all. So this time, I wanted to examine the relationship between that blank commodity and consumer ethics.

American Apparel was actually Charney's second run at making it in the garment trade. He had dropped out of college to start his first T-shirt-manufacturing business, in Columbia, South Carolina, creating a line called Classic Girl, which offered women a specific alternative to one-size-fits-all boxy cuts offered by bigger manufacturers. That brand proved no match for low-cost imported T's and went Chapter 11 in 1996. Charney moved to Los Angeles, slept on a friend's couch, and started over. He founded American Apparel in 1997 and focused on selling to the "imprintables" trade – screen printers and others who used its clothing as a canvas for original designs or band logos and so on. Basically, he became a commodity supplier. He offered a lighter, tighter cut that he felt was a throwback to a better era in T manufacture and aimed at a wholesale cost of $3 or $4, compared with the higher-end offerings that went for $6, but above the mass-oriented ones that cost $2.

In 2003, American Apparel began moving toward becoming a more directly consumer-oriented brand and opened its first retail spots, stocked with T-shirts, hoodies, and similar items in a range of colors. Back then, the company sounded to me like a marquee example of a business that had positioned itself to respond to the rising tide of ethical, antibrand consumers that I'd been reading about. At a moment when practically every clothes maker was offshoring to cut costs, American Apparel made its wares at a U.S. factory where the average industrial worker (usually a Latino immigrant) was paid $13 an hour and got medical benefits. And the company had taken out ads in arty little magazines, noting that it was "sweatshop free." That's what sparked my first meeting with Charney.

Some of what we talked about that day was in line with my assumptions. Charney remained opposed to having any kind of visible logo on his products. One of the reasons for exploitation in the apparel industry, he told me, is that apparel makers lean so heavily on logo power that they lose interest in quality issues and will put up with the problems of outsourcing in exchange for lower costs.

But it turned out that many traditional allies of socially conscious business were not embracing American Apparel. They were criticizing it for resisting a unionized workforce. *The Nation* compared the company unfavorably to a self-consciously ethical brand called SweatX, best known for being backed by the Hot Fudge venture capital fund, run by Ben & Jerry's cofounder Ben Cohen. All of SweatX's workers were members of UNITE, a garment workers union.

When I asked Charney about this, he unleashed a detailed and vigorous response that drew on everything from free market economics to the Magna Carta. There were seven thousand cut-and-sew factories in the Los Angeles area, he fumed; none were unionized, and American Apparel paid the best wages of any of them. His prounion critics would be better off criticizing factories that really did mistreat workers, he said, rather than try to score publicity points by attacking his successful business.

Indeed, the *San Francisco Chronicle* pointed out that the nonprofit Garment Worker Center, which usually supports UNITE, did not back the effort to unionize American Apparel. "The Garment Worker Center hears few complaints from American Apparel workers, and those that come up are typically minor and resolved easily," the paper wrote. In other words, unionized or not, American Apparel did not seem to have the problems with its workforce that *The Nation* had implied.

Charney's most forceful argument, however, concerned the irony of the occasion for the *Nation* piece on SweatX: The union-friendly company had just gone out of business thanks to "uneven quality," "missed delivery deadlines," and inexperienced managers. "The SweatX management team," the authors wrote, "learned too late that it could not profitably sell its products directly from the factory to individual customers or even large nonprofit organizations." Winding down from his tirade about markets and leftists, Charney got to his real point. "The article in *The Nation* was sort of saying, 'SweatX *almost* worked,'" he said, calmly. But it might have taken a different angle, he continued: that SweatX had no design expertise, not enough young people involved, and bad execution. "What that article should have said was" – and here he leapt to his feet again and slashed a pointed finger through the air – "*It fucking failed.*"

The real lesson of SweatX, to Charney, was that building a brand solely around a company's ethical practices was not a good strategy for reaching masses of consumers. The ethical sell was too limiting: It was a niche strategy, at best. Which was why American Apparel was moving away from the ethical sell to something very different.

externalities

There is plenty of evidence to suggest that Charney has a point. Despite the professed beliefs of American shoppers, the *Journal of Industrial Ecology* explained, "the actual data on 'ethical' or 'green' consumption shows that a fraction of consumers actually implement those concerns in the marketplace." It may be that a whopping majority of consumers consider themselves environmentalists, but only 10 to 12 percent "actually go out of their way to purchase environmentally sound products." Similarly, *Brandweek* (in an article separate from its fifth-column-of-eco-friendly-businesses package) reported on a survey finding that even among consumers who called themselves environmentally conscious, more than half could not name a single "green" brand. No wonder the Wirthlin survey I cited earlier, which had suggested sky-high interest in ethics among consumers, also found that only about 12 percent of corporate executives believe "corporate citizenship" has a "a lot" of influence on what shoppers choose.

Why the disconnect? Well, ask most people whether they care about the environment, and it's not particularly surprising that many would say yes. Ask whether they would back that up by "buying green" if they had the chance, and again, it's likely that very few would admit to being shallow hypocrites by saying no. Ethical virtue is easy in the context of answering a pollster's question; what we do in the marketplace is another matter.

One problem is the same real-world overload of factors we first encountered at the Magic trade show earlier in this book: price, quality, convenience, pleasure, plus the uncountable number of symbols that clutter the marketplace and the meanings they offer us as rationales to buy. Many such "externalities," as economists say, compete with our ethical concerns on any given shopping trip. "One could interpret individuals' inefficient (excessively rapid) exploitation of natural resources as evidence that they care little about future welfare," conceded one paper written collaboratively by a group of economists and ecologists. "However, we prefer the interpretation that such externalities make it impossible for individuals to express their concerns about the future in their individual production or consumption decisions." In other words, however concerned you may be about consuming ethically, the reality of the marketplace makes it dizzyingly difficult to walk your talk.

The Yale Center for Customer Insights designed an experiment to test one way this clatter of externalities can affect consumer behavior. It involved 108 subjects, divided into two groups. Members of one group were presented with a straightforward consumer choice: Would they prefer to buy a vacuum cleaner (a utilitarian object) or a pair of jeans (a bit of a luxury), each of which was assigned the same price, $50? About 73 percent chose the more practical product, the vacuum cleaner. Members of the other group, meanwhile, were told to imagine they had volunteered to spend three hours a week performing community service; they could choose teaching children in a homeless shelter or "improving the environment." They were asked to explain their choice, a process meant to prod them into engaging with the idea. Then they faced the vacuum-cleaner-or-jeans choice. In this group, a majority (57 percent) opted for the jeans.

A similar set of studies indicated that subjects were more likely to splurge on fancier sunglasses or pricier concert tickets after giving to charity. The researchers concluded: "The opportunity to appear altruistic by committing to a charitable act in a prior task serves as a license to subsequently make [the subjects] relatively more likely to choose a luxury item." In explaining their decisions after the fact, very few subjects made a direct connection between doing a good deed and their subsequent purchase decisions. Evidently, their interpreters helped them come up with other explanations. But the study strongly suggested that doing good in one area of life provided a rationale to worry less about such things in another.

There are many ways to feel you've done a good deed – and there are many ways for a consumer to feel ethical. That's why the previously mentioned LOHAS population seems so huge: This caring consumer can be someone who claims to buy ecological or "green" products or simply to be a consumer of anything from alternative health care to "personal development" offerings, including yoga or "spiritual products and services." That's a lot of options for the consumer to buy something and conclude: Hey, I've done my part.

Perhaps this is why so many big companies and brands are not so much changing their products as simply adding new alternatives to their existing lines or in some cases just carving a small donation to charity out of their profit margins. Both Nestlé and Kraft added ethical coffees to their product mixes. British chain Marks & Spencer introduced a line of clothes made from fair trade cotton, conspicuously labeled to tout this ethical production. An initiative called Product Red involved putting a special logo on products from a variety of companies, indicating that a portion of the purchase price would go to the Global Fund to Fight AIDS, Tuberculosis and Malaria. (Bono was linked to this cause, and participating companies included Gap, Armani, American Express, and Converse; there was even a Product Red version of the iPod.) Nike uses some organic cotton in some products. Even Wal-Mart – the poster brand for critics of mass consumer culture – donated money to wildlife habitat conservation, and started selling eco-conscious light bulbs. And so on.

These various efforts each add just enough options to the miles of retail shelves to give us all an ethical fix – to do our one good shopping deed. Then we can push our basket a little farther down the aisle, letting other rationales take over: Here's a bargain, here's a great product, here's something that I could probably get cheaper elsewhere, but as long as I'm here, I'll just get it – and here, yes, here is something ethical. I'll take one of those, too.

sexy t-shirts for young people

I had arranged my follow-up meeting with American Apparel's Charney specifically because his company's approach to ethical behavior in the marketplace had evolved into something so different from all of this. While more and more mass-market companies were introducing ethical-sounding subbrands or products to appeal to a concerned niche, America Apparel was attempting to move in the opposite direction: from a "sweatshop-free" image that appealed to a relatively small group of consumers to a much bigger customer base that may not know a thing about where or how the company's products are manufactured.

By the time I paid my visit to American Apparel's headquarters and factory in Los Angeles, in 2005, the company had transitioned to its new image: one soaked in youth and sex. This was apparent in its stores, where the decor often included things like *Penthouse* covers from the 1970s and 1980s, and in its print ads. Yes, some of these ads included references to quality and the sweatshop-free angle – but frequently that was in small type under a photograph of a half-naked young woman shot in a raw and vaguely decadent style reminiscent of Terry Richardson or Nan Goldin. These ads ran not in *Utne Reader,* but in *The Village Voice* and *Vice* and in more rarefied publications like *Arkitip* and *Beautiful/Decay.*

The company's (and Charney's) image was now getting so much attention that nobody seemed to bother checking into how its actual business might have changed. So I met with Marty Bailey, the company's vice president of operations. Quiet, serious, soft-spoken, and fully clothed in the presence of the media, Bailey was an industry veteran who had begun his long education in manufacturing efficiency – and the hard realities of globalization – with Fruit of the Loom more than twenty years earlier. He had come to see offshore outsourcing as more of a mixed proposition than many supposed: He believed that its promised labor savings are diluted by the costs of moving materials to the cheap labor haven and back and by sacrificed quality. He believed that with the right plan, a U.S. manufacturer could still make money.

While few were paying attention to this side of American Apparel, Bailey was playing an important role. Its factory was, he reckoned, the forty-first manufacturing facility he had walked into with the mission of revamping the system for greater efficiency. The company was producing 32,000 pieces a day and struggling to keep up with orders. In a matter of months, Bailey's system was churning out 90,000 pieces a day. In 2005, it was 190,000 pieces and heading toward 250,000. He gave me a tour of the factory, and I spent another hour or two talking with people who worked in the company's marketing and other departments. While the company was projecting an air of almost reckless decadence in its ads (and in the rather mixed PR that some of Charney's antics attracted), it was quietly building its business infrastructure to keep up with the growth it sought and that it was so far achieving.

Eventually I ended up in Charney's office, just in time, it would turn out, to witness an underwear fitting. Charney had concluded that ethical consumers were – whatever the polls might say – a niche. And he wasn't going to sell as many T-shirts as he wanted to by targeting a niche. He didn't want a niche, he wanted a *generation*.And thus: youth and sex. "We make sexy T-shirts for young people," he summarized.

As for the advertising that some people had called soft-core pornography, Charney maintained that, although the images were provocative, they communicated more than titillation. The women in them weren't models; they were people whom Charney had met and in some cases photographed himself. Many were actual American Apparel consumers, and a few were even employees. His point was that this wasn't mere imagery; it was honesty. "Young people like honesty," he said. (Earlier, a member of the company's marketing department had showed me some of the images that customers themselves sent in, essentially auditioning to be in the next squalid American Apparel ad.) Moreover, he still avoided the strategy of a logo that would broadcast status – either an eco-badge, a cool badge, or any other sort of visible badge; his T-shirts had more to do with personal narratives than with impressing strangers. Finally, as Charney pointed out, the new image had hardly alienated young women – they were the main driver of his sales.

The conversation paused when two designers working on men's underwear appeared. They had just come from the factory floor, elsewhere in the building, carrying several pairs of underwear that had been manufactured about ten minutes earlier. Charney said they'd gone through about thirty iterations of prototypes already, several of them that day. "Imagine if we were outsourcing through China!" He was anxious to get men's underwear into the stores, because "hundreds of people" had been e-mailing, asking for that addition to the product line. The designers handed Charney the newest prototypes. He took off his pants and (after checking with me) his underwear and tried them on. "I need a thin Sharpie," he said, taking off that pair and trying on the next. He wrote on the removed pair: "Good but tighter." He repeated the process with a few pairs, and there was a great deal of chatter about the legs, the waist, about taking in a half inch, about the fact that the factory shift was going to end soon. "This is a great pair that I have on right now," Charney suddenly announced.

It's easy to get distracted by the mental image of a pantsless chief executive. But the moment happens to offer a gritty Polaroid shot of the company – both its more notorious aspects and its less heralded ones. It showed things that the public image obscured: responsiveness to customer requests, his designers' excitement, the advantages of a short elevator ride from shop floor to the CEO's office.

And as we resumed the conversation, Charney pointed out that the newer and more aggressively attention-getting image did not mean that American Apparel had watered down its production practices – slashed worker wages, for example. It just made less of an effort to tell consumers about them. The benefits the company offers to its workers had, in fact, increased. And it still marketed the working conditions at American Apparel – but mostly in recruiting commercials that ran in Los Angeles, aimed at attracting the best available workers, not at consumers. (While the company continued to hire, the waiting list for a manufacturing job there is a year long.)

It's not that he cares less about treating his workers ethically, Charney insisted, it's that he doesn't think trumpeting work conditions will help him compete. Sure, he hoped quality or social consciousness or logo escapism would each attract some consumers. But he also hoped that selling a sexed-up version of youth culture to young people would attract others, and hopefully in greater numbers. If ethics draws in some consumers, great. But for others who respond to different rationales, he'll provide those, too.

The product didn't change; the rationale for buying it did.

other rationales

Making ethics central to the product, but not to the product's image, pretty much inverts the way most marketers have thought about how ethics plays in the marketplace. By and large, most have focused on something closer to a "badge" strategy – positioning eco-awareness or concern about labor issues as a form of status, through a barrage of niche products and subbrands. Sometimes all that seemed to change was the packaging – the skillful addition of a few visual signifiers (a picture of a farm) or maybe just the word *natural*, ideally leading our interpreters to fill in the blanks themselves. Boutique marketing firms popped up to help companies address the "social responsibility niche," and the upshot has been that most brand owners simply make the most they can of their best practices, rather than doing anything to change their worst ones.

Charney is not the only entrepreneur to pursue a strategy that acknowledges that, while the ethical dimensions of a product can attract some consumers, it won't attract enough to transcend niche status. Remember Method, the high-design dish soap? As I mentioned in chapter 4, Method's products have a relatively eco-friendly formulation. Given how many consumers claim they want to buy green, you would think the brand might have made that the core of its image. But Method's owners – like Charney – evidently decided that pitching their products on this basis alone (or even primarily) would not attract the audience they wanted. So instead they emphasized design, and it's likely that this approach has brought their ethical product to a far wider group of consumers than an eco-badge approach would have.

Another interesting example: Timberland. While the company's CEO, Jeffrey Swartz, is a remarkably optimistic man and clearly believes that his company ought to act in a socially responsible manner, the Timberland story I outlined earlier had very little to do with consumers seeking out ethical products. I talked to Swartz about this the day I met him in Lawrence, Massachusetts, and he surprised me. The occasion for his presence in that ramshackle town that day was his company's eighth annual "Serv-a-Palooza" event. This was part of an effort that entailed the organization of 6,500 volunteers in more than one hundred communities in the United States and twenty-six other countries, putting in forty-five thousand hours of community service. Impressive.

In 2006, Timberland began marking each of its shoeboxes with information about the "environmental impact" and "community impact" of the company and its products. The company's approach was striking: Rating the production methods involved in making the shoes inside, each box not only touted what the company was doing well, but acknowledged what it needed to improve. At a time when most efforts to reach the eco-consumer seemed to skeptics like "greenwashing," burying shortcomings underneath hype about any given product's most ethically appealing feature, that kind of candor is rare – and, again, impressive.

Yet when I had asked Swartz about what social responsibility meant for his brand in the marketplace, he seemed skeptical that it sold many boots at all. He knew that offering boots in pink and other color variations had meant a lot more to the bottom line than encouraging volunteerism. Plenty of consumers – from construction workers buying the brand's Pro line for functional reasons to kids who take their cues from rap videos buying for fashion reasons – might never know about Timberland's social causes. The big challenge his company faced, to grow revenue in the future, was creating products that were relevant to consumers as fashions shifted. Ethics might matter to a particular niche, but meanwhile Swartz was focused on creating a range of other rationales to offer to other niches as well, in hopes that a murkiest common denominator would continue to add up to mass sales.

This, of course, is something we have seen before: Red Bull, the LiveStrong bracelet, and even the iPod built a mass audience by cobbling together smaller ones. They were multiple-choice success stories, and if the rationales of different consumer groups didn't match up with one another (let alone some top-down official meaning), that didn't matter.

It's premature to suggest that American Apparel has reached that level of mainstream acceptance. Charney's personal life antics remained a bit of a wild card, and at one point he was sued by four ex-employees for sexual harassment. (Three of those suits were dropped or settled quickly, and the fourth was still pending in 2007.) But its sales were still growing, it was still opening new locations, and there was little doubt that it had become a far bigger brand through Charney's approach than it could have by following an anti-sweatshops badge strategy. Like Timberland and Method, American Apparel is an example of worrying less about creating an ethical image than about making an ethical product.

And, of course, trying to sell that product as broadly (and profitably) as possible. In one of my first conversations with Charney on this subject, he had pulled out a copy of a book called *The 48 Laws of Power* and read me number thirteen, which suggested that to get what you want, you must appeal to the self-interest of others, not to their mercy. "That's the problem with the antisweatshop movement. You're not going to get customers walking into stores by asking for mercy and gratitude." If you want to sell something, ethical or otherwise, he said, snapping the book closed, "appeal to people's self-interest."

what's the matter with wal-mart shoppers?

making goods speak to power

Among the earliest and most forceful advocates of the theory that the twenty-first-century marketing class stands essentially helpless before a mighty new breed of in-control consumers was A. G. Lafley, chief executive officer of Procter & Gamble. In 2005, he declared that the new consumers "expect more from the brands they buy and use every day." Companies like his would have no choice but to meet their demands: "Consumers have grown accustomed to having it their way," he said. "It's a consumer revolution. . . . The rise of this powerful consumer boss marks one of the most important milestones in the history of branding."

Procter & Gamble is a global marketing leviathan, with 2006 sales of about $68 billion. It owns brands ranging from Tide to Gillette, from Ivory to Crest, from Iams dog food to Pringles chips. It's no surprise that the company is intensely interested in what motivates "this powerful consumer boss." Thus it poured an estimated $200 million into the study of consumers in 2006 (five times more than it spent in 2000) and was reportedly undertaking some ten thousand formal consumer research projects annually. The firm has worked with neuroscience experts in a (successful) effort to sell more fabric spray and has, according to *USA Today*, "videotaped men taking showers at home" (with permission, one assumes) on behalf of its Old Spice brand. While the rise of the click has apparently caused the company to cut back on some television advertising, its overall marketing budget has increased. As we saw in chapter 10, it has been an aggressive murketer by way of its huge word-of-mouth programs, Tremor and Vocalpoint. Other notably postclick murketing moves by the firm have included working out a deal to seed shampoos and body sprays with teenagers at cheerleading camps; creating a network reality show about celebrities taking driving lessons from Gillette-sponsored NASCAR drivers; and setting up a Charmin-branded bank of public restrooms in Times Square, apparently inspiring at least nine consumer-made YouTube videos. Along the way, the firm's sales and profits have risen consistently; in 2005, it was even named "Marketer of the Year" by *Advertising Age*.

All in all, then, this consumer revolution seems to be going pretty well for the multinational conglomerate. Which is interesting, because while there have certainly been consumer revolutions in the past, often with ripple effects that change society in general and the very contours of American life, those revolutions usually put huge and powerful entities in the crosshairs – not in the revolutionary vanguard.

As Lizabeth Cohen, an American studies professor at Harvard, explains in her book *A Consumers' Republic,* the notion of "ethical consumption" dates back at least to the turn-of-the-twentieth-century Progressive era, when reform groups like the National Consumers League sought to leverage collective buying power in order to influence both the quality of products and the conditions under which they were made. Progressive reforms included the Pure Food and Drug Act and the Federal Trade Commission Act. Similarly, the surly "new" consumer that *Advertising Age* called an "incomprehensible ogre" back in the late 1930s (as discussed in chapter 6) was prone to organized protest and collective action in response to price hikes and consumer safety issues. Again, the goals were to check producer power and force reforms for the public good. As late as the 1970s, echoes of this more confrontational stance toward businesses and corporate production had mass appeal; Cohen notes a 1973 Harris poll finding a sizable majority agreeing that "it's good to have critics like Ralph Nader." Over the decades, the food labeling and product safety standards and other tangible victories these movements achieved have sparked some of the very improvements that helped deliver us into the world of the Pretty Good Problem.

Consumption and ethics have been linked in explicitly sociopolitical terms as well: Limiting African Americans' access to the majority marketplace was among the many injustices that inspired the protests and legal challenges (including lunch counter sit-ins and lawsuits against hotels and other businesses) of the civil rights era. In his book *The Marketplace of Revolution*, historian T. H. Breen even makes a case that collective consumer protest was crucial to nothing less than the founding of the United States itself. "The colonists' shared experience as consumers" coalesced around a surprisingly unified (and grassroots-led) refusal to purchase a variety of popular English goods (opting, in what is obviously the most famous example, to fling unfairly taxed tea into Boston Harbor) and became a means by which they "made goods speak to power."

So in charting the rise and establishment of the murketing era, I was of course looking for signs of a more genuine consumer revolution. Specifically, I was interested in shifts in the dialogue between what we buy and who we are that did not somehow turn on the assumption that we must rely on brand owners to "empower" us to express ourselves through their customized products or open-to-all marketing efforts.

We have already seen examples of consumers of everything from PBR to Timberland infusing brands with different meanings without waiting around for corporate permission. And we have even seen young entrepreneurs like Bobby Hundreds hijacking not a brand, but the whole concept of branding. Such developments may represent some long-term threat to the P&Gs of the world, in that they demonstrate that the forging of brand meanings is no longer a matter of top-down control. But ultimately, each of those developments represents a shift that plays out in the context of changing commercial persuasion tactics.

Meanwhile, it would certainly seem that plenty of American consumers would be open to bigger and more wide-ranging changes in the marketplace – changes that revolutionized something more substantial than ad delivery methods.

After all, even as the click inspired startling innovations in commercial persuasion, some headlines seemed at odds with the promises of technological progress. Recalls of pet food and toothpaste spiked with dangerous ingredients and toys covered with lead paint, along with all the environmental and labor concerns I mentioned earlier, made us uneasy about the complex global supply chain that seemed to make the things we bought somehow unfathomable and scary. Many consumers seemed to crave a clearer sense of how things are made. But while there were a few examples of somewhat greater production transparency (American Apparel is one), it remained maddeningly difficult to figure out the full backstory of a box of Iams dog treats, or a Converse sneaker, or the myriad no-name but enticingly cheap Pretty Good stuff at Wal-Mart and Target.

Today, Nader-style consumer advocates persist, but despite these concerns, they have not returned to the prominence and cultural popularity that they last saw in the 1970s. Cohen's *A Consumers' Republic* argues that that departed era marked the last phase in a shift in what consumer power was about – from "public good beyond the individual's self-interest" to something more along the lines of "Am I getting my money's worth?"

So while I did end up finding one compelling potential example of a movement that attempts to make goods speak to power in the age of murketing, perhaps it's inevitable that it turned out to be a movement that plays out strictly in the marketplace. Even so, I think it's a phenomenon that is worth consideration. It has arisen from the grass roots during the period when the click was freeing marketers to involve themselves in every aspect of our lives. Yet it has nothing to do with "collaborating" or "co-creating" or otherwise being granted power by mass producers. In fact, its roots are in something like the opposite of mass production: the handmade.

"the punk of craft"

As a high school student back in the 1990s, Jennifer Perkins was influenced by the thinking of People for the Ethical Treatment of Animals, Greenpeace, and the riot grrrl subculture of indie-punk bands, handmade zines, and alternative art that had recently emerged out of the Pacific Northwest. She even started her own "feminist- and music-slanted" zine, which she called *Scratch-n-Sniff*, filled with writing about and interviews with underground bands and artists.

She also learned how to make (as she puts it) "gi-normous, tacky jewelry" using a cast-resin process, because she could never find the kind she liked in stores. And she probably wouldn't have bought it if she could, since she preferred to keep her personal aesthetic as unique as possible.

In the Dallas suburb of McKinney where she grew up, these were not conventional traits. But Perkins found kindred spirits in college, at Southwest Texas State University, near Austin. She kept up her zine for a while there (it was part of her final project for a feminist philosophy course) but let it go when she started working a day job as a secretary. Then she learned how to make websites and started a new one that she called the Naughty Secretary Club.

Among her college friends was Tina Lockwood. Like Perkins, Lockwood was studying psychology, loved music, and liked to make things – in her case, accessories and wall hangings and other items that she gave to friends as gifts, more or less as a creative outlet. Then something exciting happened: One of Lockwood's creations was featured in *Jane* magazine. Lockwood started calling herself Tina Sparkle, and Perkins helped her make an online store called Sparkle Craft, where some of Perkins's jewelry was also sold.

Soon, Tina Sparkle got an e-mail from another young woman living in Austin, named Jenny Hart. Hart had a fine-art background but had become entranced with embroidery as a medium. In trying to figure out how to find the right audience for the kind of work she wanted to do, she had discovered a new wave of websites like GetCrafty.com, where a community was forming around the idea of reinventing traditional craft skills for a younger, hipper, "alternative" mind-set.

"Just searching online," Hart later told me, "I noticed this company Sparkle Craft was linked *everywhere*." When she realized that Tina Sparkle was based in Austin, "I immediately wrote to her and said, 'Hey, I love what you're doing, I'm thinking of starting a company myself. Would you like to get together for some coffee?'" Sparkle said yes and that she'd bring her friend Jennifer Perkins. All three had day jobs at the time, and all three had the dream of doing their own thing. "We got so excited talking about our business ideas," Hart recalls. She started her company, Sublime Stitching, in 2001. In 2003, within months of one another, all three were established enough with their new businesses to leave their day jobs behind.

Along the way, they kept meeting, trading advice, and bringing in other local women with similar ideas and ambitions, eventually forming a kind of alliance that they referred to as the Austin Craft Mafia, with nine formal members. This group also organized an annual event called Stitch, which crossed a craft fair with a fashion show and a sort of do-it-yourself version of a trade show; in the few years of its existence, it's moved from a coffeehouse to the three-thousand-person-capacity Austin Music Hall, where the 2006 iteration sold out, and "there were tons of people still wanting to come in," Tina Lockwood says.

By then, the making and selling of handmade (or DIY) objects that straddled a line between art and craft had become a minor phenomenon. For participants – the Austin Craft Mafia founders, and tens of thousands of others across the country, and increasingly the world – the act of making things had resolved the tension between individuality and belonging. A website called Etsy, lauched in 2005, positioned itself as an eBay for DIY goods; within two years, more than seventy thousand crafters had set up virtual storefronts on the site and had sold more than one million handmade items, from toys to clothing, soap to jewelry, knitted iPod cases to ceramic mugs. While independent record shops and bookstores are struggling, boutiques specializing in these independently made products are opening up all the time. Even more popular are big events with names like the Renegade Craft Fair in Chicago, Bazaar Bizarre in Boston, the Urban Craft Uprising in Seattle: Each has been around only a few years, and attendance has risen sharply with every iteration. Similar fairs have popped up from Detroit to Atlanta, Oklahoma City to Brooklyn, together drawing thousands of shoppers. The Austin Craft Mafia, meanwhile, has become the model for at least thirty similar "Mafias" (from New Orleans to Anchorage to Leeds, United Kingdom) and made the Austinites one of the most celebrated stories within the DIY product world.

To many participants, this is not a new shopping trend or

even an art movement. It is a kind of consumption revolution, a community based on celebrating individual creativity and artisanal skill – and rejecting mass-produced goods. Like the brand underground entrepreneurs such as Barking Irons and the Hundreds, the DIY practitioners prized their independent, nonmainstream status. Crafters, however, often postioned their efforts as not just an alternative to or a luxury-like refinement of mass consumer culture, but an overt challenge to it.

"Crafting is a political statement," Jean Railla, the founder of GetCrafty.com, argued in the first issue of a magazine called *Craft*, which appeared in late 2006. "With globalism, factory labor, and sweatshops as growing concerns, and giant chains like Starbucks, McDonald's and Old Navy turning America into one big mini-mall, crafting becomes a protest." Railla, whose 2004 book, *Get Crafty: Hip Home Ec*, placed self-made goods in the context of third wave feminism and a "bohemian" identity, returned in the new magazine's second issue to argue on behalf of "the punk of craft." Reiterating the political and "antiauthority" aspects of the "ethic of Do It Yourself," she mused: "In the age of hypermaterialism, Paris Hilton, and thousand-dollar 'It' bags, perhaps making stuff is the ultimate form of rebellion."

diyism

Needless to say, craft skills such as sewing and knitting never actually disappeared. Even during the decades when they became less than universal, big craft store chains were a retail staple, albeit one that catered to a fairly mainstream consumer more interested in hobbies such as scrapbooking than in starting a business or participating in a "form of rebellion." Many of the most important figures in the crafter scene that Railla was writing about are women who are in their twenties and thirties, and there was something different about what they were up to, even if it took a while for this to become clear to outsiders.

According to the owners of the online handmade bazaar Etsy .com, around 90 percent of the sellers on that site are female. Given that women have played crucial roles in every significant consumer movement in American history, it's perhaps ironic that mainstream observers of contemporary consumer culture and commercial persuasion were so slow to recognize the rise, and significance, of DIYism; they obsessed over the habits of outlaw skateboard sneaker collectors but treated crafters as an amusing fad built around girls forming hipster knitting clubs. Perhaps this happened because of the increasingly intense scrutiny and courtship of young men who are so widely seen as the epitome of tough-to-crack but influential rebels. In any case, as late as 2007, participants in the scene were still being described dismissively as "craft babes" by trend watchers such as *The New York Times* "Style" section.

Betsy Greer, a writer and crafter in Durham, North Carolina, wrote her master's thesis on the contemporary crafting phenomenon and describes it as a merger of venerable hand skills that had become "devalued" in the mass-production world and a more modern urge for creative self-expression. As she notes, many participants were influenced by the same kind of do-it-yourself punk rock ethos that motivated members of the "Beautiful Losers" scene. Or maybe by the somewhat similar, but often underappreciated, riot grrrl idea.

The riot grrrl phenomenon has been described as "an educational and revolutionary movement, partially inspired by women in alternative music," but with a variety of participants including writers and activists. The term first gained currency in fanzines associated with the independent art and music scenes in Olympia, Washington, in the early 1990s – first in a zine called *Jigsaw*, created by Tobi Vail, and then in one simply called *Riot Grrrl*, by Vail and Kathleen Hanna. (These two women were founders of a band called Bikini Kill, which along with another called Bratmobile is generally cited as the most influential band of that time and place.) The writing in those self-published booklets often dealt with politics, discrimination, and, perhaps above all, expression on one's own terms. Creating a zine or starting a band were the popular ways to do this, but as with other subcultures, there was a particular style associated with riot grrrl identity: for instance, altering cheaply bought thrift store goods – a do-it-yourself approach, making something from nothing, and rejecting mainstream consumerism.

This sentiment echoed through early manifestations of the crafting scene. Debbie Stoller, founder of the pop-culture-meets-feminism magazine *Bust* (which began as a photocopied zine), championed knitting in a book called *Stitch 'N Bitch,* which became a minor sensation in the early 2000s. *Stitch 'N Bitch* identified craft as a vehicle for both self-expression and connection. When Betsy Greer, the North Carolina writer, took up knitting around 2001, she told me, one of the things she liked about it was the conversation and interaction it sparked, even with strangers. Still, she added, few saw it as a potential big business, let alone an influential movement: "It was nothing, really. Just a bunch of people saying, 'Oh my God, you like to make stuff, too?'"

One of the most knowledgeable observers of the scene that eventually emerged is Faythe Levine, a young Milwaukee artist with a variety of tattoos peeping out from under the vintage dresses she favors. A few years ago, she attended one of the pioneering big alternative-craft fairs and was inspired. "There was no corporate backing – it was people doing things, full-on DIY," she told me. She remembers thinking: "This is where I belong." Soon she was hand-making a variety of toys and other objects under the name Flying Fish. She founded the Paper Boat Boutique & Gallery and organized an annual craft fair called Art vs. Craft. And in the summer of 2006, she and her friend Micaela O'Herlihy decided to make a documentary about crafters (titled *Handmade Nation*), spending the next nine months shooting more than eighty hours of footage in a dozen cities.

I met with Levine toward the end of their initial round of filming, in Pittsburgh, in March 2007. About sixty of the most successful and best-known DIY creators and organizers from the United States and Canada had come together in what a different era had labeled the Steel City, to convene what they were calling the first "Craft Congress." This took place in a former car dealership that has been remade into gallery space, attached to the Spinning Plate Artist Lofts. Betsy Greer was there, as was Jenny Hart, from the Austin Craft Mafia. All but two of the attendees – three if you count me – were women; most had been involved in one or another form of hand-skill creativity for years and had not imagined that what started as essentially an individual hobby could evolve into what certainly felt to participants like a huge community. Many had not previously met in person. And practically everyone agreed that without the Internet, it's unlikely that these disparate and far-flung creators ever would have found common ground with one another – and with the growing numbers of consumers who had formed a marketplace for their wares.

But as various discussions and presentations and socializing played out over the next two days, it was clear that DIYism was approaching a crossroads. Mainstream corporate attention was finally focusing on the crafters, and some of it, at least, was quite unwelcome. Handmade-*looking* products were showing up at chain stores such as Target, and some individual creators complained that their work was being knocked off by the likes of Urban Outfitters. At least one big company approached prominent crafters and craft fair organizers and offered them sponsorship: Toyota, maker of the Scion. Some had turned away big-name sponsors, but others had not. One fair, called Crafty Bastard, associated with the Washington, D.C. *City Paper,* had already done such deals, with Scion and Red Bull, among others.

Faythe Levine had been interviewing crafters about these and other issues for months and had heard a mix of responses. More interesting to her, however, wasn't the fissures, but the common ground between "political" and "small business" points of view. "Everyone agreed," she told me, "that having your own small business at this time we are at in America is a political movement in itself. Running a small business yourself and trying to separate yourself from the masses – it's a political statement." This seemed to mean that participating in the building of a different kind of marketplace, with different values, was a potent, meaningful, and possibly even ethical response to the existing marketplace.

This basic theme hovered over the Craft Congress. Discussions went back and forth from the practical dilemmas of the fledgling entrepreneur to the more philosophical challenge of "defining the movement." And there was at least as much time spent on topics like self-promotion and networking as there was on politics or ideology. As Levine had suggested, most attendees seemed to feel that these concepts were intertwined. One attendee summed it up: "If we can't have a job where we make enough money, this movement isn't sustainable."

Of course, that's a statement that entails DIYism becoming something more than simply a matter of doing it yourself. It entails selling what you do. And it means finding a significant number of buyers for what you're selling. This is what makes this phenomenon a distinctly murketing-age version of consumer revolution. Grounded in commerce, the DIY movement not only accommodates consumption and even marketing, it depends on them. It's not opposed to the meaning of objects, it's *about* the meaning of objects.

ethics vs. aesthetics

Many DIY artisan-entrepreneurs told me that craft consumers often have social motives and that they were providing in their alternatives to mass-produced, corporate-made goods not just something unique, but also a product with no murky labor or environmental impact backstory. But other consumers clearly have other motivations. By the time I attended the Craft Congress, making things and buying handmade things had gotten, for lack of a better word, trendy. There were the multiple online communities and several magazines devoted to the subject. The DIY Network, a cable channel owned by Scripps, had launched shows like *Stylelicious* and *Craft Lab* and *Knitty Gritty* (all of which happen to be hosted by members of the Austin Craft Mafia). Shopping sites such as Design*Sponge regularly touted craft creators to an audience that was likely motivated more by aesthetics than by social concerns.

After all, many crafters were making beautiful stuff. The fact that the stuff was often handmade by a specific individual made it unusual, scarce, and vaguely artlike. The possibility of a kind of personal connection between consumer and producer added another attraction. On a smaller scale, then, crafters benefited from murkiest-common-denominator rationales: Their products fit into many personal narratives, in many ways.

And the DIY/craft creators trying to quit their day jobs needed all of the consumers they could get. And even success came with unique complications. Sitting at a sewing machine for eight hours, turning out the same stuffed owl to fulfill a barrage of online orders or prepare for a craft fair, taxes the body. This can happen to crafters who have done well enough to pay the rent – but not well enough to afford health insurance. And when your customers are buying something partly out of a sense of personal connection, it can be tricky to hire another sewer – let alone cut some kind of outsourcing or licensing deal.

The Austin Craft Mafia, for instance, has become well-known enough that its members have been approached by companies with ideas about how to use that name as a brand. Jennifer Perkins joked that pursuing that strategy could mean ending up with what she called the Courtney Love syndrome: too weird for the mainstream, but successful enough to be seen as a sellout by "the underground that once loved you." In the crafting world, it's sometimes assumed that because some of the group's members are on television, they must be rolling in cash. They're not. "I've been on the same level for the last three years," Tina Lockwood told me, "because I can't physically make any more." She had recently decided to focus exclusively on making guitar straps – or, rather, on designing them. She even looked into finding a local manufacturer.

Her friend Jenny Hart, the embroiderer, had found a balance between the handmade and the volume seller by designing patterns that she sold under the Sublime Stitching name. She's also put out a couple of how-to books, which along with the patterns helps her push the spirit of actually encouraging people to do things themselves, while she earns a living and can keep up with her own creative work.

"It is 40 percent what you can do and 60 percent how you market it," Jennifer Perkins advised other crafters on her website – just as in any other business. "I know so many people in bands, and it's the same thing," Perkins said to me. "If people don't know who you are or what your band sounds like, nobody is going to buy your CD, you know what I mean? I could make the most like awesome jewelry in America, and if I didn't like push it and get it into magazines or pay to take out ads or whatever, nobody is going to know to come to Naughty Secretary. I know people that make jewelry a hell of a lot cuter than mine; they just don't know how to market it."

what backlash?

Type "iPod" into the online craft emporium Etsy.com's search engine and you get nearly a thousand product listings – all manner of nifty handmade personal things in which to encase what is, rather definitively, a mass-market object, available at big-box retailers everywhere. If you buy one of these products, you've supported an independent creator, and perhaps made a personal connection, and you can be relatively certain that there's nothing ethically slippery about your unique new purchase. But are you part of the revolution against mass production, impersonal products, and Wal-Mart? Is this really rebellion?

A few months after the Craft Congress, I talked this over with Robert Kalin, Etsy's twenty-seven-year-old founder. I met him at the company's headquarters – the rambling top floor of a repurposed industrial building in downtown Brooklyn. The shopping site has arguably become the most accessible entry point for consumers to the handmade product world. And it is, to be sure, a business: Its funding comes partly from successful Web entrepreneurs, and the site's sales were running at about $1.7 million a month and growing at the time of my visit. But to listen to Kalin, it's an odd business – the kind of business that has book club gatherings attended by the CEO, with a reading list that includes books like *The Wal-Mart Effect*, which delves into the negative social consequences of the low-low prices that have lured so many shoppers for so long.

Kalin turned out to be a more forceful advocate for the social implications of handmade goods than any actual crafter I spoke to. In another interview, I had heard him advance the theory that "it's the Baby Boomer generation that fell in love with the mass-produced aesthetic" and gave up on artisanal skills and the personal side of the material. "Blame the hippies," he had joked. DIYism is not a fad, he told me: "It's a resurgence." Etsy, he continued, enabled new versions of community that revolved around the handmade. He said his site's growing customer base was indicative of a "backlash" against the Wal-Marts and P&Gs of the world.

He envisioned setting up "Etsy Labs" where crafters could share-work "a co-op model" and building tools online and off – where best-practice entrepreneurial ideas could be swapped and community reinforced. He wanted Etsy to be an enabler, a part of the movement. "This is what all the big brands are trying to fake," he said. "Emotional connections."

But still: Buying a handmade iPod cozy doesn't sound revolutionary – it sounds more like creating new desires than finding new ways to fulfill enduring needs. Kalin replied to this point by saying he has made it a personal goal to end up with a wardrobe that consists entirely of handmade clothing. He argued that the handmade phenomenon was analogous to the recent wave of interest among many consumers in changing what they eat – away from the processed toward the organic or local.

Earlier, Faythe Levine, despite misgivings about corporate interest in the crafting phenomenon, had argued to me that there were indirect benefits from "DIY" and "craft" becoming marketing buzzwords. Perhaps, she said, such developments will spread the sorts of conversations and connections at the heart of the movement to more people. Stores like Target were selling shirts that only looked as if they were hand-silk-screened with rough, unfinished edges, she said – but maybe this helped make genuinely handmade goods "more approachable" to a wider group of consumers. "People say, 'I can buy something like this at Target for $10, how come you're selling yours for $40?' And I can tell them, 'Well, that was made in China, and I made this one myself. So maybe that actually helps the community more than it hurts it – maybe it raises awareness about the handmade."

Kalin was saying something similar with his comparison to organic foods: that DIYism's rising popularity is both emblematic of and perhaps encouraging a larger shift. In this case, the shift would be away from mindless overconsumption. "It's not just 'You are what you eat,'" he has said. "It's, 'You are what you surround yourself with.'"

limits and potential

Okay. Let's be honest. Even Kalin would admit that the handmade phenomenon is a long, long way from threatening the realities of mass production and the global supply chain. Even all rolled together, the sales of crafters pale in comparison with the profits of a Wal-Mart or a Procter & Gamble. If you're worried about tainted dog food from a foreign factory, you won't find an alternative on Etsy. Many crafters work with raw materials – beads, fabrics, and so on – that are actually products of the global supply chain.

The bottom line is that DIYism falls well short of past consumption revolutions, whose biggest effects have involved more openly collective action and which often enjoyed wide popular support and culminated in legislation that benefited *all* consumers. Frequently, those movements involved ambitious uses of boycotts or other expressions of the consumer's most powerful weapon: not buying.

Think about the parallel Kalin draws to rising consumer interest in organic foods. Perhaps the most persuasive and popular writer on that subject is Michael Pollan, who has advised his readers to pay more – and eat less. While Pollan acknowledged that the "eating less" part may be "unwelcome advice," he suggested that "quality may have a bearing on quantity: I don't know about you, but the better the quality of the food I eat, the less of it I need to feel satisfied." For Kalin's analogy to work, more consumers would have to act not only by way of what they buy – but by way of what they don't buy. That's the "eat less" part of the equation, and evidence of it in the world of material objects is hard to come by. (Indeed, evidence in the world of food consumption isn't that clear-cut, either. Sales of organic foods have risen – but so have rates of obesity.)

Of course, there are voices in America's broader consumer dialogue that do speak out for the "not buying" side of things: The so-called voluntary simplicity idea has its adherents, arguing

for reduced consumption, thoughtful recycling, and understanding the full societal and environmental impact of every
purchase. Similarly, traditional consumer advocacy groups still
play important roles – for example, in pressing for curbs on
marketing to young children or stricter rules on misleading
packaging and so on. Some collective grassroots actions, led by
activists and particularly among students, also persist and at
times achieve real changes.

I don't mean to minimize the importance of any of these
things. Surely collective grassroots consumer campaigns
represent a legitimate and useful way of reconciling the tension
between individuality and belonging. They even do so in ways
that can satisfy more stringent definitions of social capital and
community than mere mutual brand fanship does – by entailing
sacrifice, connecting back to a larger vision of society, transcending
the interests of the individual or the immediate group.

But again: Let's be honest. Given the widespread embrace of
commercial culture that I've observed over the past several years,
and laid out over the course of this book, it would be disingenuous
of me to tell you that I've found much evidence that such activities,
however valuable, are on the verge of sparking a mass movement
– particularly one that aims at creating systematic solutions.
Consider the Consumer Product Safety Commission – the
government arm that today is supposed to deal with things like
testing and mandating recalls of unsafe toys manufactured in
the far-flung global supply chain. It was established during the
last wave of old-school consumer advocacy, in 1973. Yet even as
fears about unsafe toys and other products made news, the
commission's proposed budget and staffing levels for 2008 were
roughly half the level it enjoyed in 1978.

Really, this is no surprise, given that our faith in authority
and institutions to solve problems has evidently plummeted.
While data from the market research firm Yankelovich suggesting
that we've lost trust in advertising are widely cited, it's less often

noticed that this is just one aspect of a broader shift: Not only did trust in advertising fall between 1991 and 2003 – from 8 percent to 7 percent – so did trust in doctors, religious leaders, all forms of media, the federal government, major companies, stockbrokers, car salesmen, public schools, and pharmacists. One category that remained somewhat stable is confidence in "your own abilities." We now seem to put faith in market-based solutions and to be more interested in individual actions than in collective ones. Indeed, the most popular consumer-oriented websites have more to do with finding bargains or venting about bad experiences with particular products or companies than with organizing. And even those manifestations of click culture are far less popular than cool-product-spotting sites – or, of course, shopping sites. Like Etsy.

So having been honest, let's be optimistic. If a mass movement is unlikely, perhaps murkiest-common-denominator change is possible. Maybe DIYism can draw into the broader discussion of the meaning of things a bigger audience than would ever be engaged by, say, the "simplicity" movement – or even by explicitly eco-conscious sales pitches. Maybe the fact that the crafters' handmade objects appeal to many consumers for reasons that have nothing to do with ethics is, indirectly, a strength. Maybe it really does draw those consumers into the beginning of a more wide-ranging conversation about what we buy and who we are. Maybe in some sense, the craft idea is a kind of gateway drug to a different way of thinking about material culture – and about consumer behavior that doesn't merely *feel* like being part of something larger than ourselves, but really is.

Maybe, for all its shortcomings, the craft idea is useful because it reaches us where so many of us really seem to spend our time: out there in the marketplace, acting in our own self-interest.

chapter fourteen

beyond the thing itself

YOU . . . TWO SORTS OF MATERIALISM . . . PULLING THE WOOL
OVER YOUR OWN EYES

you

"It's not about you," wrote Rick Warren, the famous pastor, in the opening sentence of his phenomenally popular book, *The Purpose Driven Life*.

It's a sentiment that seems out of step with our time. Isn't the click world *completely* about you? Giving you what you want, when you want it? Letting you say what you think and who you are? Weren't "You," in fact, *Time*'s "Person of the Year" in 2006?

Yet given Warren's popularity, there seems to be a great deal of interest in his rather different point of view. In other writings and sermons, he has sketched a self-centered and unhappy culture: Since the 1960s, Americans have gotten "increasingly anti-institutional" and ever more rootless. "People are no longer surrounded by the extended family of aunts and uncles, grandparents, and brothers and sisters that provided a safety net for previous generations." Even the core family unit has been undercut by "the high divorce rate, delayed marriages, the emphasis on individuality, alternative lifestyles, women working outside the home, and the high rate of mobility." The upshot, he has argued, is a widespread "longing for a sense of family and community" – indeed, an "epidemic of loneliness." From contemporary teenagers to "independent-minded Baby Boomers," people long for meaning and connection. "Everywhere you look there are signs that people have a deep hunger for fellowship," he has written. "Beer commercials don't sell beer – they sell fellowship."

Such a direct reference to the commercial persuasion industry is relatively rare in the evangelizing of Warren or most other contemporary religious thinkers. After all, the evangelical goal has more to do with arguing in favor of something than against something; so when Warren observes that "life is not about having more and getting more," it's followed quickly by what he really wants to say, which is what he believes life *is* about: "serving God and serving others." Contemporary "seekers," he contends, "are hungry for symbols and metaphors and experiences and stories," but of a particular kind: the kind that "reveal[s] the greatness of God."

Whether you happen to be a believer in that last idea or not, what Warren's argument suggests is nothing less than that commercial culture is a dead end – that it can never really resolve the fundamental tension of modern life, and that whatever pleasures you may find in consumerism will not last. The ultimate irony of what he has called "America's rampant individualism" is that it does not satisfy the self.

All of which, of course, is not so different from the critique offered by various university professors, simple-living fanatics, fringe culture jammers, European philosophers who favor words like "hegemony," and others who are neatly dismissed by commercial persuaders as nattering, out-of-touch elites. Critiques by religious thinkers like Warren, however, are harder to dismiss on those grounds. They are delivered not in some rarefied context, but in thoroughly populist settings, for thoroughly mainstream audiences. Warren is a particularly compelling example: He is the pastor of the megasize Saddleback Church in Lake Forest, California, with an average attendance of eighteen thousand every weekend. Whatever influential status Warren enjoys in public life today, it is a function of having built a large, grassroots following. And his thinking has been emphatically ratified by the marketplace itself: *The Purpose Driven Life* has sold more than twenty-five million copies and is said to be the best-selling hardcover book ever. He is no tenured highbrow.

In Warren's case, the commercial persuasion industry has responded to his thinking largely by ransacking it for ideas. Following his success (and the success of the movie *The Passion of the Christ* and various other cultural hits in the "Christian market"), marketers have grown increasingly fond of throwing around terms like "customer evangelist," or arguing that "brands are belief systems," or attempting to adapt the "lessons" of organized religion to the consumer marketplace.

What makes this kind of thing so misguided is that it gives short shrift to Warren's actual message. You can take or leave the belief system that Rick Warren is pushing, but you have to concede it really is a belief system. In fact, it's a belief system that calls on people – and gets people – to tithe and volunteer, to sacrifice money and time, for the benefit of others who aren't even participants in it. While he has advanced a critique of contemporary culture as overly individualistic, part of the key to his success has been an ability to offer an alternative.

As Malcolm Gladwell documented in *The New Yorker,* Saddleback has been remarkably effective not just in drawing in thousands of people, but in deploying a "small group" model that connects members in "cells" of half a dozen people or so, "who meet in one another's homes during the week to worship and pray." Warren and other religious leaders have learned that the flexible, convenient, cost-free small-group model "was an extraordinary vehicle of commitment," wrote Gladwell.

Warren has called them "affinity groups," and his own telling makes it clear how they function in part as a way to resolve the fundamental tension of modern life. While "large-group celebrations" – like worship services in arena-size churches – "give people the feeling that they are a part of something significant," they're also impersonal. "The small affinity groups, on the other hand, are perfect for creating a sense of intimacy and close fellowship. It's there that everybody knows your name. When you are absent, people notice. You are missed if you don't show up." Even Robert Putnam, the *Bowling Alone* author who has taken a dim view of watered-down notions of community building, has praised Warren's achievement. Being part of Saddleback – or a part of Christianity – reconciles the tension between individuality and belonging.

In fairness to those marketers who raid Rick Warren's success story for ideas, Warren is no stranger to the mechanics of marketing. Long before he started getting attention from *The New Yorker,* let alone getting invited onto *Larry King Live,* Warren was widely known in religious circles for his ability to fill pews. For more than fifteen years, he has taught his methods to other church leaders, through his site Pastors.com, a weekly e-mail "toolbox" (including sermon ideas) sent to 115,000 subscribers, and through a book called *The Purpose Driven Church.* That lesser-known title actually preceded *The Purpose Driven Life* by several years and is interesting, among other reasons, for framing much of its advice in consumer demographic terms.

For example, a composite profile of "the typical unchurched person your church wants to reach" is cell-phone-wielding "Saddleback Sam," who is skeptical, well educated, a contemporary-music fan, and "self-satisfied, even smug." (Saddleback happens to be in Orange County, California – the same disconnected suburban environment where Ed Templeton searched for individuality and belonging by way of the "Beautiful Losers" skateboard culture.) Warren recognizes that contemporary, younger people respond to technology and "experiential" pitches.

And on half a dozen occasions, *The Purpose Driven Life* mentions ancillary products like *The Purpose Driven Life Journal* and the Purpose Driven Life Scripture Keeper Plus, and the appendix lists more, including a twelve-song CD.

Plenty of religious thinkers think Warren and others like him are too influenced by the tactics and strategies of Madison Avenue. But the Purpose Driven products are material objects ginned up to reflect a belief system, not the other way around. They are not meant to serve as conspicuous status markers. Participants in a belief system finding material ways to express their connection to it is something quite different from trying to extract a belief system from the mere fact that a lot of people have bought a particular sort of car or MP3 player. Again, you can take or leave Warren's belief system, but it isn't successful because Saddleback sells cool "badges," as modern-day marketers might put it. It's successful because participation is its own reward. If there's a badge involved, it's internal – an *invisible* badge.

Like so much else in the secret dialogue between what we buy and who we are, the line between objects and beliefs has become murkier. This is the reason I think it's important to consider Warren's critique now, in this age muddled by murketing and fractured by the click. It's important not just for businesses and not just for the culture at large, but for the individual. With apologies to Warren: In many ways, it *is* about you.

two sorts of materialism

You are what you surround yourself with.

This remark by Robert Kalin, the Etsy founder, has stuck with me. Consumer Economicus might resist the idea: It sounds a little frivolous to make such a blunt connection between material objects and identity. Somehow it reminds one of Miuccia Prada's warning about showing "weakness" in buying a $5,000 handbag. Surely we are much more than what we surround ourselves with or the "badges" of the commercial marketplace. Surely, for example, my identity does not hang in the balance as I work out what sort of sneakers I should buy now that I'm no longer willing to align myself with the Converse brand.

Yet Kalin's sentiment reflects and speaks to some basic facts about the relationship between people and things, and to the reality of how that relationship plays out in the world we live in now.

Back in the late 1970s, academics Mihály Csíkszentmihályi and Eugene Rochberg-Halton conducted lengthy interviews with several dozen families about their possessions, asking them a battery of detailed questions about which of their possessions were most important to them and why. A number of their subjects insisted that the researchers had their priorities out of whack – material objects and symbols aren't important, people and human relationships are.

But one of the themes that eventually emerged from their work, described in their 1981 book, *The Meaning of Things: Domestic Symbols and the Self,* is that some objects matter a great deal – not least because of their relationships to other people or larger ideas. In other words, the things that mattered had meaning precisely *because* they were symbols: The crucifix, the wedding ring, the diploma, and the trophy are some obvious examples of things that exist purely to join us to – to symbolize – something else (a belief system, a union, an achievement, a memory).

Csíkszentmihályi and Rochberg-Halton interviewed members of three generations of eighty-two families, asking their subjects: "What are the things in your home which are special to you?" Their interviewees mentioned a total of 1,694 objects, which were divided into forty-one categories. Objects in the top ten categories accounted for around half of the total mentioned: visual art, photographs, books, stereo, musical instruments, TV, sculpture, plants, and plates. The subjects gave 7,875 reasons why their chosen things were special, and these were divided into eleven broad "meaning classes," such as "memories."

Part of what the authors found was that – not surprisingly – the most meaningful objects were rarely chosen on the basis of some intrinsic, rational property, like marketplace value, cutting-edge quality, simple aesthetic pleasure, or anything that an economist might describe as "utility." They were chosen instead for connections to something else: family or social ties, a particular episode in the narrative of the subject's life, perhaps religious faith or some other belief system affiliation. That is to say, their "meaning" tended to be a function of what the thing represented.

Csíkszentmihályi has continued to address materialism in some of his work, extending ideas from that earlier study, in particular by way of something he calls "psychic energy." This essentially means attention, or simply what we choose to think about. "Objects are generally tools," he wrote in his contribution to a 2004 book called *Psychology and Consumer Culture: The Struggle for a Good Life in a Materialistic World.* "We attend to them in order to achieve some goal or experience beyond the thing itself."

Devoting "psychic energy" to objects can make sense, he argued, if it is part of an effort to "transcend self-interest" and "reach outside [our] own needs and goals and invest in another system, thus becoming a stakeholder in an entity larger than [our] previous selves." In other words, when the material object is a reflection of who we are.

Problems arise when people use "material goals and material experiences" not to reflect who they are, but to construct who they are. Not to reflect a self, but to *build* a self. *The Meaning of Things* drew a distinction between "instrumental" materialism and "increasingly expensive symbolic demonstrations of our autonomy and power," which the authors gave the scary label "terminal materialism."

If you are a terminal materialist, you surround yourself with what you *wish* you were. And that's what leads to the conclusion that Warren suggested: self-focused materialism that fails to satisfy the self.

Early in this book, I mentioned the pleasure we often feel at the anticipation of acquiring some new object. Later, I noted the "mere ownership effect," describing the tendency to assign greater value to a thing we've obtained than an objective observer would. You might wonder how this squares with all the junk in your closet that you lost interest in long ago – if you can even remember what it is or why you bought it. One way to think about the answer is to understand adaptation, another term borrowed from psychology.

There's been a great deal of research into adaptation, and you can probably guess what it means: Human beings have a remarkable capacity to get used to things. This means a capacity to get used to miserable situations. And it means a tendency to become bored with stuff that used to thrill us: to overestimate how much pleasure any given purchase will give and for how long. Thus the iPod eventually gets taken for granted, the visually thrilling high-end kitchen appliance simply becomes your stove, and the LiveStrong bracelet ends up in the back of a drawer.

We all know that novelty fades. But Jon Gertner, my colleague at *The New York Times Magazine,* has boiled down the key insight that adaptation research strongly suggests. "It isn't that we get the big things wrong," he wrote. "We know we will experience visits to le Cirque and to the periodontist differently; we can accurately predict that we'd rather be stuck in Montauk than in a Midtown elevator." What we're not good at judging is the "intensity and duration" of our feelings about events that haven't happened yet: The BMW, or the Nike Shima Shima 2 Air Max 1's, or the Viking Range stove, or whatever, will not make us as happy as we believe it will, and certainly not for as long as we guess. More to the point, what adaptation research suggests is not that we don't know novelty fades, but that we're not good at figuring out how to factor this knowledge into our decision making: "Thus, when we find the pleasure derived from a thing diminishing, we move on to the next thing or event, almost certainly make another error of prediction, and then another, ad infinitum." This is easily done, as the vast data set of commercial novelty proliferates endlessly, giving our interpreter more options every day. There's always another choice to spark that anticipation of pleasure, inspire that fresh rationale. Ad infinitum.

And there it is: terminal materialism.

pulling the wool over your own eyes

Those two versions of materialism that Csíkszentmihályi and Rochberg-Halton suggested seem vastly different, but in practice they are easily confused. We are thirsty for meaning, for connection, for individuality, for ways to tell stories about ourselves that make sense. Meanwhile, what brand makers generally have to sell is a Pretty Good product that is hardly equipped to fulfill those needs. What can they do?

If they can't *literally* make what we need – to feel a part of something big or to feel like a Magic Person, and so on – well, then they can at least position what they make *as* what we need, as though it might quench some other, deeper thirst.

Apparent solutions to those needs can, with some effort, be tied to almost any commodity. The job of commercial persuasion is to add to the awesome data set we confront every day, hoping our interpreter will tease out the relevant patterns – whether those patterns really exist or not. We know customized sneakers or a new car or deodorant can't *really* make us more of an individual; we know that mutual admiration of the same T-shirt brands or opportunities to tout Procter & Gamble products to your neighbors aren't *really* forms of community. But they're easily available, salient options. And it's the job of the commercial persuasion business to keep them that way. As one contemporary ad agency executive has put it: "Few stronger emotions exist than the need to belong and make meaning. And brands are poised to exploit that need."

There's no point, however, in demonizing people who are simply doing their jobs as effectively as they can. Of course, commercial persuasion adjusts – and will adjust forever – to sell us what we need, even when it's not quite the same thing as what we actually end up buying. That's just the profit motive in action, a thing that is much older than Hamlin's Wizard Oil, let alone taurine, and will last much longer than either.

While the rhetoric of the all-controlling consumer rings false, it's undeniable that the murketing pros could never do what they do without us. When murketing works, it does so because far from rejecting it or resisting it or being immune to it, we're part of it. It's easy to move from surrounding yourself with what you are to surrounding yourself with what you wish you were. Surely instrumental and terminal tendencies are alive in almost all of us.

I decided to talk all of this over with Andrew Andrew – the two iPod fans to whom I attached the label "consumption artists" back in chapter 4. Since first meeting them several years ago, I've kept in touch with them, always fascinated and surprised by their latest projects. Andrew Andrew might be thought of as addressing consumer culture from a kind of trickster tradition, descended more from Duchamp and Warhol than, say, Tom Peters and Seth Godin. This, of course, is exactly why I find their perspective interesting and useful. Plus, they have a sense of humor.

Eventually, I convinced them to meet me in a Roosevelt Island diner (they live on that little sliver of land in the East River) to talk to me about their work, their lives – and their consumption. These things are all the same, and all different, and maybe a little confusing at first. "We're dissatisfied with the idea of art being able to make any change," Andrew said early in the conversation. "So it's about products, marketing, selling people things to change their minds."

This sounds a bit crass, but bear with them. "I think it's like in an anthropology text," Andrew chimed in. "Like on an island in New Guinea, their whole lives are centered around yams, because it's their main crop, they eat yams, it's their currency, they base the phases of the year around the yam season, and you pay tribute in yams. And we're the same way, except we deal in products, not yams."

The foundation of the Andrew Andrew project was their fashion line. Their first "season" consisted of adhesive labels that read "Respect Me." Two or three times a week, they would walk into Old Navy or Gap locations, Kmarts, H&M stores, and other mass merchants and affix their stickers to the clothing. "Someone would buy the shirt," Andrew explained. "They would get home, they would look at the shirt, and they would see this sticker that said 'Respect Me.' We were trying to conform their product into our line."

In all, they stuck around a thousand stickers on mass-produced clothing. They never made an announcement or public explanation of any kind. "We kind of wanted to get caught, because we felt it would be good marketing," Andrew added. "But we never did."

For their second season, they experimented with labels again. This time, they set up a sewing machine at a store in SoHo. "You would bring in a robe, or you'd give us your sweater, and we would sew this oversized label onto your sweater, making your shirt part of our line." They charged different prices for different thread colors – $50 for black thread, $100 for gold, and so on. The department store Barneys was impressed with this and wanted to work with Andrew Andrew but suggested that next season it would be good to come up with "something you can hang on a rack," Andrew recalled.

And?

"We made coat hangers." Elaborately sculpted coat hangers, with gold leafing and so on. "You put your clothing on the hanger and it becomes our line. Once you remove it, it is no longer part of the line." At its most fundamental level, the line was unwearable, unattainable. Barneys passed on this idea, as Andrew Andrew knew perfectly well the store would.

By now, the basic theme should be clear: The Andrew Andrew fashion line had never included an actual article of clothing. "That's the whole point," Andrew said. But from their perspective, it's perfectly consistent with the way consumption now works. People do not buy objects, they buy ideas about products.

"The only thing you need is clothing and food," Andrew said. "Everything else is just –"

"And the thing about that is we're in such an absurd place with clothing and food," Andrew interrupted. "We don't buy food for its nutritional value, nor do we buy clothing for its protective value. It's entirely – we buy for all the wrong reasons."

But, I asked, what exactly does it mean to say "the wrong reasons"? If someone creates a symbol that has meaning, if it's Polo or Ecko, and I buy into it and it makes me feel more classy or urban, isn't that okay?

"Yeah," they answered in unison, and Andrew clarified: "You're spending the money to pay for the advertising that they paid for to make you believe that. That's the snake-eating-its-own-tail of it all."

The Andrews are very funny. But they're saying something here that's actually true: By and large, we find value and meaning where we have created it ourselves.

Think of a wedding ring. Could there be a more meaningful object (to someone in a happy marriage, I mean)? And does that meaning have anything to do with economic market value? Is the no-frills $500 wedding ring of a happily married person less meaningful to its owner than a "well designed" one that cost ten times more is to its owner? I don't think so. The real meaning and value of the thing is invisible – like the satisfaction that Rick Warren's congregants seem to find in their belief system. The object's power as a "badge," as it were, is something only the owner can truly see.

Consumer Economicus might not understand any of this. But I don't think that matters. As the authors of *The Meaning of Things* put it: "An effective symbol need not be logically or empirically understood." Andrew – or perhaps it was Andrew – gave this same sentiment a more memorable formulation: "As long as you're pulling the wool over your own eyes," he said, "then it's okay."

Maybe this is where "consumer control" begins.

If we tell ourselves we are "immune" to murketing and brands simply by virtue of living in the clicky world of the twenty-first century, it's that much easier to slip into rationale thinking as we confront the increasingly murky line between commercial persuasion and everyday life. But the significance of the material things and symbols that mean the most has always flowed from us to the object, not the other way around. If we know that meaning and value are things we give to symbols, not things we get from them, the dynamic changes – even in the distracting context of consumer culture. In different ways, I think that Rick Warren and Mihály Csíkszentmihályi and various behavioral psychologists have all made similar points, but I happen to like the version from Chuck D that I quoted earlier in this book. The Public Enemy front man, talking about the making-something-from-nothing culture that he believed marked the early days of hip-hop, said: "It was *you* that was important, and everything else would define you *after* you defined yourself. It wasn't like a brand defined you, *you* defined the brand."

Maybe, then, the secret dialogue between what we buy and who we are should go like this. You are only what you surround yourself with? No. You surround yourself only with who you are.

Imagine that.

acknowledgments

Some of the material in this book was gathered in the course of writing articles for *The New York Times Magazine, Slate, GQ, Inc.,* and *Outside;* thank you to all the editors, copy editors, and fact checkers I worked with. I also wish to thank Elyse Cheney, Tim Bartlett, Vera Titunik, Nicholas Varchaver, James Gaddy, Jonathan Karp, Gerry Marzorati, Alex Heard, Hugo Lindgren, Andreas Campomar and Michael Kinsley, some for reasons they know, others for reasons they might not guess.

Thank you, M&D, for endless love and support and patience and encouragement.

Thank you, E., again and again, and for everything, and always.

additional source notes

By and large, this book is based on firsthand interviews and observations that are – along with most of the books and other materials that I relied on – generally indicated within the text itself. Additional noteworthy source material (plus a few more detailed citations of mentioned sources) follows.

introduction

"A Profit Gusher of Epic Proportions," by Shawn Tully, *Fortune*, April 30, 2007. "Look – Up in the Sky! Product Placement!" by Brian Steinberg, *The Wall Street Journal*, April 18, 2006. "Anywhere the Eye Can See, It's Likely to See an Ad," by Louise Story, *The New York Times*, January 15, 2007, "Neural Correlates of Behavioral Preference for Culturally Familiar Drinks," by Samuel M. McClure, Jian Li, et al., *Neuron* 44, (October 14, 2004). U.S. Department of Commerce, Bureau of Economic Analysis website (www.bea.gov/briefrm/saving.htm). *The Power of Persuasion: How We're Bought and Sold*, by Robert Levine.

part one | the desire code

one . . . the pretty good problem

"Consumers Cite Past Experience as the No. 1 Influencer When Buying," by Bradley Johnson, *Advertising Age*, November 20, 2006.

"MLB and NHL Brands Strike Out in Fashion Index," *Retail Merchandiser*, April 7, 2005. "Wardrobe Malfunction," by Teri Agins, *The Wall Street Journal*, February 4, 2005. "Prada vs. Prada: Overcoming Fashion Phobia," by Alessandra Galloni, *The Wall Street Journal*, January 18, 2007. "Ranges: More on the Menu," *Consumer Reports*, May 2005. "Rockin' to a T," by Bruce Ward, *Gazette*, July 31, 2007. "Between Punk Rock and a Hard Place," by Keith Gessen, *New York* magazine, June 20, 2005. "Other Marketing for Uplifting Guerillas," by Jim Edwards, *Brandweek*, November 21, 2005. "Barbie, Kitty Age for Mom," by Stephanie Thompson, *Advertising Age*, June 21, 2004. "Barbie's New Clothes," by Queena Sook Kim and Ichiko Fuyuno, *The Wall Street Journal*, January 30, 2004. Tokion Creativity Now Conference, September 2003, transcript in *Tokion* 39 (January/ February 2004). "How Hello Kitty Commodifies the Cute, Cool and Camp: 'Consumutopia' versus 'Control' in Japan," by Brian J. McVeigh, *Journal of Material Culture* 5, no. 2 (2002). *Point of Purchase: How Shopping Changed American Culture*, by Sharon Zukin. *The White T*, by Alice Harris. *Hello Kitty: The Remarkable Story of Sanrio and the Billion Dollar Feline Phenomenon*, by Ken Belson and Brian Bremner.

two . . . the straw man in the gray flannel suit

"The Ghosts of Dogtown: A Quarter-Century Later, the Zephyr Competition Skate Team Still Rules," by Joe Donnelly, *L.A. Weekly*, August 24–30, 2001. "Sk8er Girl in Z-Boy Land," by Joe Donnelly, *L.A. Weekly*, June 3–9, 2005. "Dogtown East," by David Browne, *New York* magazine, June 13, 2005. "Dogtown, U.S.A.," by Damien Cave, *The New York Times*, June 12, 2005. "Skating to the Top," by Shannon McMahon, (San Diego) *Union-Tribune*, September 25, 2005. "Sky's the Limit," by Eric Fetters, (Everett, Washington) *Herald*, July 10, 2005. "A Sport So Popular, They Added a Second Boom," by Matt Higgins, *The New York Times*, July 25, 2005. "How the Yes Man Learned to Say No," by Alan Ehrenhalt, *The New York*

Times, November 26, 2006."Rebellions and Reasonable, the Yin and Yang of Design," by Robin Givham, *The Washington Post,* February 10, 2006. Powell Peralta/Bones Brigade website (www.bonesbrigade.com). "Brand Community," by Albert M. Muniz Jr. and Thomas C. O'Guinn, *Journal of Consumer Research* 27 (March 2001). "Brand Communities and Personal Identities: Negotiations in Cyberspace," by Hope Jensen Schau and Albert M. Muniz Jr., *Advances in Consumer Research* 29, 2002. "Communal Consumption and the Brand," by Thomas C. O'Guinn and Albert M. Muniz Jr., in *Inside Consumption: Consumer Motives, Goals, and Desires,* edited by S. Ratneshwar and David Glen Mick (2005). *Beautiful Losers: Contemporary Art and Street Culture,* edited by Aaron Rose and Christian Strike.

three . . . rationale thinking

"It's the Purpose Brand, Stupid," by Clayton M. Christensen, Scott Cook, and Taddy Hall, *The Wall Street Journal,* November 29, 2005. " 'Cognitive Dissonance' Became a Milestone in 1950s Psychology," by Cynthia Crossen, *The Wall Street Journal,* December 4, 2006. "The Marketplace of Perceptions," by Craig Lambert, *Harvard* magazine, March–April 2006. "Subliminal Seduction," by Carrie McLaren, *StayFree!* 22 (2004). "Why Hawks Win," by Daniel Kahneman and Jonathan Renshon, *Foreign Policy* (January/February 2007). "This Is Your Brain at the Mall: Why Shopping Makes You Feel So Good," by Tara Parker-Pope, *The Wall Street Journal,* December 6, 2005. "The Voices in My Head Say 'Buy It!' Why Argue?" by John Tierney, *The New York Times,* January 16, 2007. "The Stove Groupies' Pilgrimage," by Taylor Holliday, *The New York Times,* November 5, 2004. "Big and Bad," by Malcolm Gladwell, *The New Yorker,* January 12, 2004. "Make My Memory: How Advertising Can Change Our Memories of the Past," by Kathryn A. Braun, Rhiannon Ellis, and Elizabeth F. Loftus. *Psychology & Marketing* 19, no. 1 (January 2002): 1–23. "Memory Change: An

Intimate Measure of Persuasion," by Kathryn A. Braun-LaTour and Gerald Zaltman, working paper. "Rich False Memories: The Royal Road to Success," by Elizabeth F. Loftus and Daniel M. Bernstein, in *Experimental Cognitive Psychology and Its Applications*, edited by A. F. Healy (2005). "Postexperience Advertising Effects on Consumer Memory," by Kathryn A. Braun, *Journal of Consumer Research* 25, no. 4 (March 1999). "Assessing the Long-Term Impact of a Consistent Advertising Campaign on Consumer Memory," by Kathryn A. Braun-LaTour and Michael S. LaTour, *Journal of Advertising* 33, no. 2 (Summer 2004). "Neural Predictors of Purchases," by Brian Knutson, Scott Rick, et al., *Neuron* 53 (January 4, 2007). "The Totalitarian Ego: Fabrication and Revision of Personal History," by Anthony G. Greenwald, *American Psychologist* 35, no. 7 (July 1980). "Sophisticated by Design: Non-conscious Influences on Consumer Choice," by T. Andrew Poehlman, Eric Louis Uhlmann, Ravi Dhar, and John A. Bargh, working paper. *Descartes' Error: Emotion, Reason, and the Human Brain*, by Antonio R. Damasio. *Satisfaction: The Science of Finding True Fulfillment*, by Gregory Berns.

four . . . ignoring the joneses

"Apple's 'Breakthrough' iPod," by Brad King and Farhad Manjoo, *WiredNews*, October 23, 2001. "Inside the Apple iPod, Design Triumph," by Erik Sherman, *Design Chain* (Summer 2002). "Heard on the Street: Apple's E-Music Store Isn't the Next Beatles," by Pui-Wing Tam, *The Wall Street Journal*, October 9, 2003. "Apple's Not Thinking Different," by Beth Snyder Bulik, *Advertising Age*, June 25, 2007. "Apple Settles Patent Dispute with a Rival," by Laurie J. Flynn, *The New York Times*, August 24, 2006. "How Glaxo Marketed a Malady to Sell a Drug," by Jeanne Whalen, *The Wall Street Journal*, October 25, 2006. "This Is Your Brain on a Strong Brand: MRIs Show Even Insurers Can Excite," by Kevin Helliker, *The Wall Street Journal*, November 28, 2006. "Putting Drug Ads

Back in the Bottle," by Arlene Weintraub, *BusinessWeek*, August 13, 2007. "Color Coded Causes," by Nancy Coltun Webster, *Advertising Age*, June 13, 2005. "LiveStrong and Prosper," by Christopher Keyes, *Texas Monthly*, March 2005. "Tunes, a Hard Drive and (Just Maybe) a Brain," by Rachel Dodes, *The New York Times*, August 26, 2004. "The Green Method," Bertha Coombs, CNBC, March 23, 2007. "Running Through the Legs of Goliath," by Stephanie Clifford, *Inc.* magazine, February 2006. "Eric Ryan: The Method to His Madness," by Jack Neff, *Point* (supplement to *Advertising Age*), October 2005. "Petrochemicals in Cleaners?" by Emily Main, *Green Guide*, posted June 6, 2006, (plus correspondence). "Agencies Don Lab Coats to Reach Consumers," by Suzanne Vranica, *The Wall Street Journal*, June 4, 2007. "Trying to Get into the Minds of Consumers," by Alan Mitchell, *Financial Times*, January 15, 2007. "Assessing the Long-Term Impact of a Consistent Advertising Campaign on Consumer Memory," by Kathryn A. Braun-LaTour and Michael S. LaTour, *Journal of Advertising* 33, no. 2 (Summer 2004). "Advertising's Misinformation Effect," by Kathryn A. Braun and Elizabeth F. Loftus, *Applied Cognitive Psychology* 12 (1998): 569–591. "Mindfulness and Consumerism," by Erika L. Rosenberg, in *Psychology and Consumer Culture: The Struggle for a Good Life in a Materialistic World*, edited by Tim Kasser and Allan D. Kanner. *The Cult of Mac*, by Leander Kahney. *Luxury Fever: Money and Happiness in an Era of Excess*, by Robert H. Frank.

part two | murketing

"Content's King," by Staci D. Kramer, *Cableworld*, April 29, 2002. "More U.S. Homes Have Outhouses Than TiVos," by Bradley Johnson, *Advertising Age*, November 4, 2002. "Will This Machine Change Television?" by Bill Carter, *The New York Times*, July 5, 1999. "The Fast-Forward, On-Demand, Network-Smashing Future of Television," by Frank Rose, *Wired*, October 2003. "Person of the

Year: You," by Lev Grossman, *Time,* December 13, 2006. "Adages," by Ken Wheaton, *Advertising Age,* July 18, 2005.

five . . . chuck taylor was a salesman

"The Flop Heard Round the World," by Peter Carlson, *The Washington Post,* September 4, 2007. "Timberland Hits Its Stride," by John Greenwald, *Time* magazine, November 29, 1993. "Timberlands," by Justin Monroe, *Vibe,* September 2005. "Out of the Woods," by Michel Marriott, *The New York Times,* November 7, 1993. "Nike Takes Chuck Taylors from Antifashion to Fashionista," by Stephanie Kang, *The Wall Street Journal,* June 23, 2006. "Advertising of, by and for the People," by David Kiley, *BusinessWeek,* July 25, 2005. "Marketers' New Idea: Get the Consumer to Design the Ads," by Suzanne Vranica, *The Wall Street Journal,* December 14, 2005. "Nike Drafts an All Star: Purchase of Converse Dismays Fans of Classic Chucks," by Joshua Partlow, *The Washington Post,* July 18, 2003. "Nike to Gain Possession of Rebounding Rival Converse," by Leslie Earnest, *The Los Angeles Times,* July 10, 2003. "Pros and Cons," by Noah Rubin, *Mass Appeal* 26. "Rise and Fall Again of Converse Chuck Taylor All Star Sneakers," by Frank DeFord, NPR, July 16, 2003. Converse website (www.converse.com). Timberland annual reports: 1999–2006. "Style Is Everywhere: So Where Does It Start Anyway?" by Kim Hastreiter, in *20 Years of Style: The World According to Paper. Madison Avenue, U.S.A.,* by Martin Mayer. *The Influentials,* by Ed Keller and Jon Berry. *For God, Country and Coca-Cola: The Unauthorized History of the Great American Soft Drink and the Company That Makes It,* by Mark Pendergrast. *Rising Tide: Lessons from 165 Years of Brand Building at Procter & Gamble,* by Davis Dyer, Frederick Dalzell, and Rowena Olegario. *Soap Opera: The Inside Story of Procter & Gamble,* by Alecia Swasy. *Bling Bling: Hip Hop's Crown Jewels,* by Minya Oh. *Back in the Days,* by Jamel Shabazz. *Yes Yes Y'all: The Experience Music Project Oral History of Hip-Hop's First Decade,* by Jim Fricke and Charlie Ahearn.

six . . . rebellion, unsold

"The Consumer Movement," by Kenneth Dameron, *Harvard Business Review* (Spring 1939). "Marketing Myopia," by Theodore Levitt, *Harvard Business Review* (1960). "Business Week Reports to Executives on the Consumer Movement," *Business Week*, April 22, 1939. "What About the Consumer Movement?" *Advertising Age*, January 8, 1940. "Brand Me," by Tom Van Riper, *Forbes*, February 10, 2006. "Savvy Gen Y Isn't Buying Traditional Sales Pitches," by Kim Peterson, *Seattle Times*, May 17, 2004. "At School, Labels a Runway Hit," by Ylan Q. Mui, *The Washington Post*, November 29, 2004. "Teen Talk Is, Like, Totally Branded," by Kenneth Hein, *Brandweek*, August 6, 2007. "Does Your 'Research' Embrace the Boy of Today?: The Modern Youth Is Far Different from the Youth of Yesterday," by Jess H. Wilson, *Printers' Ink*, March 16, 1922, as reprinted in *Primary Documents* #6, "Dealing in Futures," 1996. "Professional Youth," *The Saturday Evening Post*, April 28, 1923, collected in *Dorothy Parker: Complete Stories*. "The New Hucksterism," by Mary Kuntz, Joseph Weber, and Heidi Dawley, *BusinessWeek*, July 1, 1996. "It's Morning After in America," by Kay S. Hymowitz, *City Journal* (Spring 2004). "Beyond Demographics," by James Atlas, *The Atlantic Monthly*, October 1984. "Merchants of Cool," *Frontline*, 2001. *Listening In: Radio and the American Imagination*, by Susan J. Douglas. *A Consumers' Republic: The Politics of Mass Consumption in Postwar America*, by Lizabeth Cohen.

seven . . . click

"Questions for Faith Popcorn," by Suzanne Vranica, *The Wall Street Journal*, January 7, 2004. "The Business of Faith," by Ruth Shalit, *The New Republic*, April 18, 1994. "Putting Faith in Trends," by Annetta Miller, *Newsweek*, June 15, 1987. "Trend-Surfing in the USA," by Andrew Serwer, *Fortune*, April 15, 1996. "Cool Hunting

Goes Corporate," by Beth Snyder Bulik, *Advertising Age*, August 1, 2005. "Tylenol Remedy Sees Results," by Rich Thomaselli, *Advertising Age*, February 9, 2004. "The Pill Whose Name Goes Unspoken," by Julia Boorstin, *Fortune*, September 20, 2004. "Ad Campaigns for Your Tiny Cellphone Screen Get Bigger," by Paul Davidson, *USA Today*, August 8, 2006. "Television's New Joy of Text," by Li Yuan, *The Wall Street Journal*, July 20, 2006. "Dial 'M' for Marketing," by Kenneth Hein, *Brandweek*, January 8, 2007. "Madison Avenue Calling," by Louise Story, *The New York Times*, January 20, 2007. "TV Is Corralling 'Clutter,'" by Brian Steinberg, *The Wall Street Journal*, April 24, 2007. "The Prime-Time Product Placement Boom," by Lacey Rose, Forbes.com, June 5, 2007. "Time-Shifted Viewing Figures Offer Dramatic Reality Check," by Jim Edwards, *Brandweek*, December 11, 2006. "Spreading 'Branded' Shows Overseas," by Suzanne Vranica, *The Wall Street Journal*, June 6, 2007. "'Lonelygirl15' Cozies Up to Promo Deal," by Marc Graser, *Variety*, June 19, 2007. "How to Sell Body Sprays to Teenagers? Hint: It's Not Just Cleanliness," by Julie Bosman, *The New York Times*, October 28, 2005. "Children of the Web: How the Second-Generation Internet Is Spawning a Global Youth Culture – And What Business Can Do to Cash In," by Steve Hamm, *BusinessWeek*, July 2, 2007. "Analyzing 'Axe Man,'" by Jack Neff, *Advertising Age*, June 4, 2004. "Unilever's Lesson to P&G: Embrace the Nitty-Gritty," by Jack Neff, *Advertising Age*, February 27, 2006. "Unilever, BA Work Pushes BBH to Top," by Emma Hall and Laurel Wentz, *Advertising Age*, January 9, 2006. "Television and Radio," by Gilbert Seldes, *The Atlantic*, May 1937 (reprinted in *The Atlantic*, September 2006). The following as reprinted in *Primary Documents* #5, "The March of Radio," 1996: "The Future of Radio Advertising in the United States," by Roy S. Durstine, BBD&O Annals of *The American Academy*, January 1935. "The National Radio Home-Maker's Club," by Ida Bailey Allen, introduction to *One Hundred Radio Four Prize Radio Recipes*. "Do They Earn Their Pay?" by Robert Eichberg, read into the *Congressional Record*, June

1, 1934, v. 78, pt. 9, 10180–81. "What Radio Reports Are Coming To," *New York Sun*, 1926. *Branding Unbound*, by Rick Mathieson. *Fables of Abundance*, by Jackson Lears. *Confessions of an Advertising Man*, by David Ogilvy. *Soft Soap, Hard Sell: American Hygiene in an Age of Advertising*, by Vincent Vinikas.

eight . . . very real

"Perpetual Motion: A Survey of the Car Industry," *The Economist*, September 4, 2004. "The Car Company in Front," *The Economist*, January 29, 2005. "A Box of Dreams," by Michael Joseph Gross, *The New York Times Magazine*, September 28, 2003. "Scion Plays Hip-Hop Impresario to Impress Young Drivers," by Norihiko Shirouzu, *The Wall Street Journal*, October 5, 2004. "Scion Finds a Way to Tap Oh-So-Cool Counterculture," by Tamara Audi, *Detroit Free Press*, February 13, 2007. "Scion's Dilemma: Be Hip – But Avoid the Mainstream," by Mark Rechtin, *Autoweek*, May 23, 2006. "Marketer of the Year: Toyota," by Jean Halliday, *Advertising Age*, November 13, 2006. "Scion's Marketing Goal: To Attract Non-Car Buyers?" by Scott Burgess, *Detroit News*, May 2, 2007. "A Way Cool Strategy: Toyota's Scion Plans to Sell Fewer Cars," by Gina Chon, *The Wall Street Journal*, November 10, 2006. *Strangers to Ourselves: Discovering the Adaptive Unconscious*, by Timothy D. Wilson.

nine . . . the murkiest common denominator

"Red Bull Charging Ahead," by Kenneth Hein, *Brandweek*, October 15, 2001. "Coke, Pepsi Expend More Energy to Fight Red Bull," by Kenneth Hein, *Brandweek*, September 26, 2005. "When Coffee Doesn't Do It, Turning to Canned Energy," by Vicky Lowry, *The New York Times*, May 11, 2004. "The Energy-Drink Buzz Is Unmistakable. The Health Impact Is Unknown," by Michael Mason, *The New York Times*, December 12, 2006. "Herr Mateschitz Wants to Juice You Up," by Bryan Curtis, *The New York Times*

Magazine/Play, October 29, 2006. "For Red Bull, It's Here, There and Everywhere; Energy Drink Maker Corners the Marketing," by Melanie Ho, *The Washington Post,* August 23, 2006. "Placebo Effects of Marketing Actions: Consumers May Get What They Pay For," by Baba Shiv, Ziv Carmon, and Dan Ariely, *Journal of Marketing Research* 42 (November 2005). E-mail from Lawrence Spriet, December 14, 2005, with abstract: "The Effect of Acute Taurine Ingestion on Endurance in Well Trained Cyclists." *The Origin of Brands: Discover the Natural Laws of Product Innovation & Business Survival,* by Al and Laura Ries. *Popular Culture & High Culture: An Analysis and Evaluation of Taste,* by Herbert J. Gans. *Quack, Quack, Quack: The Sellers of Nostrums in Prints, Posters, Ephemera & Books,* by William H. Helfand. *For God, Country and Coca-Cola,* by Mark Pendergrast.

ten . . . the commercialization of chitchat

"Word Games," by Todd Wasserman, *Brandweek,* April 24, 2006. "P&G Provides Product Launchpad, a Buzz Network of Moms," by Jack Neff, *Advertising Age,* March 20, 2006. "Kid Nabbing," by Melanie Wells, *Forbes,* February 2, 2004. "Welcome to the Anti-Social Club," by Matthew Creamer, *Advertising Age,* August 7, 2006. "Marketers Seek Out Today's Coolest Kids to Plug into Tomorrow's Mall Trends," by Roger Ricklefs, *The Wall Street Journal,* July 11, 1996. "The Quest for Cool," by Lev Grossman, *Time* magazine, August 30, 2003. "Buzz-Seeking Marketers Mingling with Mixtapes," by Todd Wasserman, *Brandweek,* May 23, 2005. "Word of Mouth Gaining Respect of Marketers," by Matthew Creamer, *Advertising Age,* January 23, 2006. "FTC Moves to Unmask Word-of-Mouth Marketing," by Annys Shin, *The Washington Post,* December 12, 2006. "On the Social Nature of the Nonsocial Perception: The Mere Ownership Effect," by James K. Beggan, University of Louisville, *Journal of Personality and Social Psychology* 62, no. 2, (1992). "Effort for Payment: A Tale of

Two Markets," by James Heyman and Dan Ariely, *Psychological Science* 15, no. 11 (2004). "To Tell or Not to Tell?" by Walter J. Carl, January 2006.

eleven . . . the brand underground

Adcult USA, by James B. Twitchell.

part three | invisible badges

"U.S. Consumer – Like No Other on the Planet," by Peter Franchese, *Advertising Age*, January 2, 2006. "Luxury or Necessity? Things We Can't Live Without: The List Has Grown in the Past Decade," Pew Research Center, a Social Trends Report (pewresearch.org/pubs/323/luxury-or-necessity).

twelve . . . murketing ethics

"Living on the Edge at American Apparel," by Christopher Palmeri, *BusinessWeek*, June 27, 2005. "And You Thought Abercrombie & Fitch Was Pushing It?" by Jaime Wolf, *The New York Times Magazine*, April 23, 2006. "Meet Your New Boss," by Claudine Ko, *Jane* magazine, June/July 2004. "The Young Garmentos," by Malcolm Gladwell, *The New Yorker*, April 24 and May 1, 2000. "SweatX Closes Up Shop," by Richard Applebaum and Peter Dreier, *The Nation*, July 19/26, 2004. "Made in the U.S.A.," by Jenny Strasburg, *San Francisco Chronicle*, July 4, 2004. "Companies Find It's Not Easy Marketing Green," by Wendy Melillo and Steve Miller, *Brandweek*, July 24, 2006. "Be It Ever So Homespun, There's Nothing Like Spin," by Kim Severson, *The New York Times*, January 3, 2007. "Agency Finds Social Responsibility Niche," by Stephanie Kang, *The Wall Street Journal*, August 17, 2007. "Progressive Business," by Matthew Grimm, *Brandweek*, November 28, 2005. JC Report website (www.jcreport.com/mailer/issue81/interview/).

"Social Responsibility: Key to Building Reputation and Regaining Trust," *Wirthlin Report* 13, no. 2 (April 2004). These articles from the *Journal of Industrial Ecology* 9, nos. 1–2, (Winter/Spring 2005): "Consumption and Industrial Ecology," by Edgar G. Hertwich. "The World Behind the Product," by Bas de Leeuw. "Transitions to Sustainability in Production-Consumption Systems," by Louis Lebel. "Consumption: It Is Time for Economists and Scientists to Talk," by Betsy Taylor. "Market Movements: Nongovernmental Organization Strategies to Influence Global Production and Consumption," by Dara O'Rourke. "Are We Consuming Too Much?" by Jon Christensen, *Conservation in Practice*, April–June 2005. "Are We Consuming Too Much?" by Kenneth Arrow, Partha Dasgupta, et al., *Journal of Economic Perspectives* 18, no. 3 (Summer 2004): 147–172. "Licensing Effect in Consumer Choice," by Uzma Khan and Ravi Dhar, *Journal of Marketing Research*, May 2006.

thirteen . . . what's the matter with wal-mart shoppers?

"Getting Along with the New Boss – The Consumer," by A. G. Lafley, *Advertising Age*, March 28, 2005. "Marketers Take a Close Look at Your Daily Routines," by Bruce Horovitz, *USA Today*, April 29, 2007. "Penetrating the Mind by Metaphor," by Emily Eakin, *The New York Times*, February 23, 2002. "P&G Kisses Up to the Boss: Consumers," by Jack Neff, *Advertising Age*, May 2, 2005. "Gimme an Ad!: Brands Lure Cheerleaders," by Brian Steinberg, *The Wall Street Journal*, April 19, 2007. "New TV Reality Series a Gillette Brand Showcase," Associated Press, June 6, 2007. "Well-Balanced Plan Allows P&G to Soar," by Jack Neff, *Advertising Age*, December 12, 2005. "Procter & Gamble Takes Marketing into a New Era," by Renuka Rayasam, *U.S. News & World Report*, March 27, 2007. "Why Making Stuff Is Fashionable Again," by Jean Railla, *Craft* 1. "Unhappy Meals," by Michael Pollan, *The New York Times Magazine*, January 28, 2007. "Obesity Rate in U.S. Still Climbing," by Amanda Gardner, *The Washington Post*, August 27, 2007. "Reviving a

Consumer Watchdog," by Ann Brown and Pamela Gilbert, *The Washington Post*, August 26, 2007. *Coming to Concurrence*, by J. Walker Smith, Ann Clurman, and Craig Wood. *Get Crafty: Hip Home Ec*, by Jean Railla.

fourteen . . . beyond the thing itself

"When Would Jesus Bolt?" by Amy Sullivan, *Washington Monthly*, April 2006. "Veneration Gap: A Popular Strategy for Church Growth Splits Congregants Across U.S.," by Suzanne Sataline, *The Wall Street Journal*, September 5, 2006. "The Cellular Church: How Rick Warren's Congregation Grew," by Malcolm Gladwell, *The New Yorker*, September 12, 2005. "Can Money Buy Happiness?" by David Futrelle, *Money*, August 2006. "The Futile Pursuit of Happiness," by Jon Gertner, *The New York Times Magazine*, September 7, 2003. The following from Rick Warren's *Ministry Toolbox* on Pastors.com: "Turning Attendees into Part of the Family," Issue #225, September 21, 2005. "Leading Your Teen Toward a Purpose Driven Life," Issue #206, May 11, 2005. "Sharing Eternal Truth with an Ever-Emerging Culture," Issue #214, July 6, 2005. "Small Groups Give Every Member Personal Care and Attention," Issue #220, August 17, 2005. "Materialism and the Evolution of Consciousness," by Mihály Csíkszentmihályi, in *Psychology and Consumer Culture: The Struggle for a Good Life in a Materialistic World*, edited by Tim Kasser and Allan D. Kanner. *PyroMarketing: The Four-Step Strategy to Ignite Customer Evangelists and Keep Them for Life*, by Greg Stielstra. *Primalbranding: Create Zealots for Your \\Brand, Your Company, and Your Future*, by Patrick Hanlon. *The Culting of Brands: When Customers Become True Believers*, by Douglas Atkin. *The Paradox of Choice: Why More Is Less*, by Barry Schwartz.

Index

DO YOU WORK FOR A PSYCHOPATH?

The Corporation
ISBN: 9781845291747
RRP £6.99

Are they grandiose, manipulative and unable to feel remorse?

Do they relate to others superficially, presenting themselves in ways that are appealing but deceptive?

If so, you might well be working for a corporation. Required by law to maximize returns to shareholders, the publicly traded corporation enjoys an inhuman clarity of purpose. As Bakan argues in what is both a diagnosis and a course of treatment, it is time to see corporations for what they are, and to take steps to defend ourselves against them.

This fine book was virtually begging to be written. With lucidity and verve, expert knowledge and incisive analysis, Bakan unveils the history and character of a devilish instrument that has been created and is nurtured by modern states.' Noam Chomsky

'Unlike much of the soggy thinking peddled by too many anti-globalizers, *The Corporation* is a surprisingly rational and coherent attack on capitalism's most important institution.'
Economist

'Fahrenheit 9/11 for people who think.' *Independent*

YOU CAN SHOP ANYWHERE YOU LIKE,
AS LONG AS IT'S TESCO

Tescopoly
ISBN: 9781845295110
RRP £7.99

The inexorable rise of supermarkets is big news but have we taken on board what it really means for our daily lives, and those of our children? In this searing analysis Andrew Simms, director of the acclaimed think-and-do-tank the New Economics Foundation and the person who introduced the term 'Clone Towns' into the language, tackles a subject that none of us can afford to ignore.

Simms traces the supermarket disease back to its American roots and charts the moment when the promise of supermarket choice turned into something altogether different. *Tescopoly* shows how the supermarkets have brought:

Banality – homogenized high streets chock-full of cloned chain stores

Ghost towns – out-of-town superstores have drained the life from our town centres

A Supermarket State – new services (health, banking, telecommunications, legal) spell the rise of a new commercial nanny state that knows more about you than you think

Profits from poverty – shelves full of global plunder, produced for a pittance

Parasitic retail – the loss of local retail unpicks the fabric of community

The beginnings of global food domination – as big US and European superstores expand overseas

How Rich Countries Got Rich and Why Poor Countries Stay Poor
ISBN: 9781845298746
RRP £12.99

Erik S. Reinert is a key figure in the growing worldwide movement against neoclassical economic theory. He argues that rich countries have developed through a combination of government intervention, protectionism, and strategic investment, yet, when it comes to today's poorer nations, the orthodoxy insists on unqualified and absolute standards of free trade.

Reinert's strongly revisionist history reveals how economic theory has long been torn between the continental Renaissance tradition and the free market ideas of English and later American economics. Our economies were founded on protectionism and state activism and could only later afford the luxury of free trade, so when our leaders come to lecture poor countries on the right road to riches they do so in almost perfect ignorance of the real history of mass affluence. His book mounts a strong challenge and opens up the debate on why free trade is not the best answer for our hopes of worldwide prosperity.

"Unlike much of the writing produced by opponents of contemporary globalization [this is] a serious book, by a serious person. [It] deserves to be read." —Martin Wolf, *Financial Times*

"A heavyweight assault on the smug post-Cold War consensus of neo-cons and neo classical economists..." —Martin Vander Weyer, *Daily Telegraph*